T0128276

My Golf Balls Grew Eyes

Can an Inanimate Object Become Alive?

This book may never change your mind but it
is guaranteed to make you think.

Edward Robinson

WESTBOW
PRESS®
A DIVISION OF THOMAS NELSON
& ZONDERVAN

WestBow Press books may be ordered through booksellers or by contacting:

WestBow Press
A Division of Thomas Nelson & Zondervan
1663 Liberty Drive
Bloomington, IN 47403
www.westbowpress.com
844-714-3454

Scripture taken from the New King James Version® Copyright © 1982
by Thomas Nelson. Used by permission. All rights reserved.

ISBN: 978-1-6642-0850-6 (sc)
ISBN: 978-1-6642-0851-3 (hc)
ISBN: 978-1-6642-0849-0 (e)

Library of Congress Control Number: 2020920149

Print information available on the last page.

WestBow Press rev. date: 11/05/2020

CONTENTS

Acknowledgment 1

Foreword.. 2

Solitudes 4

Who was Charles Darwin?..11

Who was William Paley?..16

    Can we see Deity through His creation?....................................17

Genetics Introduced...21

    Letty's Garden:...21

Who was Gregor Johann Mendel?.. 23

    Experiments in Plant-Hybridisation 26

Darwin and Genetics 31

    Hybrids and Mongrels compared, independently of their fertility.... 34

    Difficulty with Classification - The Natural System 37

Similar but Not Same 39

Complexity of Life 41

    The Cell...41

    What is a Cell? 42

    What is a Chromosome?... 44

    What is DNA? 45

    What is a gene?.. 46

    How do genes direct the production of proteins? 46

    How do cells divide?... 47

    Recombination 48

    What is a gene mutation and how do mutations occur?.................. 49

    Genes can be turned on and off..51

    What are the homeobox genes?..51

Irreducible Complexity...53

    Sex - where acquired? 55

    The Mousetrap... 57

    The Eye.. 59

    Walking 62

    Teeth... 63

    Human Brain 66

    Hearing 66

Life was and is Changing 69

On the Imperfection of the Geological Record 70

Human Advent - Creation or Evolution? 79

The Neanderthal 82

Piltdown Man 84

Lucy 87

Deduction 88

Charles Darwin's World View and Lack of Faith 89

Consciousness 91

Emotions 92

What did Darwin say? 100

Geographical Distribution 104

Facts and Theories 109

Variation under Domestication 111

Effects of Habit and of the Use or Disuse of Parts 113

Laws regulate variation 114

Character of Domestic Varieties 117

Unconscious Selection 124

Variation Under Nature 127

Struggle for Existence and Natural Selection 132

Geometrical Ratio of Increase 133

Nature of the Checks to Increase 134

Natural Selection - the Survival of the Fittest 137

Sexual Selection? 140

Survival of the Fittest 145

On the Inhabitants of Oceanic Islands 147

Absence of Batrachians and Terrestrial Mammals on
Oceanic Islands 149

Extinction caused by Natural Selection 154

Darwin's Tree 157

On the Degree to which Organisation tends to advance 160

Incredible Organization Needs an Organizer 161

Convergence of Character 168

Laws of Variation 170

Effects of the increased Use and Disuse of Parts 172

Correlated Variation 175

Of the Animal Structure Regarded as a Mass 177

Compensation and Economy of Growth 180

Rudimentary, Atrophied [withered], and Aborted Organs 182
Specific Characters more Variable than Generic Characters 187
Difficulties of the Theory 193
Organs of Extreme Perfection and Complication 207
Development and Embryology..217
Special Difficulties of the Theory of Natural Selection 219
     Beauty how acquired 222
Miscellaneous Objections to the Theory of Natural Selection.............. 227
     Mammary Glands... 234
     Climbing Plants 237
     Instincts 240
     Special Instincts 248
     Morphology - Structure of Organisms..252
Recapitulation and Conclusion 255
     Charles Darwin...255
     William Paley..261
Can We Trust the Judaic Christian Bible?...265
     Fulfillment of Prophecy...265
     More Than a Carpenter... 267
     Christ has Risen 267
     Salvation in Christ 269
     My Boss is More Than a Carpenter... 269
Final Conclusion... 271
Works Cited..274

ACKNOWLEDGMENT

Many thanks to Letty - my loving, lovely, supportive wife. I am also thankful to my daughters Rachel Anne and Hannah Ruth.

At the beginning of this project, I told Letty I intended to write a book. She laughed until she almost fell on the floor. Just to stop the laughing I told her, "a children's book!" Ten-year-old Rachel then spoke up to offer "I want to help. I want to help. I want to help!"

The truth was that I was thinking of a book that was much broader - perhaps extreme. I intended to compare "creation" according to the Christian bible to the "Darwinian Evolution" according to Charles Darwin where all organic life develops from pre-existing life forms.

That meant I hadn't been truthful in saying it would be a children's book and I felt bad for much of that day. Was this a white lie or a downright lie? I confessed to God for my digression and was determined to do better. When I confessed to my wife, she started laughing all over again.

Since that shaky beginning, Letty has been more than supportive. I worked on this book as a non-paying job so our main family income was her day-care business. She also kept me focused. She would tell me to keep at the task at hand rather than taking other job offers - that she was making enough money to pay the on-going expenses.

I wish to give a special thanks to my daughter Rachel Anne. as one of the editors of this book. Once again, thank you.

I wish to also thank WestBow Press for their patience, and recommendations through numerous phone calls and emails.

FOREWORD

Much of what follows contains portions taken from Charles Darwin's book, *"On the Origin of Species by Means of Natural Selection"*; in comparison *to* William Paley's, *"Natural Theology* or *Evidences of the Existence and Attributes of the Deity"*. You will readily see similarities in structure, and subject matter within both Charles Darwin's and William Paley's writings but with vastly divergent conclusions. I also added comments throughout - (I AM WALKING IN THE SHOES OF GIANTS).

Can something come from nothing such as eyes on gulf balls?

Since our universe and all organic life did not exist eternally, then where did we come from? The two prevailing worldviews are that there is a Creator God and the other that everything came into existence by natural causes. There are perhaps many other views for our existence like being seeded from outer space, or that God initially created and evolution produced species

We cannot ignore obvious scientific realities: mutations do exist, and deviations and natural selection do happen, but does this negate the existence of a creator God? To answer this question, I included a little science, and since Gregor Johann Mendel is known as the father of modern genetics, I have included some of his work.

There has been a tremendous increase in scientific knowledge since Charles Darwin's time. This added knowledge is often used by some as further proofs in support for Darwinian evolution, even to the extent in denying the existence of a Creator God. To others, these same scientific facts add credence to intelligent design. Can we perceive a Creator through His creation?

Scientists are still looking for missing links (apes to human etc.) I have added some fossil examples to illustrations change and extinction over time. Do these changes demonstrate Darwinian evolution where, with time, new creatures are created such as ape like creatures to human?

The origin of consciousness would be hard if not impossible to explain by means of Darwinian evolution, and without consciousness we would be no better than scare-crows in a corn patch. From where did our consciousness originate?

Empathy for deceased relatives would also be difficult to explain through Darwinian evolution since it does not have any survival benefits. I added my wife's family in the Philippines and the extinct Neanderthal for consideration. Where does compassion come from?

For many Christians, their Bible is the emphatic word of God. This same Bible states that God created the cosmos and every creature distinct. Christ said, "I came to fulfill the law not destroy it". Does the Judaic Christian Bible stand up to scrutiny? Is it accurately copied?

For those of us who believe God is the Creator, it is difficult to believe that all biological complex structures were produced in a Darwinian gradual systematic fashion. Can it be that even with all the facts which Charles Darwin provides that he is wrong where it matters most? And if so, would it not be that all who think like Darwin are wrong as well?

These are enormous considerations so I have tried to add humor throughout. I trust that what follows is both enjoyable and insightful.

SOLITUDES

There can be no middle ground. Either God created the heavens and the earth and all living thing as separate entities or He didn't.

Many people trust that God is as real as the ground we all walk on, and to others this belief is ludicrous —Eyes to see and ears to hear, but see and hear differently. For Christians, a belief in the life, death and resurrection of Jesus Christ changes everything. "So then faith comes from hearing and hearing by the word of God."[1] Many Christians also come to a belief in the Christian bible as factual, and thus accept the credence that there is a Creator God who formed each species as a separate entity.

William Paley communicated that we can perceive the creator through His creation. For others, they believe that William Paley has been discredited by Darwinian evolution which teaches that all life derived and evolved through natural causes.[2]

Frequently, our pre-conceived and divergent beliefs can be so entrenched that many do not even want to listen to another's point of view. For example, when a guest mentioned 'creation', on a popular call in radio talk show, the moderator asked, "Why revisit that question again? It has already been proven." On another occasion when someone mentioned 'the bible', this same person said, "Well that old book — is it not full of contradictions; why would anyone go there?"

Our family went to visit a nurse whose job is to take care of elderly and dying. I asked Jane (not her real name) whether she believed in God. Her answer surprised me. I always thought she was a complete atheist. She said that sometimes she believes in God, but it doesn't last long. My daughter then asked her, "Where do you think you will be when you die?"

---

[1] Romans 10:17 (Scripture taken from the New King James Version. Copyright @ 1982 by Thomas Nelson, Inc. Used by permission. All rights reserved. [All scripture taken from the NKJV unless otherwise marked]

[2] (For Christians, there is much to be gleaned through Paley's writings.)

Jane responded, "Well, I wish I could offer my patients something more, something to hope for when they are dying." She also added, "There is one thing I just cannot stand, and that is those religious people who say that they are right and everyone else is wrong".

An atheist or an agnostic can view the universe in an internally different way than individual who believers in a Creator God. It is not unusual to hear a person say, "I believe in science – not God". This is frequently expressed as science versus religion. To a non-believer, science can have one domain and religion or spirituality, another. With a believer in a Creator God, it is impossible to separate science and religion (faith) since God is the creator of the universe, and therefore all the laws of which science are based are within God's sphere as well.

Is God's existence just wishful thinking? Can talking to God be likened to crying in the night, and no one out there to listen? Without a God, there is no hope. No future. We are all destined for eventual oblivion. Our moon is slowly drifting away from the earth[3] and our sun will, in the end, become a super nova engulfing our little planet. Amazingly, a total destruction by fire was foretold over two thousand years ago in the Christian bible.

The apostle Peter writes:

10. But the day of the Lord will come as a thief in the night, in which the heavens will pass away with a great noise and the elements will melt with fervent heat; both the earth and the works that are in it will be burned up.

11. Therefore, since all these things will be dissolved, what manner of persons ought you to be in holy conduct and godliness?

12. Looking for and hastening the coming of the day of God because of which the heavens will be dissolved being on fire and the elements will melt with fervent heat? (2 Peter 3:10-13)[4]

---

[3] Our moon is drifting away from the earth at 3.8 centromeres per year. Mirrors were placed on the moon by Apollo 11, 14, and 15 to reflect laser light making it possible in measuring the distance between the earth and moon.

[4] Scripture taken from the New King James Version. Copyright © 1982 by Thomas Nelson, Inc. Used by permission. All rights reserved.

Belief does not always equate truth, but if truths are based on reliable opinion polls, then there is a God in heaven and we are his creation. Polls have consistently shown that a belief in God has been close to 90% and above for many years.

Evolution seems to be taught everywhere. We cannot deny the obvious: mutations exist, and also the crossing of species' varieties produces change. Evolution is not necessarily at odds with belief in a God. Where there is the greatest discrepancy of belief is in life's origin. Did an Intelligent Designer God create life as independent entities with much commonality (links among all living things)? Or alternatively, did all organic life come into existence by natural causes?

Charles Darwin and others thought that as evolution would become better known, it would replace the belief that species were independently created. Many people then and now believe that the Judaic Christian bible is archaic and evolution is more scientific and modern. It has been over a hundred and fifty years since the introduction of evolution by Charles Darwin, yet the belief in a Creator God has not disappeared. Why? Could it be that Charles Darwin had the correct evidence and wrong conclusion?

Darwin:

..."I am well aware that this doctrine of natural selection ... is open to the same objections which were first urged against Sir Charles Lyell's noble views on "the modern changes of the earth, as illustrative of geology;" but we now seldom hear the agencies which we see still at work, spoken of as trifling or insignificant, when used in explaining the excavation of the deepest valleys or the formation of long lines of inland cliffs. Natural selection acts only by the preservation and accumulation of small inherited modifications, each profitable to the preserved being; and as modern geology has almost banished such views as the excavation of a great valley by a single diluvial wave, [biblical flood][5] so will natural selection banish the belief of the continued creation of new organic beings, or of any great and sudden modification in their structure." (Darwin C., 1872, pp. 76-77)[6]

---

[5] I have inserted box brackets for clarity throughout this book. i.e. [...]

[6] All excerpts are from the sixth edition of "Origin of Species". unless otherwise stated

To equate the belief in Sir Charles Lyell views on change in the earth to that of creation is flawed. Changes in the earth's geography are obvious; while there is no proof that God did not create individual species, "biblically called kinds", with the ability to change. Evolution and natural selection do not explain first causes [life's origin].

Darwin from Descent of Man vol-1:

"Whether primeval man, when he possessed very few arts of the rudest kind, and when his power of language was extremely imperfect, would have deserved to be called man, must depend on the definition which we employ. In a series of forms graduating insensibly from some ape-like creature to man as he now exists, it would be impossible to fix on any definite point when the term "man" ought to be used. But this is a matter of very little importance. So again, it is almost a matter of indifference whether the so-called races of man are thus designated, or are ranked as species or sub-species; but the latter term appears the most appropriate. Finally, we may conclude that when the principles of evolution are generally accepted, as they surely will be before long, the dispute between the monogenists [from a single pair] and the polygenists [having many] will die a silent and unobserved death." (Page235)

Another apparent axiom of truth is from James Watson book, "DNA":

... "There are those who will continue to believe humans are creations of God, whose will we must serve. ... It could be that as knowledge grows in centuries to come, with ever more individuals coming to understand themselves as products of random throws of the generic dice–chance mixtures of their parents' genes and a few equally accidental mutations-a new gnosis in fact much more ancient than today's religions will come to be sanctified. Our DNA, the instruction book of human creation may well come to rival religious scripture as the keeper of the truth."... (Watson, 2004, p. 404)

No one can argue that what is referred to as the Ten Commandments are not good.

Christ said in John 13:33 "a new commandment I give to you, that you love one another, as I have loved you, that you also love one another." (NKJV)

Edward Robinson

It is thought-provoking that what follows was written by William Paley before Charles Darwin published, "Origin of Species"

Can golf balls grow eyes or with time, can round balls acquire wings?

William Paley:

… "Another system, which has lately been brought forward, and with much ingenuity, is that of *appetencies*. The principle, and the short account of the theory, is this: Pieces of soft, ductile matter, being endued with propensities [tendencies] or appetencies [strong desires] for particular actions, would, by continual endeavours, carried on through a long series of generations, work themselves gradually into suitable forms; and at length acquire, though perhaps by obscure and almost imperceptible improvements, an organization fitted to the action which their respective propensities [tendencies]led them to exert. A piece of animated matter, for example, that was endued with a propensity to fly, though ever so shapeless, though no other we will suppose than a round ball, to begin with, would, in a course of ages, if not in a million of years, perhaps in a hundred millions of years, (for our theorists, having eternity to dispose of, are never sparing in time, acquire wings. The same tendency to locomotion in an aquatic animal, or rather in an animated lump which might happen to be surrounded by water, would end in the production of fins; in a living substance, confined to the solid earth, would put out legs and feet; or, if it took a different turn, would break the body into ringlets, and conclude by trawling upon the ground." … (Paley W., "Natural Theology or Evidences of the Existence and Attributes of the Deity", 1829, pp. 244-245)

An interesting footnote on page 244 of this same book follows: "I trust I may be excused for not citing, as another fact which is to confirm the hypothesis, a grave assertion of this writer, that the branches of trees upon which the stag feeds, break out again in his horn such facts merit no discussion."

Paley:

… "If we could suppose joints and muscles to be gradually formed by action and exercise, what action or exercise could form a skull, or fill it with brains? No effort of the animal could determine the clothing of its skin. What *co-natlus* (sic) could give prickles to the porcupine or hedgehog or to the sheep its fleece? In the last place: What do these appetencies mean when applied to plants? I am not able to give a signification to the term, which can be transferred from animals to plants; or which is common to both. Yet a no less successful organization is found in plants, than what obtains in animals. A solution is wanted for one as well as the other. Upon the whole; after all the schemes and struggles of a reluctant Philosophy, the necessary resort is to a Deity. The marks of design are too strong to be gotten over. Design must have had a designer. That designer must have been a person. That person is God." ... (Paley W., "Natural Theology or Evidences of the Existence and Attributes of the Deity", 1829, p. 249)[7]

Darwin:

... "Changed habits produce an inherited effect, as in the period of the flowering of plants when transported from one climate to another. With animals the increased use or disuse of parts has had a more marked influence; thus I find in the domestic duck that the bones of the wing weigh less and the bones of the leg more, in proportion to the whole skeleton, than do the same bones in the wild-duck; and this change may be safely attributed to the domestic duck flying much less, and walking more, than its wild parents. The great and inherited development of the udders in cows and goats in countries where they are habitually milked, in comparison with these organs in other countries, is probably another instance of the effects of use. Not one of our domestic animals can be named which has not in some country drooping ears; and the view which has been suggested that the drooping is due to the disuse of the muscles of the ear, from the animals being seldom much alarmed, seems probable." ... (Darwin C., 1872, p. 8) [8]

The two prevailing worldviews are that there is a Creator God and the other that everything came into existence by natural causes. There are perhaps many other views for our existence like being seeded from outer space, or that God initially created and evolution produced species. Etc.

---

[7] Derived from William Paley's "Natural theology" or, "Evidences of the existence and attributes of the Deity, collected from the appearances of nature" (Darwin and Paley's works are not indented in this book because they are numerous)

[8] Derived from Charles Darwin's, "The Origin of Species by Means of Natural Selection" or "Preservation of Favoured Races in the Struggle for Life." [Darwin–year–page number]

There is another view, or an alternate idea — A belief in a Creator God and evolution. Yes! A belief that God created the heavens, the earth, and every creature [kind] distinct—and changing; when varieties cross, we have evolution — we have change. New varieties are created — all the time.[9] There are also species and varieties going extinct — all the time. This view does not contradict the Christian bible version that humankind and other creatures were created distinct, or what is obvious — that varieties change. This belief also leaves room for mutations.

Seek the Lord while he may be found; call on him while he is near. (Isaiah 55:6)

Two solitudes with no middle ground; either God created the universe and everything in it or He didn't. What follows is only some of the evidence for the existence of a creator God.

---

[9] [The creation of a new species can be debatable because this can be dependent on one's classification of what constitutes a species or kind I.E. zebra – horse etc.]

WHO WAS CHARLES DARWIN?

Charles Darwin (1809-1882) is best known for his controversial book, *"On the Origin of Species by Means of Natural Selection or The Preservation of Favoured Races in the Struggle for Life"*. This book was first published in 1859 with a sixth edition in 1872.

Darwin was a self-proclaiming agnostic. He also believed that natural causes shaped life. His lack of faith is obvious in some of his letters and portions of his autobiography titled, "Recollections of the Development of my Mind". His autobiography was written for his family, but later edited and published in 1887 by his son Frances. There were several omissions from the original autobiography doe to the wishes of Charles Darwin's wife Emma. These omissions were replaced by Darwin's granddaughter, 'Norma Barlow', in a 1958 version of Darwin's memoirs.

Darwin:

… "Beautiful as is the morality of the New Testament, it can hardly be denied that its perfection depends in part on the interpretation which we now put on metaphors and allegories." ... "The old argument of design in nature, as given by Paley[10], which formerly seemed to me so conclusive, fails, now that the law of natural selection has been discovered. We can no longer argue that, for instance, the beautiful hinge of a bivalve shell must have been made by an intelligent being," ... (Darwin C., pp. 66-67)

In omissions from the original autobiography, Darwin states that he, "slowly began to disbelieve Christianity". He also questions the bible's miracles, the eyewitness accounts, the time of the writings to the events etc. (ibid p 86)

His beliefs are quite similar to what many believe today. In a letter written to William Graham dated July 3 1881, Darwin writes:

... "But I have had no practice in abstract reasoning and I may be all astray. Nevertheless, you have expressed my inward conviction, though far more vividly and clearly than I could have done, that the Universe is not the result of chance. But then with me the horrid doubt always arises whether the convictions of man's mind, which has been developed from the mind of the lower animals, are of any value or at all trustworthy. Would any one trust in the convictions of a monkey's mind, if there are any convictions in such a mind?" ... (Darwin C.) or (Darwin, 1887)-(found in either source)

Perhaps here, Darwin gives a little leeway for the existence of a Divine. But he also infers that our minds have been developed from lower animals.

In this same letter, Darwin also defends 'natural selection' for progress: ... "The more civilized so-called Caucasian races have beaten the Turkish hollow in the struggle for existence. Looking to the world at no very distant date, what an endless number of the lower races will have been eliminated by the higher civilized races throughout the world". ... (Ibid-NP)

This belief of a superior race beating down the inferior obviously appealed to Adolf Hitler and his followers before and during the Second World War. In this persuasion would not the more violent destroy the less fortunate? This is totally at odds with what Christ said, *"The meek shall inherit the earth".*

---

[10] William Paley is best known for his watchmaker analogy.

In his letter to John Fordyce, 7 May 1879, Charles Darwin describes himself as a self-proclaimed agnostic:

... "I think that generally (& more and more so as I grow older) but not always, that an agnostic would be the most correct description of my state of mind". ... (Darwin C., Darwin Correspondence Database, entry-12041, 1876)

Excerpt from Darwin's letter to Boole, M. E. 14 Dec 1866:

... "I cannot see how the belief that all organic beings including man have been genetically derived from some simple being, instead of having been separately created bears on your difficulties.—These as it seems to me, can be answered only by widely different evidence from Science, or by the so called "inner consciousness" ... (Darwin C.)

Creation or Darwinian evolution—these two solitudes are evident in this letter. Perhaps "inner consciousness" in quotation marks implying that evidence for "God's creation" (in Darwin's view) lacks proof.

Excerpts from Darwin's letter to Gray, Asa, 22 May 1860:

... "There seems to me too much misery in the world. I cannot persuade myself that a beneficent & omnipotent God would have designedly created the Ichneumonidae with the express intention of their feeding within the living bodies of caterpillars, or that a cat should play with mice. Not believing this, I see no necessity in the belief that the eye was expressly designed". ... (Darwin, Darwin Correspondence Database, entry-2814, 1860)

With pain and suffering in the world, Darwin is questioning the very existence of God. Is it possible to put God in a box of our own making and if He doesn't fit dismiss Him as non-existent?

Why does a loving God allow suffering? There seems to be no satisfactory answer. This biblical perspective is taken from "The Bible Knowledge Commentary by John F Walvoord and Roy B. Zuck" – page 935: "The problem of human suffering, even for a limited time, has always perplexed faithful Christians. Suffering can be expected for the ungodly, but why should the godly suffer? The Scriptures give a number of reasons. Suffering may be (1) disciplinary (1 Cor. 11:30-32; Heb. 12:3-13), (2) Preventive (as Paul's thorn in the flesh, 2Cor. 12:7, (3) The learning of obedience (as Christ's suffering, Heb. 5:8; cf. Rom. 5:3-5) or (4) The providing of a better testimony for Christ (as in Acts 9:16)."

Suffering can be a test of faith by satanic forces: Job in the Christian bible had wealth and a loving family. He lost all including his health in a satanic test of his faith. Through all his suffering, Job remained blameless. Another example is in a letter written to Smyrna from the book of Revelation: "Do not fear any of those things which you are about to suffer. Indeed, the devil is about to throw some of you into prison that you may be tested and you will have tribulation ten days. Be faithful until death, and I will give you the crown of life." (Revelation 2:10)

In the Old Testament, the prophet Habakkuk asked God why He allowed the wicked to prosper. God replied that He was going to send the Babylonians to punish Juda. Habakkuk then did not understand why a more wicked people would be sent to punish the Jews. He was informed that in due time the Babylonians would also be punished. God also stated that, "the just shall live by faith". -- God did not say that the righteous would not suffer, but they would live by faith. (Habakkuk 1:1-2:20)

The passage that follows is taken from Charles Darwin's autobiography published in 1887.

Darwin:

… "In order to pass the B.A. examination, it was also necessary to get up Paley's 'Evidences of Christianity and his 'Moral Philosophy.' This was done in a thorough manner, and I am convinced that I could have written out the whole of the 'Evidences' with perfect correctness, but not of course in the clear language of Paley. The logic of this book and, as I may add, of his 'Natural Theology,' gave me as much delight as did Euclid. The careful study of these works, without attempting to learn any part by rote, was the only part of the academical course which, as I then felt and as I still believe, was of the least use to me in the education of my mind. I did not at that time trouble myself about Paley's premises; and taking these on trust, I was charmed and convinced by the long line of argumentation. By answering well the examination questions in Paley, by doing Euclid well, and by not failing miserably in Classics, I gained a good place among the oi polloi or crowd of men who do not go in for honours." … (Darwin C.)

Charles Darwin used a great deal of William Paley's work without giving credit. Also, he was definitely not a humble man and his ideas about a superior race support this big ego. Surprisingly Today, Charles Darwin is well known (in some circle a cultist figure) while William Paley is almost forgotten.

WHO WAS WILLIAM PALEY?

William Paley (1743-1805) was an Anglican priest who graduated from Christ's College, Cambridge, who wrote several books on philosophy and Christianity. Paley was a bible-believing Christian whose writings reflected his Christian worldview that God created and controls everything. A major theme of his book, *"Natural Theology, or Evidences of the Existence and Attributes of the Deity"*, is that we can not only know that God exists, but also understand His nature through His creation.

Paley is perhaps best recognized for his watchmaker analogy. (Can a great work of art exist without an architect?). Paley's "Natural Theology or Evidences of the Existence and Attributes of the Deity" (1802) was written before Darwin's book, "On the Origin of Species by Means of Natural Selection or The Preservation of Favoured Races in the Struggle for Life", (1859). William Paley's 'happy world' in his book, 'Natural Theology' is in stark contrast to Darwin's fraught world in 'Origin'. Their books are very different, and yet possessing many areas similar in theme and style. It has even been surmised by some that Darwin replaced Paley's *'God or Deity'* in 'Natural Theology' with *'evolution'* in 'Origin of Species.

CAN WE SEE DEITY THROUGH HIS CREATION?

Paley:

"IN (sic) crossing a heath, suppose I pitched my foot against a stone, and were asked how the stone came to be there, I might possibly answer, that, for any thing I knew to the contrary, it had lain there forever: nor would it perhaps be very easy to show the absurdity of this answer. But, suppose I had found a watch upon the ground, and it should be inquired how the watch happened to be in that place, I should hardly think of the answer which I had before given, that, for any thing I knew, the watch might have always been there. Yet why should not this answer serve for the watch, as well as for the stone? Why is it not as admissible in the second case, as in the first? For this reason, and for no other, viz. that, when we come to inspect the watch, we perceive (what we could not discover in the stone) that its several parts are framed and put together for a purpose, e. g. that they are so formed and adjusted as to produce motion, and that motion so regulated as to point out the hour of the day ; that, if the several parts had been differently shaped from what they are, or of a different size from what they are, or placed after any other manner, or in any other order, than that in which they are placed, either no motion at all would have been carried on in the machine, or none which would have answered the use that is now served by it. To reckon up a few of the plainest of these parts, and of their offices, all tending to one result" … (Paley W., "Natural Theology or Evidences of the Existence and Attributes of the Deity", p. 5)

Paley describes the many parts of a watch, which are dissimilar in shape and size and fashioned from different materials. Each part of the watch is independent and yet functions for the overall purpose for which the watch was made. The obvious analogy here is that the watch was man-made and our universe was God made.

Paley:

… "We take notice that the wheels are made of brass, in order to keep them from rust; the springs of steel, no other metal being so elastic; that over the face of the watch there is placed a glass, a material employed in no other part of the work; but in the room of which, if there had been any other than a transparent substance, the hour could not be seen without opening the case.

This mechanism being observed (it requires indeed an examination of the instrument, and perhaps some previous knowledge of the subject, to perceive and understand it; but being once, as we have said, observed and understood,) the inference, we think, is inevitable; that the watch must have had a maker ; that there must have existed, at some time and at some place or other, an artificer or artificers, who formed it for the purpose which we find it actually to answer ; who comprehended its construction, and designed its use." ... Ibid p.6

Paley:

... "It is an immense conclusion, that there is a God; a perceiving, intelligent, designing Being; at the head of creation, and from whose will it proceeded. The attributes of such a Being, suppose his reality to be proved, must be adequate to the magnitude, extent, and multiplicity of his operations: which are not only vast beyond comparison with those performed by any other power, but, so far as respects our conceptions of them, infinite, because they are unlimited on all sides." ... (Ibid 249-250)

Christians believe they have a future beyond death since God is the architect of all life and inheritance.

The universe did not exist eternally. An estimate for our universe is 13 billion years. The probability for our universe being created by chance has been compared to tossing Leo Tolstoy's book 'War and Peace'[11] with over a thousand pages into the wind time after time, until at some point, all pages land on the ground in proper order. This desired result may take billions of years, or on the first toss, or never. If we combine the complexity of our universe and organic life, the probability of our existence could be likened to tossing pages of a large book into the air and having it come together on the very first toss.

"You art worthy, O Lord, to receive glory and honour and power: For You created all things, And by Your will they exist and were created." (Revelation 4:11) NKJV

---

[11] War and Peace is a novel by the Russian author Leo Tolstoy, which is regarded as a central work of world literature and one of Tolstoy's finest.

What follows is an account of creation taken from the Judaic Christian Bible.

Genesis 1:24-27

24 Then God said, "let the earth bring forth the living creature according to its kind: cattle and creeping thing and beast of the earth, each according to its kind"; And it was so.

25 And God made the beast of the earth according to its kind, cattle according to its kind, and everything that creeps on the earth according to its kind. And God saw that it was good.

26 Then God said. "Let Us make man in Our image, according to Our likeness: let them have dominion over the fish of the sea, over the birds of the air, and over the cattle, over all the earth and over every creeping thing that creeps on the earth."

27 So God created man "in His own image; in the image of God He created him; male and female He created them.

28 Then God blessed them. And God said to them. "Be fruitful and multiply; fill the earth and subdue it; have dominion over the fish of the sea, over the birds of the air, and over every living thing that moves on the earth." (NKJV)[12]

The Darwinian credence that all organic life was created and evolved exclusively through natural causes is totally at odds with the belief that God created humankind unique and each species as a separate entity.

What follows are biblical passages which infer God's existence, with the uniqueness of humankind. Matthew 6:25-34

25 "Therefore I say to you, "do not worry about your life, what you will eat or what you will drink; nor about your body, what you will put on. Is not life more than food and the body more than clothing?

---

26 "Look at the birds of the air. For they neither sow nor reap nor gather into barns; yet your heavenly Father feeds them. Are you not of more value than they?

27 -Which of you by worrying can add one cubit to his stature?

28 "So why do you worry about clothing? Consider the lilies of the field, how they grow: they neither toil nor spin:

29 "and yet I say to you that even Solomon in all his glory was not arrayed like one of these.

30 "Now if God so clothes the grass of the field, which today is and tomorrow is thrown into the oven, will He not much more clothe you. O you of little faith?

31 "Therefore do not worry, saying, 'What shall we eat?' or 'What shall we drink?' or 'What shall we wear?'

32 "For after all these things the Gentiles seek. For your heavenly Father knows that you need all these things.

33 "But, seek first the kingdom of God and His righteousness. and all these things shall be added to you.

34 "Therefore do not worry about tomorrow, for tomorrow will worry' about its own things. Sufficient for the day is its own trouble. (NKJV)

Although William Paley looked at creation from a position of faith, he had an open mind and examined evidence in support of a Creator God. Darwin in contrast, missed the mark where it mattered most. He does not have an answer for the source of all life and its complexity.

GENETICS INTRODUCED

There has been an enormous proliferation in scientific knowledge in the last one hundred and fifty years since Charles Darwin wrote "On the Origin of Species by Means of Natural Selection". Does this added knowledge further support that all life derived by chance from pre-existent life forms, or is there additional evidence for a "Creator God"? To answer this question, we have to have some elementary knowledge of science, and what better way to introduce genetics then in a homegrown garden.

LETTY'S GARDEN:

My wife Letty has a passion for gardening. She loves to water, weed, and pick. Every year she has created a large garden that takes up much of the front, one side and back of our house. This garden is always magnificent with heaps of color and variety - much appreciated!

She planted two kinds of bean plants. One was a climbing variety and the other a low or sitting type. For last year's crop of climbing beans, she acquired the seed from her cousin, and for the sitting verity she bought them from a store. She planted the climbing beans all around the fences and at the house. For the sitting variety, she planted a small cluster at our back fence that separates us from a school yard. Last year, the bean crop was beautiful. The shells of the climbing type were long and full of seeds and the sitting variety were a little smaller but also very good. We had a continual abundant crop from both types of bean plants; we had more than enough for ourselves and plenty to give away to neighbors and friends.

Last fall my wife saved seeds from both varieties for this year's crop. This year's crop was planted in much the same way as last except she added a few pumpkin plants to the climbers. The pumpkin plants were doing just fine, but the bean crop was more than a disappointment. Letty told me that some of her sitting plants wanted to climb although she did not mix the seeds. The sitting plants were such a disaster that my wife completely removed them from the garden. The climbing variety was not a complete calamity. The pods were not of uniform length but varied from about a puny one half to a grand six inches. We had beans for supper but less to give away.

This was a mystery! Why was there such a difference in my wife's bean crop this year as compared to last? Also, why is it that my wife's cousin, whom she obtained her original seed, has had a fantastic crop growing in her back yard, while Letty's garden was such a dismal failure? My wife complained saying, "Well, I am going to have to fertilize more." Also, "I need to water more." She sometimes said, "This year we have had a lot of rain." Letty had also shown me how the seeds from this year's crop were different in size and color from her original stock. How could this be?

It finally dawned on me that inadvertently my wife was carrying on a home-grown experiment in our back yard. I went and got a book that has the experiments of Gregory Mendel (1822-1884). Mendel crossed varieties of peas and explained what happens and why. The mystery was solved in that my wife's two varieties of sitting and climbing plants had cross-pollinated with help from the bugs and bees, and then the next generation became very unproductive and often looked different than either parent varieties.

WHO WAS GREGOR JOHANN MENDEL?

Gregor Johann Mendel (1822-1884) was born in Heinzen Dorf. Austria. He became an Augustinian friar, and from his monastery garden, worked out the mathematical laws of genetics Today, Mendel is best known as, "the father of modern genetics".

Mendel performed thousands of crosses with garden peas. He discovered for example, that with a cross of tall to short plants tall would always mask or dominate short. Thus in the first generation from the parental, the plants were all tall. When Mendel crossed the offspring, of the first generation, the progeny was tall and short as parental in a three-to-one ratio. The results were not a blend or intermediate of parental; the plants were tall or short as parental. This is quite different than a Darwinian vision where change happens progressively in a step by step fashion over time.

Mendel's factors are new called genes. There are two characteristics [alleles] in each factor. In formation of Gametes [sex cells] these alleles separate out and only one allele from each parent contribute to a zygote [fertilized egg cell]

Edward Robinson

Mendel's Law of Segregation states that when gametes [reproductive cells] form, alleles are separated so that each gamete carries only one allele for each gene

Mendel's law of independent assortment states that his factors [today called genes] for different traits are dispersed to sex cells independently of one another, thus height does not influence color or texture etc.

Mendel's experiments were carried out about the same time as Charles Darwin was writing, *"The origin of Species",* yet Darwin's work became well known while Mendel was forgotten and ignored for over 35 years.

William Bateson's assessment of why Mendel's works was not appreciated for so long follows:

… "One may naturally ask, how can these results be brought into harmony with the facts of hybridisation hitherto known; and, if all this is true, how is it that others who have carefully studied the phenomena of hybridisation have not long ago perceived this law? The answer to this question is given by Mendel at some length, and it is, I think, satisfactory. He admits from the first that there are undoubtedly cases of hybrids and crossbreds which maintain themselves pure and do not break up. Such examples are plainly outside the scope of his law.

Next, he points out, what to anyone who has rightly comprehended the nature of discontinuity in variation is well known that the variations in each character must be separately regarded. In most experiments in crossing, forms are taken which differ from each other in a multitude of characters some continuous, others discontinuous, some capable of blending with their contraries, while others are not. The observer on attempting to perceive any regularity is confused by the complications thus introduced. Mendel's law, as he fairly says, could only appear in such cases by the use of overwhelming numbers, which are beyond the possibilities of practical experiment. Lastly, no previous observer had applied a strict statistical method.

It may seem surprising that a work of such importance should so long have failed to find recognition and to become current in the world of science. It is true that the journal in which it appeared is scarce, but this circumstance has seldom long delayed general recognition. The cause is unquestionably to be found in that neglect of the experimental study of the problem of Species which supervened [appeared] on the general acceptance of the Darwinian doctrines. The problem of Species, as Kreutzer, Gartner, Naudin, Wichura, and the other hybridists of the middle of the nineteenth century conceived it, attracted thenceforth no workers. The question, it was imagined, had been answered and the debate ended. No one felt much interest in the matter. A host of other lines of work were suddenly opened up, and in 1865 the more original investigators naturally found those new methods of research more attractive than the tedious observations of the hybridizers, whose inquiries were supposed, moreover, to have led to no definite result. …

… When several naturalists of the first rank were still occupied with these problems, should have passed wholly unnoticed, will always remain inexplicable, the more so as the Brünn Society exchanged its publications with most of the Academies of Europe, including both the Royal and Linnaean Societies. …

… Naudin's views were well known to Darwin and are discussed in Animals and Plants (ed. 1885, n., p. 23); but, put forward as they were without full proof, they could not command universal credence. Gartner, too, had adopted opposite views; and Wichura, working with cases of another order, had proved the fact that some hybrids breed true. Consequently, it is not to be wondered at that Darwin was sceptical. Moreover, the Mendelian idea of the "hybrid-character," or heterozygous form, was unknown to him, a conception without which the hypothesis of dissociation sociation of characters is quite imperfect.

Had Mendel's work come into the hands of Darwin, it is not too much to say that the history of the development of evolutionary philosophy would have been very different from that which we have witnessed." … (Bateson, 1902, pp. 38-40)

A generation after Mendel published his papers; three botanists Hugo DeVries, Carl Correns and Erich von Tschermak independently rediscovered Mendel's work. The three Europeans, unknown to each other, were working on different plant hybrids when they each worked out the laws of inheritance. When they reviewed the literature before publishing their own results, they were startled to find Mendel's old papers spelling out those laws in detail.

Each man announced Mendel's discoveries and his own work as confirmation of them.

By 1900, cells and chromosomes were sufficiently understood to give Mendel's abstract ideas a physical context. (Roberts) "Courtesy: National Human Genome Research Institute" https://www.genome.gov/.

We owe considerable to the work of Gregor Johann Mendel for our understanding of genetics which is taught in high school science courses. What follows is my quick overview from his 'Experiments in Plant-Hybridisation' read at the Meetings of the 8th February and 8th of March, 1865. I have kept out much of the comparing counting and numbers on which the statistical results are based. For clarity I also added some Punnet squares and comments. I trust that the reader will gain an appreciation for Gregor Mendel in this contraction.

EXPERIMENTS IN PLANT-HYBRIDISATION

SELECTION OF THE EXPERIMENTAL PLANTS.

The value and utility of any experiment are determined by the fitness of the material to the purpose for which it is used, and thus in the case before us it cannot be immaterial what plants are subjected to experiment and in what manner such experiments are conducted.

The selection of the plant group which shall serve for experiments of this kind must be made with all possible care if it be desired to avoid from the outset every risk of questionable results. Experiments which were made with several members of this family led to the result that the genus Pisum [pea family] was found to possess the necessary conditions.

In all, thirty-four more or less distinct varieties of Peas were obtained from several seedsmen and subjected to a two years' trial... no essential difference was observed during two trial years. For fertilisation twenty-two of these were selected and cultivated during the whole period of the experiments. They remained constant without any exception.

The characters which were selected for experiment relate: 1. The ripe seed: round or wrinkling. 2. The color or the albumen (endosperm): yellow or green. 3. The color of the seed-coat: white with white flowers or gray to brown with purple flower.4. The form of the ripe pods: inflated or contracted. 5. The color of the unripe pods: green or yellow. 6. Position of the flower: axial (along the main stem) or terminal (bunched at the top). 7. Length of the stem: tall or short

The plants were grown in garden beds, a few also in pots, and were maintained in their naturally upright position by means of sticks, branches of trees, and strings stretched between. For each experiment a number of pot plants were placed during the blooming period in a green-house, to serve as control plants for the main experiment, one of the two parental characters was so preponderant [more significant] that it was difficult, or quite impossible, to detect the other in the hybrid [offspring]. …

This is illustrated in a "punnet square". An offspring derives an allele from each parent and thus its genotype (genetic makeup) contains tall and short, [T and t] but since tall is the dominant and masks the recessive, the phenotype [appearance] is all tall.

The cross TTxtt	Tall Parent TT	Tall Parent TT
Short Parent tt	Progeny Tall Tt	Progeny Tall Tt
Short Parent tt	Progeny Tall Tt	Progeny Tall Tt

By crossing a tall purebred plant with a short purebred plant, the resulting offspring is not a blend of the two-parent stocks but surprisingly all tall.

For convenience, uppercase letters are used to denote dominant and tall. Thus TT=tall. To illustrate the short and recessive the lowercase is used. Thus tt=short. A cross of TTxtt=Tt. The hybrids were all tall plants since tall is dominant and short is recessive. (Tall masks short)

TtxTt	Tt	Tt
Tt	TT	Tt
Tt	Tt	tt

By crossing a hybrid with genotype Tt with another hybrid Tt, the observable resulting phenotype is a three to one ratio of tall to short.

One TT [tall plant]; Two Tt [tall plant]; One tt [short plant]. There is a 3:1 ratio of tall to short

THE SECOND GENERATION [BRED] FROM THE HYBRIDS

Those forms, which in the first generation maintain the recessive character, do not further vary in the second generation as regards this character; they remain constant in their offspring. It is otherwise with those which possess the dominant character in the first generation [bred from the hybrids]. Of these, two-thirds yield offspring which display the dominant and recessive characters in the proportion of 3 to 1, and thereby show exactly the same ratio as the hybrid forms, while only one-third remains with the dominant character constant.

The ratio of 3 to 1, in accordance with which the distribution of the dominant and recessive characters results in the first generation, resolves itself therefore in all experiments into the ratio of 2: 1: 1 if the dominant character be differentiated [separated] according to its significance as a hybrid character or a parental one. Since the members of the first generation spring directly from the seed of the hybrids, it is now clear that the hybrids form seeds having one or other of the two differentiating characters, and of these, one-half develop again the hybrid form, while the other half yield plants which remain constant and receive the dominant or recessive characters [respectively] in equal numbers.

THE SUBSEQUENT GENERATIONS [BRED] FROM THE HYBRIDS.

The proportions in which the descendants of the hybrids develop and split up in the first and second generations presumably hold good for all subsequent progeny [offspring]. ...

THE OFFSPRING OF HYBRIDS IN WHICH SEVERAL DIFFERENTIATING CHARACTERS ARE ASSOCIATED

"In the experiments above, described plants were used which differed only in one essential character. The next task consisted in ascertaining whether the law of development discovered in these applied to each pair of differentiating [separate] characters when several diverse characters are united in the hybrid by crossing. As regards the form of the hybrids in these cases, the experiments showed throughout that this invariably more nearly approaches to that one of the two parental plants which possesses the greater number of dominant characters. If, for instance, the seed plant has a short stem, terminal white flowers, and simply inflated pods; the pollen plant, on the other hand, a long stem, violet-red flowers distributed along the stem, and constricted pods; the hybrid resembles the seed parent only in the form of the pod; in the other characters it agrees with the pollen parent. Should one of the two parental types possess only dominant characters, then the hybrid is scarcely or not at all distinguishable from it. …

… In addition, further experiments were made with a smaller number of experimental plants in which the remaining characters by twos and threes were united as hybrids: all yielded approximately the same results. There is therefore no doubt that for the whole of the characters involved in the experiments, the principle applies that the offspring of the hybrids in which several essentially different characters are combined represent the terms of a series of combinations, in which the developmental series for each pair of differentiating characters are associated. It is demonstrated at the same time that the relation of each pair of different characters in hybrid union is independent of the other differences in the two original parental stocks." … (Bateson, 1902)

Varieties of species can be so very different than their lineages and it was Gregor Johann Mendel who has given us our understanding of how this change takes place. Novel varieties can be created by crossing existing varieties of the same species. This process can be repeated with the same result if both parental varieties are still in existence; if there is extinction in one or both parent stock, then there is no way of repeating from the original varieties to create the same results.

Gregor Johann Mendel's work and modern genetics can explain what happened in my wife Letty's garden. She began with a sitting and climbing plants which cross pollinated, thus creating many plants with low yield and looking different from her original parental stock.

Mendel did not know how a cell worked or why his factors functioned as they did. He did not realize that his peas have seven chromosomes, and his factors were on separate chromosomes. Mendel also selected peas with clear dominant or recessive characteristics. For example, the plants were either tall dominant or short recessive, wrinkled or smooth, yellow or green etc. However, in nature some traits blend. Some examples of incomplete dominance are the Andalusia fowl in which the crossing of homozygous white and black birds obtains a blue hybrid. Also, the four o'clock garden flower can be either red or white and the hybrid is pink.

Today, Gregor Johann Mendel is known as the father of modern genetics. He published his work 1866. Darwin's Origin was first published in 1858 with a sixth edition in 1872.

Darwin became well known while Mendel was almost forgotten. It took another thirty years before others took up the mantel and Gregor Johann Mendel was recognized for his genius.

There may have been many reasons why Mendel's work was not accepted: Darwinian creation without a god appealed to the scientific community. Also, Mendel could have published his work more aggressively and followed up with many other experiments. Mendel may have been bogged down with other duties and he was also known for bouts of depression.

DARWIN AND GENETICS

Darwin had seemingly no knowledge of genetics or George Mendel. Much of what Darwin expressed as change can be explained through variety change and not species created through time. For example, what is referred to as "Darwin's Finches" - are they not all varieties of finches found on the Galapagos Islands, - no more and no less?

Darwin in 1896 had his own incorrect theory of inheritance that he called pangenesis. He presented his hypothesis in his 1868 work, "The Variation of Animals and Plants under Domestication".

Darwin:

It is almost universally admitted that cells, or the units of the body, propagate themselves by self-division or proliferation [multiplying], retaining the same nature, and ultimately becoming converted into the various tissues and substances of the body. But besides this means of increase I assume that cells, before their conversion into completely passive or "form-material," throw off minute granules or atoms, which circulate freely throughout the system, and when supplied with proper nutriment multiply by self-division, subsequently becoming developed into cells like those from which they were derived. These granules for the sake of distinctness may be called cell-gemmules, or, as the cellular theory is not fully established, simply gemmules. They are supposed to be transmitted from the parents to the offspring, and are generally developed in the generation which immediately succeeds, but are often transmitted in a dormant state during many generations and are then developed. Their development is supposed to depend on their union with other partially developed cells or gemmules which precede them in the regular course of growth. Why I use the term union, will be seen when we discuss the direct action of pollen on the tissues of the mother-plant. Gemmules are supposed to be thrown off by every cell or unit, not only during the adult state, but during all the stages of development. Lastly, I assume that the gemmules in their dormant state have a mutual affinity for each other, leading to their aggregation either into buds or into the sexual elements. Hence, speaking strictly, it is not the reproductive elements, nor the buds, which generate new organisms, but the cells themselves throughout the body. These assumptions constitute the provisional hypothesis which I have called Pangenesis. (Darwin C., TheVariation of Animals and Plants Under Domestication, 1868) (pp 448-449)

"Soon after Darwin's pangenetic theory was published, Francis Galton designed a series of blood transfusion experiments on differently pigmented rabbits to test its validity. He found no evidence in support of the existence of Darwin's gemmules and the concept of Pangenesis was largely abandoned." … (Yongsheng, 2008) A new perspective on Darwin's Pangenesis. *Cambridge Philosophical Society, 83*, pp 148-149. Retrieved, 2016.

Paley:

… The rational animal does not produce its offspring with more certainty or success than the irrational animal; a man than a quadruped, a quadruped than a bird; nor (for we may follow the gradation through its whole scale) a bird than a plant; nor a plant than a watch, a piece of dead mechanism, would do, upon the supposition which has already so often been repeated. Rationality therefore has nothing to do in the business. If an account must be given of the contrivance [device or machine] which we observe; if it be demanded, whence arose either the contrivance by which the young animal is produced, or the contrivance manifested in the young animal itself, it is not from the reason of the parent that any such account can be drawn. He is the cause of his offspring in the same sense as that in which a gardener is the cause of the tulip which grows upon his parterre, and in no other. We admire the flower; we examine the plant; we perceive the conduciveness [contribution] of many of its parts to their end and office; we observe a provision for its nourishment, growth, protection, and fecundity [fertility]; but we never think of the gardener in all this. We attribute nothing of this to his agency; yet it may still be true, that without the gardener we should not have had the tulip: just so it is with the succession of animals even of the highest order. … (Paley W., Natural Theology or Evidences of the Existence and Attributes of the Deity, 1829, p. 33)

Darwin:

… "The laws governing inheritance are for the most part unknown. No one can say why the same peculiarity in different individuals of the same species, or in different species, is sometimes inherited and sometimes not so; why the child often reverts in certain characters to its grandfather or grandmother or more remote ancestor; why a peculiarity is often transmitted from one sex to both sexes, or to one sex alone, more commonly but not exclusively to the like sex. It is a fact of some importance to us, that peculiarities appearing in the males of our domestic breeds are often transmitted, either exclusively or in a much greater degree, to the males alone. A much more important rule, which I think may be trusted, is that, at whatever period of life a peculiarity first appears, it tends to re-appear in the offspring at a corresponding age, though sometimes earlier. In many cases this could not be otherwise; thus, the inherited peculiarities in the horns of cattle could appear only in the offspring when nearly mature; peculiarities in the silkworm are known to appear at the corresponding caterpillar or cocoon stage. But hereditary diseases and some other facts make me believe that the rule has a wider extension, and that, when there is no apparent reason why a peculiarity should appear at any particular age, yet that it does tend to appear in the offspring at the same period at which it first appeared in the parent. I believe this rule to be of the highest importance in explaining the laws of embryology. These remarks are of course confined to the first which may have acted on the ovules or on the male element; in nearly the same manner as the increased length of the horns in the offspring from a short-horned cow by a long-horned bull, though appearing late in life, is clearly due to the male element" … (Darwin C., 1872, pp. PP 10-11) [13]

Darwin:

… "The whole subject of inheritance is wonderful. When a new character arises, whatever its nature may be, it generally tends to be inherited, at least in a temporary and sometimes in a most persistent manner. What can be more wonderful than that some trifling peculiarity, not primordially attached to the species, should be transmitted through the male or female sexual cells, which are so minute as not to be visible to the naked eye, and afterwards through

---

[13] All excerpts are taken from the sixth edition unless otherwise stated

the incessant changes of a long course of development, undergone either in the womb or in the egg, and ultimately appear in the offspring when mature, or even when quite old, as in the case of certain diseases? Or again, what can be more wonderful than the well-ascertained fact that the minute ovule of a good milking cow will produce a male, from whom a cell, in union with an ovule, will produce a female, and she, when mature, will have large mammary glands, yielding an abundant supply of milk, and even milk of a particular quality? Nevertheless, the real subject of surprise is, as Sir H. Holland has well remarked, not that a character should be inherited, but that any should ever fail to be inherited. In a future chapter, devoted to a hypothesis which I have termed pangenesis, an attempt will be made to show the means by which characters of all kinds are transmitted from generation to generation." ... (Darwin C., Animals and Plants Under Domestication, 1875, p. 448)

The following is an interesting read in comparing what we know today of Mendelian genetics and Darwin's observation. It is obvious that Darwin observed the properties of genetics, and interpreted their causes and effects. It is a fair statement to say that Darwin *observed* while Mendel *counted*. What follows also demonstrates the confusion in labeling species as well as varieties.

Darwin:

HYBRIDS AND MONGRELS COMPARED, INDEPENDENTLY OF THEIR FERTILITY.

"Independently of the question of fertility, the offspring of species and of varieties when crossed may be compared in several other respects. Gärtner, whose strong wish it was to draw a distinct line between species and varieties, could find very few, and, as it seems to me, quite unimportant differences between the so-called hybrid offspring of species, and the so-called mongrel [mixed breed] offspring of varieties. And, on the other hand, they agree most closely in many important respects.

I shall here discuss this subject with extreme brevity. The most important distinction is, that in the first-generation mongrels [offspring of mixed breed] are more variable than hybrids [offspring of pure breed]; but Gärtner admits that hybrids from species which have long been cultivated are often variable in the first generation; and I have myself seen striking instances of this fact. Gärtner further admits that hybrids between very closely allied species are more variable than those from very distinct species; and this shows that the difference in the degree of variability graduates away. When mongrels [already a mix] and the more fertile hybrids are propagated for several generations, an extreme amount of variability in the offspring in both cases is notorious; but some few instances of both hybrids and mongrels long retaining a uniform character could be given. The variability, however, in the successive generations of mongrels is, perhaps, greater than in hybrids.

This greater variability in mongrels than in hybrids does not seem at all surprising. For the parents of mongrels are varieties, and mostly domestic varieties (very few experiments having been tried on natural varieties), and this implies that there has been recent variability, which would often continue and would augment that arising from the act of crossing. The slight variability of hybrids in the first generation, in contrast with that in the succeeding generations, is a curious fact and deserves attention. For it bears on the view which I have taken of one of the causes of ordinary variability; namely, that the reproductive system from being eminently sensitive to changed conditions of life, fails under these circumstances to perform its proper function of producing offspring closely similar in all respects to the parent-form. Now hybrids in the first generation are descended from species (excluding those long-cultivated) which have not had their reproductive systems in any way affected, and they are not variable; but hybrids themselves have their reproductive systems seriously affected, and their descendants are highly variable.

But to return to our comparison of mongrels and hybrids: Gärtner states that mongrels are more liable than hybrids to revert to either parent-form; but this, if it be true, is certainly only a difference in degree. Moreover, Gärtner expressly states that hybrids from long cultivated plants are more subject to reversion than hybrids from species in their natural state; and this probably explains the singular difference in the results arrived at by different observers: thus, Max Wichura doubts whether hybrids ever revert to their parent-forms, and he experimented on uncultivated species of willows; whilst Naudin, on the other hand, insists in the strongest terms on the almost universal tendency to reversion in hybrids, and he experimented chiefly on cultivated plants. ...

Edward Robinson

… When two species are crossed, one has sometimes a prepotent power of impressing its likeness on the hybrid. So, I believe it to be with varieties of plants; and with animals one variety certainly often has this prepotent [predominant] power over another variety. Hybrid plants produced from a reciprocal cross, generally resemble each other closely; and so, it is with mongrel plants from a reciprocal cross. Both hybrids and mongrels can be reduced to either pure parent-form, by repeated crosses in successive generations with either parent. …

… Much stress has been laid by some authors on the supposed fact, that it is only with mongrels that the offspring are not intermediate in character, but closely resemble one of their parents; but this does sometimes occur with hybrids, yet I grant much less frequently than with mongrels. Looking to the cases which I have collected of cross-bred animals closely resembling one parent, the resemblances seem chiefly confined to characters almost monstrous in their nature, and which have suddenly appeared—such as albinism, melanism, deficiency of tail or horns, or additional fingers and toes; and do not relate to characters which have been slowly acquired through selection. A tendency to sudden reversions to the perfect character of either parent would, also, be much more likely to occur with mongrels, which are descended from varieties often suddenly produced and semi-monstrous in character, than with hybrids, which are descended from species slowly and naturally produced. On the whole, I entirely agree with Dr. Prosper Lucas, who, after arranging an enormous body of facts with respect to animals, comes to the conclusion, that the laws of resemblance of the child to its parents are the same, whether the two parents differ little or much from each other, namely, in the union of individuals of the same variety, or of different varieties, or of distinct species.

Independently of the question of fertility and sterility, in all other respects there seems to be a general and close similarity in the offspring of crossed species, and of crossed varieties. If we look at species as having been specially created, and at varieties as having been produced by secondary laws, this similarity would be an astonishing fact. But it harmonises perfectly with the view that there is no essential distinction between species and varieties." … (Darwin C., The Origin of Species by Means of Natural Selection. 6th ed., 1872, pp. 259-263)

It is obvious from the above that Charles Darwin, and others, did not know Mendelian genetics but observed its affects. (If you find the above rather convoluted and difficult to follow, you are not alone.)

DIFFICULTY WITH CLASSIFICATION - THE NATURAL SYSTEM

Darwin:

"From the most remote period in the history of the world organic beings have been found to resemble each other in descending degrees, so that they can be classed in groups under groups. This classification is not arbitrary like the grouping of the stars in constellations. ...

Naturalists, as we have seen, try to arrange the species, genera, and families in each class, on what is called the Natural System. But what is meant by this system? Some authors look at it merely as a scheme for arranging together those living objects which are most alike, and for separating those which are most unlike; or as an artificial method of enunciating, as briefly as possible, general propositions,—that is, by one sentence to give the characters common, for instance, to all mammals, by another those common to all carnivora, by another those common to the dog-genus, and then, by adding a single sentence, a full description is given of each kind of dog. The ingenuity and utility of this system are indisputable. But many naturalists think that something more is meant by the Natural System; they believe that it reveals the plan of the Creator; but unless it be specified whether order in time or space, or both, or what else is meant by the plan of the Creator, it seems to me that nothing is thus added to our knowledge. ... .

Finally, with respect to the comparative value of the various groups of species, such as orders, sub-orders, families, sub-families, and genera, they seem to be, at least at present, almost arbitrary. Several of the best botanists, such as Mr. Bentham and others, have strongly insisted on their arbitrary value. Instances could be given amongst plants and insects, of a group first ranked by practised naturalists as only a genus, and then raised to rank of a sub-family or family; and this has been done, not because further research has detected important structural differences, at first overlooked, but because numerous allied species with slightly different grades of difference, have been subsequently discovered.

All the foregoing rules and aids and difficulties in classification may be explained, if I do not greatly deceive myself, on the view that the Natural System is founded on descent with modification;—that the characters which naturalists consider as showing true affinity between any two or more species, are those which have been inherited from a common parent, all true classification being genealogical;—that community of descent is the hidden bond which naturalists have been unconsciously seeking, and not some unknown plan of creation, or the enunciation of general propositions, and the mere putting together and separating objects more or less alike." ... (Darwin C., 1872, pp. 263-369) (pp 263-369)

Darwin had seemingly no knowledge of genetics or George Mendel. Darwin and Mendel had fundamentally different ideas. Mendel believed that heredity was constant or static while Darwin believed in evolution where inheritance is continually changing Darwin tried to back up his ideas with many false assumptions such as his 'pangenesis hypotheses' and 'the use and disuse of parts' etc.

SIMILAR BUT NOT SAME

The "Systema Naturae" is one of the major works of the Swedish botanist, zoologist and physician Carl Linnaeus (1707–1778). The first edition was published in 1735 and in 1766–1768 Linnaeus published his 12th and last edition.

… "Linnaeus developed his classification of the plant kingdom in an attempt to describe and understand the natural world as a reflection of the logic of God's creation.". …

… "Linnaeus believed in God's creation and that there were no deeper relationships to be expressed. He is frequently quoted to have said. "God created, Linnaeus organized". The classification of animals was more natural. For instance, humans were for the first time placed together with other primates, as Anthropomorpha." (Wikipedia, Systema Naturae)

Today, we are still influenced by Linnaean classification in which he organized plants and animals in a descending hierarchy of categories: kingdom, phylum, class, order, family, genus, and species.

Both Hymans and Apes are in the Animal Kingdom: organisms that can move on their own. Both are in the Chordates Phylum: Animals with the same body plan; a backbone and nerve cords. Both are in the Mammals Class: Chordates with fur or hair and milk glands; the females have milk-secreting organs for feeding the young. Both are in the Primates Order: Mammals with collar bones and grasping fingers. Both are in the Hominids Family: Primates with relatively flat faces and three-dimensional vision. Humans are in the Homo Genus: Hominids with upright posture and large brains. Apes are in the Hylobates Genus: Its name means 'forest walker'. Species can reproduce but cannot interbreed with other species, thus Apes and humans are two distinct species. Homo is a Latin word that means man, or human. The genus that includes modern humans is called Homo, thus "Homo sapiens" are modern humans. Our ancestors had names like "Homo Neanderthal" and "Homo Erectus".

Did Homo sapiens derive from ape like creatures, and are we related to the barnyard cow and chicken? All organic life has much in common but commonality does not mean same. One example is that Homo sapiens normally have forty-six chromosomes, apes have forty-eight. It would be ludicrous to say that an airplane is a modified automobile and an automobile a modified bike, a bicycle a modified tricycle etc. They all have commonality but are vastly different.

Today, doctors can even transplant a pig or calf heart valve for a damaged human heart valve.

(You will always know whether a person has received a pig or calf heart valve because they will have a tendency to say Oink ... Oink, Or Moo ... Moooo...)! If anyone believes this, they will believe anything.

My oldest daughter (ten at the time) was sitting at our computer when I told her some scientists say she could be likened to the computer and no more than a bunch of chemical reactions. My daughter, no doubt, took exception to what I had said and replied, "I am not just a bunch of chemicals. .... I am a girl."

Is my daughter's belief that she is more than chemical reactions true, or can she and we be likened to a computer where our free will is no more than responses to our environment based upon how we are wired and programmed? ... Is a computer not just an extension of a human; a tool in the hands of a craftsperson? A computer cannot reflect back on itself; it cannot reason; it has no free will, or motivation; no goals; no emotion. A computer cannot reproduce itself. In addition, a computer cannot think; it cannot love or hate — garbage in — garbage out.

Computers are obviously man-made. Is it not as obvious to conclude that humans are God-made since organic life is much more than physical existence?

COMPLEXITY OF LIFE

If we examine a watch and its many irreducible parts, do we not determine that it is crafted by humans? The human body is much more complex than any watch. Can we not look at our own bodies and recognize intelligent design?

Our knowledge has increased tremendously over the last one hundred and fifty years since Darwin, Paley and Mendel. Does increased knowledge of organic life further prove Darwinism[14] or the existence of a Creator God? To answer this question, we need to know at least some basic science. Much of the basic science that follows is taught to students in high school science courses.

THE CELL

The basic unit of life is the cell. For a cell to survive as in all life, it has to take in food excrete waste and multiply. There are single celled as well as multi celled organisms; A large organism is comprised of trillions of cells, while an amoeba is a one celled creature. Cells are also in various shapes and sizes often determined by their function; the cells in our body are diversified into over 200 different kinds such as blood, bone, skin, muscle etc. We also have brain cells that can last a lifetime while skin cells are continually replaced. (A dead organism has cells that have stopped working).

The cell can be likened to a small factory. For example, there is a membrane surrounding each cell that functions as a selective barrier controlling substances in and out. In the cell, the cytoplasm is a thick liquid holding all the cell's internal sub-structures (called organelles). Each organelle in the cell works separately and yet each is essential for the function of the whole.

A motor of an automobile could also be likened to a human cell in that they are both irreducible complex [structures with essential independent parts]. I once tore apart and reassembled the engine of an old automobile. I placed

---

[14] Darwinism – A belief that all life including humankind deriving from per existing forms.

the nuts, bolts and small parts in a container and when I put the engine back together, I had a few small parts left over. I could never figure out what these left-over parts were used for or where they went in the engine. However, they could not have been essential because my automobile worked quite well for some time without them. Like a motor of an automobile, the cell also has essential parts that have to be in place and functioning for a cell to work.

If we inspect the complexity of an engine of any automobile (or a watch), would we not say that these are all man-made? The cell and the human body are also very complex. Can we examine the cell, perceive the working of design, and recognize the existence of a Creator God? For many, this is William Paley's old analogy in a new guise, but to others, it is an old truth in a new light

What follows is derived from 'US National Library of Medicine':[15] For further information and diagrams please refer to: (https://ghr.nlm.nih.gov/primer/basics/cell).

WHAT IS A CELL?

"Cells have many parts, each with a different function. Some of these parts, called organelles, are specialized structures that perform certain tasks within the cell.

Cytoplasm

Within cells, the cytoplasm is made up of a jelly-like fluid (called the cytosol) and other structures that surround the nucleus.

Cytoskeleton

The cytoskeleton is a network of long fibers that make up the cell's structural framework. The cytoskeleton has several critical functions, including determining cell shape, participating in cell division, and allowing cells

---

[15] Placed in Public Domain

to move. It also provides a track-like system that directs the movement of organelles and other substances within cells.

Endoplasmic reticulum (ER)

This organelle helps process molecules created by the cell. The endoplasmic reticulum also transports these molecules to their specific destinations either inside or outside the cell.

Golgi apparatus

The Golgi apparatus packages molecules processed by the endoplasmic reticulum to be transported out of the cell.

Lysosomes and peroxisomes

These organelles are the recycling center of the cell. They digest foreign bacteria that invade the cell, rid the cell of toxic substances, and recycle worn-out cell components.

Mitochondria

Mitochondria are complex organelles that convert energy from food into a form that the cell can use. They have their own genetic material, separate from the DNA in the nucleus, and can make copies of themselves.

Nucleus

The nucleus serves as the cell's command center, sending directions to the cell to grow, mature, divide, or die. It also houses DNA (deoxyribonucleic acid), the cell's hereditary material. The nucleus is surrounded by a membrane called the nuclear envelope, which protects the DNA and separates the nucleus from the rest of the cell.

Plasma membrane

The plasma membrane is the outer lining of the cell. It separates the cell from its environment and allows materials to enter and leave the cell.

Edward Robinson

Ribosomes

Ribosomes are organelles that process the cell's genetic instructions to create proteins. These organelles can float freely in the cytoplasm or be connected to the endoplasmic reticulum." (U.S. National library of Medicine)

WHAT IS A CHROMOSOME?

"In the nucleus of each cell, the DNA molecule is packaged into thread-like structures called chromosomes. Each chromosome is made up of DNA tightly coiled many times around proteins called histones that support its structure.

Chromosomes are not visible in the cell's nucleus—not even under a microscope—when the cell is not dividing. However, the DNA that makes up chromosomes becomes more tightly packed during cell division and is then visible under a microscope. Most of what researchers know about chromosomes was learned by observing chromosomes during cell division.

Each chromosome has a constriction point called the centromere, which divides the chromosome into two sections, or "arms." The short arm of the chromosome is labeled the "p arm." The long arm of the chromosome is labeled the "q arm." The location of the centromere on each chromosome gives the chromosome its characteristic shape, and can be used to help describe the location of specific genes. DNA and histone proteins are packaged into structures called chromosomes" ... (Ibid)

WHAT IS DNA?

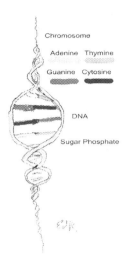

"DNA, or deoxyribonucleic acid, is the hereditary material in humans and almost all other organisms. Nearly every cell in a person's body has the same DNA. Most DNA is located in the cell nucleus (where it is called nuclear DNA), but a small amount of DNA can also be found in the mitochondria (where it is called <u>mitochondrial DNA</u> or mtDNA).

The information in DNA is stored as a code made up of four chemical bases: adenine (A), guanine (G), cytosine (C), and thymine (T). Human DNA consists of about 3 billion bases, and more than 99 percent of those bases are the same in all people. The order, or sequence, of these bases determines the information available for building and maintaining an organism, similar to the way in which letters of the alphabet appear in a certain order to form words and sentences.

DNA bases pair up with each other, A with T and C with G, to form units called base pairs. Each base is also attached to a sugar molecule and a phosphate molecule. Together, a base, sugar, and phosphate are called a nucleotide. Nucleotides are arranged in two long strands that form a spiral called a double helix. The structure of the double helix is somewhat like a ladder, with the base pairs forming the ladder's rungs and the sugar and phosphate molecules forming the vertical sidepieces of the ladder.

An important property of DNA is that it can replicate, or make copies of itself. Each strand of DNA in the double helix can serve as a pattern for duplicating the sequence of bases. This is critical when cells divide because each new cell needs to have an exact copy of the DNA present in the old cell.

DNA is a double helix formed by base pairs attached to a sugar-phosphate backbone." (Ibid)

WHAT IS A GENE?

A gene is the basic physical and functional unit of heredity. Genes, which are made up of DNA, act as instructions to make molecules called proteins. In humans, genes vary in size from a few hundred DNA bases to more than 2 million bases. The Human Genome Project has estimated that humans have between 20,000 and 25,000 genes.

Every person has two copies of each gene, one inherited from each parent. Most genes are the same in all people, but a small number of genes (less than 1 percent of the total) are slightly different between people. Alleles are forms of the same gene with small differences in their sequence of DNA bases. These small differences contribute to each person's unique physical features. Genes are made up of DNA. Each chromosome contains many genes. (Ibid)

HOW DO GENES DIRECT THE PRODUCTION OF PROTEINS?

"Most genes contain the information needed to make functional molecules called proteins. (A few genes produce other molecules that help the cell assemble proteins.) The journey from gene to protein is complex and tightly controlled within each cell. It consists of two major steps: transcription and translation. Together, transcription and translation are known as gene expression.

During the process of transcription, the information stored in a gene's DNA is transferred to a similar molecule called RNA (ribonucleic acid) in the cell nucleus. Both RNA and DNA are made up of a chain of nucleotide bases, but they have slightly different chemical properties. The type of RNA that contains the information for making a protein is called messenger RNA (mRNA) because it carries the information, or message, from the DNA out of the nucleus into the cytoplasm.

Translation, the second step in getting from a gene to a protein, takes place in the cytoplasm. The mRNA interacts with a specialized complex called a ribosome, which "reads" the sequence of mRNA bases. Each sequence of three bases, called a codon, usually codes for one particular amino acid. (Amino acids are the building blocks of proteins.) A type of RNA called transfer RNA (tRNA) assembles the protein, one amino acid at a time. Protein assembly continues until the ribosome encounters a "stop" codon (a sequence of three bases that does not code for an amino acid).

The flow of information from DNA to RNA to proteins is one of the fundamental principles of molecular biology. It is so important that it is sometimes called the "central dogma".

Through the processes of transcription and translation, information from genes is used to make proteins". (U.S. National Library of Medicine)

HOW DO CELLS DIVIDE?

"There are two types of cell division: mitosis and meiosis. Most of the time when people refer to "cell division," they mean mitosis, the process of making new body cells. Meiosis is the type of cell division that creates egg and sperm cells.

Mitosis is a fundamental process for life. During mitosis, a cell duplicates all of its contents, including its chromosomes, and splits to form two identical daughter cells. Because this process is so critical, the steps of mitosis are carefully controlled by a number of genes. When mitosis is not regulated correctly, health problems such as cancer can result.

The other type of cell division, meiosis, ensures that humans have the same number of chromosomes in each generation. It is a two-step process that reduces the chromosome number by half—from 46 to 23—to form sperm and egg cells. When the sperm and egg cells unite at conception, each contributes 23 chromosomes so the resulting embryo will have the usual 46. Meiosis also allows genetic variation through a process of DNA shuffling while the cells are dividing." (Ibid)

RECOMBINATION

As illustrated above, a baby has characteristics derived from both parents. Imagine (a tie like structures representing chromosomes in meiosis) Crossing over is the swapping of genetic material during the formation of egg and sperm cells in meiosis. Chromosomes from each parent align so that similar DNA sequences from the paired chromosomes cross over one another. This shifting of genetic material is an important cause of the genetic variation seen among offspring. Genetic recombination or crossing over assures brothers from the same family are not genetically identical and the same for sisters. It would be a crazy world if all males were genetically identical. You would not be able to tell the difference between your brother from your neighbour who lives next door or across the street. If all women were the same, what a mixed-up world we would live in! With crossing over, an individual acquires more inherited traits from a mother or father, and thus a son in appearance could be more like his mother's side of his family then his dad's and a daughter vice-versa. Etc.

For any permanent hereditary change to occur, a mutation has to happen in the sex cells. A somatic [body] cell mutation after birth would not be passed on to a future generation.

WHAT IS A GENE MUTATION AND HOW DO MUTATIONS OCCUR?

"A gene mutation is a permanent alteration in the DNA sequence that makes up a gene, such that the sequence differs from what is found in most people. Mutations range in size; they can affect anywhere from a single DNA building block (base pair) to a large segment of a chromosome that includes multiple genes.

Gene mutations can be classified in two major ways:

Hereditary mutations are inherited from a parent and are present throughout a person's life in virtually every cell in the body. These mutations are also called germline mutations because they are present in the parent's egg or sperm cells, which are also called germ cells. When an egg and a sperm cell unite, the resulting fertilized egg cell receives DNA from both parents. If this DNA has a mutation, the child that grows from the fertilized egg will have the mutation in each of his or her cells.

Acquired (or somatic) mutations occur at some time during a person's life and are present only in certain cells, not in every cell in the body. These changes can be caused by environmental factors such as ultraviolet radiation from the sun, or can occur if a mistake is made as DNA copies itself during cell division. Acquired mutations in somatic cells (cells other than sperm and egg cells) cannot be passed on to the next generation.

Genetic changes that are described as de novo (new) mutations can be either hereditary somatic. In some cases, the mutation occurs in a person's egg or sperm cell but is not present in any of the person's other cells. In other cases, the mutation occurs in the fertilized egg shortly after the egg and sperm cells unite. (It is often impossible to tell exactly when a de novo mutation happened.) As the fertilized egg divides, each resulting cell in the growing embryo will have the mutation. De novo mutations may explain genetic disorders in which an affected child has a mutation in every cell in the body but the parents do not, and there is no family history of the disorder.

Somatic mutations that happen in a single cell early in embryonic development can lead to a situation called mosaicism. These genetic changes are not present in a parent's egg or sperm cells, or in the fertilized egg, but happen a bit later when the embryo includes several cells. As all the cells divide during growth and development, cells that arise from the cell with the altered gene will have the mutation, while other cells will not. Depending on the mutation and how many cells are affected, mosaicism may or may not cause health problems.

Most disease-causing gene mutations are uncommon in the general population. However, other genetic changes occur more frequently. Genetic alterations that occur in more than 1 percent of the population are called polymorphisms. They are common enough to be considered a normal variation in the DNA. Polymorphisms are responsible for many of the normal differences between people such as eye color, hair color, and blood type. Although many polymorphisms have no negative effects on a person's health, some of these variations may influence the risk of developing certain disorders". (U.S. National Library of Medicine, 2016)

Mutations do occur. The question is, do mutations create change in the right direction and to the extent that new species or 'kinds' were created from existing species such as people from ape-like creatures? (Are we really related to the common barnyard pig?) [If you call your brother a pig, you would have to be a pig as well to be telling the truth].

A Darwinian model of change is a slow step-by-step process including the destruction of the old in favour of the new. Mendelian Genetic change does not really work this way. We already knew that crossing a variety with a different variety of the same species may create a novel variety. This process of producing this novel variety can be repeated if the original varieties still exist. There are also some examples where creatures cross with difficulty, such as the horse and zebra. However, they both belong to the same 'kind' the horse family.

GENES CAN BE TURNED ON AND OFF

"Each cell expresses, or turns on, only a fraction of its genes. The rest of the genes are repressed, or turned off. The process of turning genes on and off is known as gene regulation. Gene regulation is an important part of normal development. Genes are turned on and off in different patterns during development to make a brain cell look and act different from a liver cell or a muscle cell, for example. Gene regulation also allows cells to react quickly to changes in their environments. Although we know that the regulation of genes is critical for life, this complex process is not yet fully understood.

Gene regulation can occur at any point during gene expression, but most commonly occurs at the level of transcription (when the information in a gene's DNA is transferred to mRNA). Signals from the environment or from other cells activate proteins called transcription factors. These proteins bind to regulatory regions of a gene and increase or decrease the level of transcription. By controlling the level of transcription, this process can determine the amount of protein product that is made by a gene at any given time." (U.S. National Library of Medicine, 2016)

Amazing Genes: Our bodies are created and controlled by genes. In addition, just as we turn on and off light switches or turn a tap to control the water flow in our homes, genes can have similar biological functions. Doesn't all this order need an organizer? How can these things be without a creator God?

WHAT ARE THE HOMEOBOX GENES?

"Homeobox genes are a large family of similar genes that direct the formation of many body structures during early embryonic development. In humans, the homeobox gene family contains an estimated 235 functional genes and 65 pseudogenes (structurally similar genes that do not provide instructions for making proteins). Homeobox genes are present on every human chromosome, and they often appear in clusters. Many classes and subfamilies of homeobox genes have been described, although these groupings are used inconsistently.

Homeobox genes contain a particular DNA sequence that provides instructions for making a string of 60 protein building blocks (amino acids) known as the homeodomain. Most homeodomain-containing proteins act as transcription factors, which means they bind to and control the activity of other genes. The homeodomain is the part of the protein that attaches (binds) to specific regulatory regions of the target genes.

Genes in the homeobox family are involved in a wide range of critical activities during development. These activities include directing the formation of limbs and organs along the anterior-posterior axis (the imaginary line that runs from head to tail in animals) and regulating the process by which cells mature to carry out specific functions (differentiation). Some homeobox genes act as tumor suppressors, which means they help prevent cells from growing and dividing too rapidly or in an uncontrolled way.

Because homeobox genes have so many important functions, mutations in these genes are responsible for a variety of developmental disorders. For example, mutations in the HOX group of homeobox genes typically cause limb malformations. Changes in PAX homeobox genes often result in eye disorders, and changes in MSX homeobox genes cause abnormal head, face, and tooth development. Additionally, increased or decreased activity of certain homeobox genes has been associated with several forms of cancer later in life." (U.S. National Library of Medicine, 2012)

"It is striking that several of the genes of the two *Drosophila* homeotic-gene clusters (ANT-C and BX-C) have homologues within the mouse (and human) genomes, and the order of the homologues is retained within the gene clusters in both the insects and mammals. This observation suggests that the ancestor of arthropods and vertebrates … must have possessed a similar cluster of genes that determined its body plan during embryonic development." (Gerald Karp, 1996, p. 557)

The homeobox Genes do not determine the segment themselves but control their placement. Amazingly, especially in vertebrates, the genes on the chromosome are in similar sequence as their expression –head to toe alignment. This amazing order - does it not indicate the existence of a Creator God? And, couldn't this same God create species independently on a common template? A great painter and sculptor, like Michelangelo for example, would he not use the same style and type of materials for his many masterpieces?

IRREDUCIBLE COMPLEXITY

To a creationist, God built all life on a similar template and if we admit that complexity displays a designer, and if this designer is the God of the Judaic Christian bible, then God created Homo sapiens as a distinct creature from the dust of the ground.

Humans have unique features which are additional credence for the existence of an Intelligent Creator God. With Darwinian evolution, our ancestors could have had fur which slowly changed by accident to conveniently placed eyebrows lashes and hair on our heads. How can all this happen by chance?

What follows is so obvious and yet its application so profound:

A bicycle has essential parts that work independently for the function of the whole bike. For example, the frame, handlebars, spokes, wheels, chain, gears, peddles, seat, etc. and to make the bicycle work, we add a rider. Take away any essential part and the entire structure does not function.

We can add non-essential parts such as a horn and light, but any rider knows that a lost or broken chain renders a bicycle functionless. In addition, many independent and essential parts could have been made in another place from where the bicycle has been assembled.

A bike also comprises order – most parts have to be assembled appropriately or a bicycle would be useless for its function of transporting a rider. For example, the seat and handlebars cannot be interchanged. A bike is also assembled with a specific number of parts. It has a front and back wheel – not six or eight. It has one set of front spokes and handlebars, one chain etc... Is it not ludicrous to say that a bicycle (or a watch) (or a cell) (or a human) came together by chance through time with all essential parts functioning in proper order?

A bike assembly has parallels in nature. Genetics controls what an organism becomes. Just as a bicycle is assembled in a factory, we were assembled within our mother's womb. We were formed with a certain number of necessary parts arranged in a practical order. For example, our ribs are arranged in a given pattern. Our head is on one end of our body with our buttocks on the other. We have a specified number of parts placed in an optimum position, such as two legs for walking – not one, three, or more. We have only two hands with fingers and thumbs for grasping. There are exceptions to the rule, but these exceptions highlight the norm. Can all this order be created by chance over time in a Darwinian step-by-step fashion?

Can inanimate objects come together and form a functional unit? With human-made structures, there would be very little or no useless parts added. With biological structures created by chance, there could be as many, if not more, non-functional or useless parts as useful. If we examine the cell or any organism of the human body this is not so. Therefore, does all this not add credence for the existence of a Creator?

In summary: As well as having the cell as the basic unit of life, many animals have analogous genes. It is interesting that humans and primates are alike in appearance and structure. To a Darwinian evolutionist, this is additional indication that all life has a common origin, but there are vast differences as well. For example, humans walk upright while apes walk on all fours and for a human to walk upright requires the necessary inherited instincts and powerful hip muscles that other primates lack. Does not all this complexity combined with human intelligence demonstrate Intelligent Design? I have yet to see an ape driving an automobile on a busy highway, or an ape-like creature driving an airplane!

SEX - WHERE ACQUIRED?

One day, while passing my wife when she was sweeping the stairs, she jokingly said, "what more could you ask for in a wife that takes such good care of you?"

Not to be outdone I replied, "Well, I will have to advertise in Kijiji — that's all."

Then I got thinking; what kind of advertisement could this be? Why settle for one wife when I could advertise for five. This ad might read as follows: "Man seeking five wives —only those with the specified qualifications may apply. One wife for my social needs - accompany me to all necessary social events; a second for domestic needs - clean the house and all my messes; a third for psychological needs - laugh at all my jokes, even if they are not funny; a fourth - to massage all my little aches and pains, and last but not least, a fifth - to fulfill all my sexual desires. Then I got thinking - Letty is correct. Who would want five wives? Better still, who in their right mind would answer such a silly ad?

(I have to admit, that my wife Letty is an amazing lady. I am very blessed and would not trade her for any number of others.)

For some Christians our biological differences are another proof of the existence of a creator God. (Male and female He created them.) (Genesis 1:27)

Paley:

"But relation perhaps is never so striking, as when it subsists, not between different parts of the same thing, but between different things. The relation between a lock and a key is more obvious than it is between different parts of the lock. A bow was designed for an arrow, and an arrow for a bow; and the design is more evident for their being separate implements. Nor do the works of the Deity want this clearest species of relation. The *sexes* are manifestly made for each other They form the grand relation of animated nature universal, organic, mechanical; subsisting like the clearest relations of art, in different individuals: unequivocal, inexplicable without design. So much so, that were every other proof of contrivance in nature dubious or obscure, this alone would be sufficient. The example is complete. Nothing is wanting to the argument. I see no way whatever of getting over it." (Paley W., 1829, p. 156)

What came first—the chicken or egg?

One day my daughter Rachel was heartily laughing as she recalled the story of what had happened at a friend's place and school.

Rachel was invited for lunch to her friend Helen's[16], and Helen's uncle John was there as well. Helen is a vegetarian, and John asked her whether she eats eggs. Helen answered, "yes – because an egg is not a chick."

John asked, "Why is it not a chick?"

She answered, "Because the rooster has to sit on the egg before it becomes a chick."

Everyone laughed except Helen who then said, "I know what I am talking about. The rooster has to sit on the egg before it becomes a chick."

Rachel replied "No, you just don't get it, do you?"

When they arrived back at school, Rachel told her other friends who all laughed, except for Ann. Then they turned to Ann and said, "you just don't get it either, do you?" Ann then said that it was Tim who told them that a rooster has to sit on the egg to become a chick.

The other girls responded, "Tim doesn't know anything"!

And now they all know — a rooster has to sit on a hen — for an egg to become a chick.

Male and female; we are so different and yet the same species. Sex is necessary for our very existence and if we consider just some of what is essential for procreation, would it not confirm some kind of Master Planner? What follows is so obvious, and yet it can be used as further proof of the existence of a designer God.

---

[16] Not her real name

We have specialized organs for reproduction and without sex there is no future generation. For the male, he has to produce sperm in specialized organs called—testes. And for fertilization, the sperm has to be delivered to the reproductive tract of the female. For the female, she has to produce eggs, receive the sperm, and for mammals, the production of milk is both gender and time specific. Also, for both sexes the age or timing of sexual maturity is appropriately governed. The origin of sex by means of Darwinian evolution is highly problematic because sex has to be in existence in the first place. Without unique sexual characteristics we would not even be here.

A good question often asked is why do men have nipples? The answer to that question seems to be that we are similar at the beginning and later change with the production of hormones, especially estrogen and testosterone. Keep in mind that what we are to become "male" or "female" is determined at fertilization before the development of nipples.

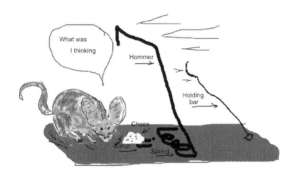

THE MOUSETRAP

Darwin from (Origin of Species): "If it could be demonstrated that any complex organ existed which could not possibly have been formed by numerous, successive, slight modifications, my theory would absolutely break down."

For many, what follows is William Paley's old analogy in a new guise, and to others, it is an old truth in a new light.

"Irreducible-complexity" is a term used in Michael Behe's book "Darwin's *Black Box*" (1996). The principal that Behe makes is that many systems with irreducible complexity needs all their parts in place in order to function. Since Darwin's theory is built on numerous successive slight modifications, his theory is problematic.

Michael J. Behe uses a mousetrap analogy in his book, "Darwin's *Black Box*":

"The first step in determining irreducible complexity is to specify both the function of the system and all system components. An irreducible complex object will be composed of several parts, all of which contribute to the function. To avoid the problems encountered with extremely complex objects (such as eyes, beetles, or other multicellular biological systems) I will begin with a simply Mechanical example: the humble mousetrap."[17] ... (Behe, 1996, p. 42)

Michal Behe's mousetrap and its irreducible parts are as follows: the flat board, metal hammer, a spring, a catch, a metal bar that connects to the catch.

... "The second step in determining if a system is irreducible complex is to ask if all the components are required for its function. In this example the answer is clearly yes. ... If the hammer were gone, the mouse could dance all night on the platform without becoming pinned to the wooden base." ... (ibid) 42

Michael Behe's mousetrap analogy has its critics. For example, Professor Kenneth R Miller writes, "Behe's evidence that biochemical pathways are intelligently designed is that Behe can't imagine how they could function without all of their parts, but given how easy it is to reduce the complexity of a mousetrap, I'm not convinced." ... (http://udel.edu/~mcdonald/oldmousetrap.html)

Michael Behe in his article, *"A Mousetrap Defended: Response to Critics"* writes:

..." Professor McDonald started with a complete mousetrap and then showed ones with fewer parts. I will reverse that order, start with his simplest trap, and show the steps that would be necessary to convert it into the next more complex trap in his series. That, after all, is the way Darwinian evolution would have to work. If we are to picture this as a Darwinian process, then

---

[17] Mousetrap image and references to Behe are used by permission.

each separate adjustment must count as a "mutation." If several separate mutations have to occur before we go from one functional trap to the next, then a Darwinian process is effectively ruled out, because the probability of getting multiple unselected mutations that eventually lead to a specific complex structure is prohibitive." … (Behe, 2000)

Behe's model of a mousetrap works very well. (I have used this model myself). The individual parts of a mousetrap can be used for other purposes, but one would not go to a hardware store and buy pieces of wire or springs to do the job of a fully assembled mousetrap. Behe could have used another mousetrap model or other mechanical structures for his analogy, but he picked the simple mousetrap as he explains:

… "To avoid the problems encountered with extremely complex objects (such as eyes, beetles, or other multicellular biological systems) I will begin with a simple mechanical example: The humble mousetrap. … (ibid 42)

Another reality of a Darwinian process is that it is a slow step-by-step progression where the most, if not all, old systems are replaced by new and improved. Where is the evidence for the existence and eventual death of thousands or millions of steps needed for this theory to be correct?

THE EYE

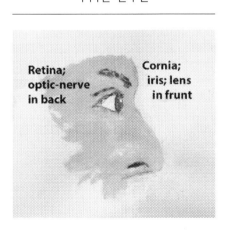

This model of a mousetrap analogy can have many parallels in nature. For example, I went to get my eyes checked for new glasses. The eye specialist told me we see with our brain. 'Yes! We see with our brain', and not just with our eyes. Our eyeballs are only one part of a complex system. There are many component parts working as a unit for one purpose – sight. Described simplistically, to see properly we need the eyeballs to receive the information, the optic nerve delivers this information to the brain, and the brain processes it. Impaired sight is where one or many independent parts are not working properly. Take away the optic nerve, for example, and we are blind.

Also, why do we have two eyes; not one; not three or more? With two eyes, the brain can decipher distance since triangulation between two eyes and the object viewed changes with distance. Thus, we see in 3D. Is this reality not additional proof of a creator designer God?

Paley:

"Relation of parts to one another accompanies us throughout the whole animal economy. Can any relation be more simple, yet more convincing, than this, that the eyes are so placed as to look in the direction in which the legs move and the hands work? It might have happened very differently if it had been left to chance. There were at least three-quarters of the compass out of four to have erred in. Any considerable alteration in the position of the eye, or the figure of the joints, would have disturbed the line, and destroyed the alliance between the sense and the limbs." (Paley W., Natural Theology or Evidences of the Existence and Attributes of the Deity, 1829, p. 156)

Darwin:

… "To suppose that the eye with all its inimitable contrivances for adjusting the focus to different distances, for admitting different amounts of light, and for the correction of spherical and chromatic aberration, could have been formed by natural selection seems, I freely confess, absurd in the highest degree." … (Darwin C., 1872, p. 143)

Paley:

… "Thus, in comparing the eyes of different kinds of animals, we see, in their resemblances and distinctions, one general plan laid down, and that plan varied with the varying exigencies [requirements] to which it is to be applied.

There is one property, however, common, I believe, to all eyes, at least to all which have been examined, namely, that the optic nerve enters the bottom of the eye, not in the centre or middle, but a little on one side; not in the point where the axis of the eye meets the retina, but between that point and the nose. The difference which this makes is, that no part of an object is unperceived by both eyes at the same time.

In considering vision as achieved by the means of an image formed at the bottom of the eye, we can never reflect without wonder upon the smallness, yet correctness, of the picture, the subtilty of the touch, the fineness of the lines. A landscape of five or six square leagues is brought into a space of half an inch diameter; yet the multitude of objects which it contains, are all preserved; are all discriminated in their magnitudes, positions, figures, colors. The prospect from Hampstead-hill is compressed into the compass of a sixpence [small British coin], yet circumstantially represented. A stage-coach, travelling at its ordinary speed for half an hour, passes, in the eye, only over one-twelfth of an inch, yet is this change of place in the image distinctly perceived throughout its whole progress; for it is only by means of that perception that the motion of the coach itself is made sensible to the eye. If anything can abate our admiration of the smallness of the visual tablet compared with the extent of vision, it is a reflection, which the view of nature leads us, every hour, to make, viz. that in the hands of the Creator, great and little are nothing." (Paley W., pp. 21-22)

WALKING

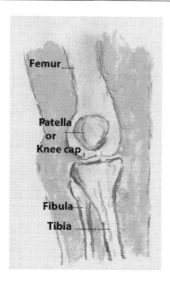

For most of us, walking from one step to another seems to happen automatically. However, walking is a very irreducible complex system. For example, we need at least two legs for walking, each consist of a femur which is the upper bone that connects to the Pelvic girdle, the patella or knee cap, the tibia and fibula which or lower bones and also the bones of the ankle and foot. Also, our brain controls our balance which is essential for walking upright.

Because walking is a very irreducible complex system, remove any essential component and we cannot walk. The knee cap and its muscles are ideally located where the joints bend. Take away the knee cap and walking, as we know it, is impossible. I have a friend who fell on a hard floor and shattered her kneecap — she could not walk for six months.

It is also incredible how the body heals itself. For some of us, if we cut ourselves shaving, we bleed and create a terrible mess, but within minutes the bleeding stops, and in a few days the nick we created on our face has completely healed without a trace. How can this be? Did this ability to heal evolve, or is it all part of a master plan from a Creator God?

TEETH

What are the origins of teeth, 'accidental' or by 'design'?

Darwin:

… "Aristotle, in his 'Physicae Auscultationes' (lib. 2, cap. 8, s. 2), after remarking that rain does not fall in order to make the corn grow, any more than it falls to spoil the farmer's corn when threshed out of doors, applies the same argument to organisation; and adds (as translated by Mr. Clair Grece, who first pointed out the passage to me), "So what hinders the different parts [of the body] from having this merely accidental relation in nature? As the teeth, for example, grow by necessity, the front ones sharp, adapted for dividing, and the grinders flat, and serviceable for masticating the food; since they were not made for the sake of this, but it was the result of accident. And in like manner as to the other parts in which there appears to exist an adaptation to an end. Wheresoever, therefore, all things together (that is all the parts of one whole) happened like as if they were made for the sake of something, these were preserved, having been appropriately constituted by an internal spontaneity; and whatsoever things were not thus constituted, perished, and still perish." We here see the principle of natural selection shadowed forth, but how little Aristotle fully comprehended the principle, is shown by his remarks on the formation of the teeth." … (Darwin C., 1872, p. XV)

By stating that ordinary acts of rain and different parts of the body are accidental denies the sovereignty of God over His creation.

Our teeth are only one part of an organism called the human body. What is the statically possibility of our teeth being created by chance in conjunction with all our other body part functioning as a unit?

Paley:

"I can hardly imagine to myself a more distinguishing mark and consequently [as a result] a more certain proof of design, than preparation, i. e. the providing of things beforehand which are not to be used until a considerable time afterwards; for this implies a contemplation of the future, which belongs only to intelligence. ...

The human teeth afford an instance, not only of prospective [future] contrivance [device], but of the completion of the contrivance being designedly suspended...They are formed within the gums, and there they stop: the fact being, that their farther advance to maturity would not only be useless to the new-born animal, but extremely in its way; as it is evident that the act *of sucking,* by which it is for some time to be nourished, will be performed with more ease both to the nurse and to the infant, whilst the inside of the mouth, and edges of the gums, are smooth and soft, than if set with hard pointed bones. By the time they are wanted, the teeth are ready. They have been lodged within the gums for some months past, but detained as it were in their sockets, so long as their farther protrusion would interfere with the office to which the mouth is destined. Nature, namely, that intelligence which was employed in creation, looked beyond the first year of the infant's life; yet, whilst she was providing for functions which were after that term to become necessary, was careful not to incommode those which preceded them. What renders it more probable that this is the effect of design, is, that the teeth are imperfect, whilst all other parts of the mouth are perfect. The lips are perfect, the tongue is perfect; the cheeks, the jaws, the palate, the pharynx, the larynx, are all perfect. The teeth alone are not so. This is the fact with respect to the human mouth: the fact also is, that the parts above enumerated are called into use from the beginning; whereas the teeth would be only so many obstacles and annoyances, if they were there. When a contrary order is necessary, a contrary order prevails. In the worm of the beetle, as hatched from the egg, the teeth are the first things which arrive at perfection. The insect begins to gnaw as soon as it escapes from the shell, though its other parts be only gradually advancing to their maturity.

What has been observed of the teeth is true of the *horns* of animals, and for the same reason. The horn of a calf or a lamb does not bud, or at least does not sprout to any considerable length, until the animal be capable of browsing upon its pasture; because such a substance upon the forehead of the young animal, would very much incommode the teat of the dam in the office of giving suck.

But in the case of the teeth, of the human teeth, at least the prospective contrivance looks still farther. A succession of crops is provided, and provided from the beginning; a second tier being originally formed beneath the first, which do not come into use till several years afterwards. And this double or suppletory provision meets a difficulty in the mechanism of the mouth, which would have appeared almost insurmountable. The expansion of the jaw (the consequence of the proportionable growth of the animal, and of its skull,) necessarily separates the teeth of the first set, however compactly disposed, to a distance from one another, which would be very inconvenient. In due time, therefore, i. e. when the jaw has attained a great part of Its dimensions, a new set of teeth springs up (loosening and pushing out the old ones before them,) more exactly fitted to the space which they are to occupy, and rising also in such close ranks, as to allow for any extension of line which the subsequent enlargement of the head may occasion." (Paley W., 1829, pp. 146-148)

The last teeth to develop in the human jaw are the wisdom teeth. They usually develop at around 16 to 18 years when our jaws are larger. One of my daughter's wisdom teeth was coming in before her sixteenth birthday (She must have been very wise!)

Can the existence of wisdom teeth be explained through Darwinian evolution where they first arrive by chance and develop in a step by step fashion over time? Could it be that all those who didn't have these "wise teeth" died out because they lived with a disadvantage, or isn't it obvious that our teeth are irreducible complex and part of an irreducible complex structure called the human body - indicating intelligent Design?

It is also thought-provoking that we have an upper and lower set of teeth with fount teeth for cutting and back teeth grinding together to process our food. This is all so very organized. ... How can this be without a Designer?

HUMAN BRAIN

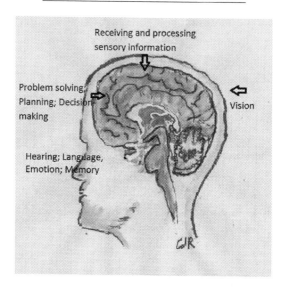

Our brains - amazingly well organized, and quite possibly the most complex system found in nature. Our heads and brains are symmetrical left to right, while many of the brain's functions are asymmetrical. How can this be explained by chance without a Creator God?

"The association areas of the cerebral cortex, unlike the primary motor and sensory areas, are not bilaterally symmetric; each side of the brain controls different functions. Speech, language, and calculation, for example, are centered in the left hemisphere, while the right hemisphere controls artistic ability and spatial perception." ... (Campbell, p. 1009)

With left-handed people, this order may be reversed.

HEARING

For hearing, as with our sight, we have two ears, not one, three, or more. Our brains decipher information given to it through the hearing nerves such as loudness and frequency. Our brains also indicate direction and distance through triangulation. Yes, we have 3D sound because our ears are placed on both sides of our heads. Thus, through triangulation our brain determines direction and distance.

I know firsthand that our brains use our two ears to determine direction. I am quite deaf and I have two hearing aids with approximately equal strength. When I use only one hearing aid, sound is amplified for one ear only and I find it difficult to determine where the sound is coming from. With two hearing aids, I can easily distinguish direction.

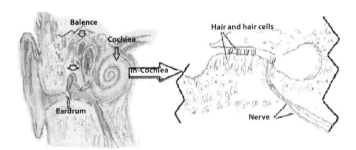

Our hearing is a very irreducible complex system. For hearing, there is the outer ear (which we see), the auditory canal, and the eardrum. From the eardrum, sound is transmitted to the inner ear that consists of three small bones (hammer, anvil, and stapes). From here, sound is transferred to the cochlea of the inner ear. The cochlea is a coiled snail-like structure containing two chambers called the vestibular and tympanic canals. These chambers are separated by a smaller cochlear-duct. Within this smaller duct area are tiny hairs of different length. Volume and pitch are transmitted through the movement of these hairs. Cells then transmit information through the auditory nerves to the brain where it is deciphered as sound. It is thought-provoking that we have many other hair follicles throughout our body and not one transmits sound. To hear, we need our ears with all essential parts functioning correctly; If not, our hearing is impaired, or we are deaf.

Paley:

… "The ear, it is probable, is no less artificially and mechanically adapted to its office than the eye. But we know less about it: we do not so well understand the action, the use, or the mutual dependency of its internal parts. Its general form, however, both external and internal, is sufficient to show that it is an instrument adapted to the reception of sound; that is to say, already knowing that sound consists in pulses of the air, we perceive, in the structure of the ear, a suitableness to receive impressions from this species of action, and to propagate these impressions to the brain. For of what does this structure consist? ...

... This assemblage of connected parts constitutes together an apparatus, plainly enough relative to the transmission of sound, or of the impulses received from sound, and only to be lamented in not being better understood." (Paley, Natural Theology or Evidences of the existence and Attributes of the Deity, 1829, pp. 26-27)

Our bodies comprise many complex parts (each part functioning for the purpose of the whole organism). If we combine sight, walking, hearing, chewing, and the great organization of our brain as just a small sample of the complexity of a whole body, does this not indicate that there must be an organizer, and this organizer must stand as a Creator God?

LIFE WAS AND IS CHANGING

The fossil evidence (meager as it is) shows that deviation is a normal process. There is plenty of evidence confirming that varieties change; crossing of existing varieties continually creates new varieties. In meiosis, the process of crossing over creates change. A mutation also creates change. And also, species and varieties are becoming extinct – all the time.

Scientists are still looking for missing links.

To find fossils one has to know where to look. My father was a farmer and whenever an animal died, for whatever reason, they were moved to a hollow area quite a distance away from our home and farm buildings. They were left to the maggots and the elements. The bones would be the last to go, but it would not take long before the whole animal would disappear without a trace.

… "The rarity of direct traces of life in the oldest rocks is partly due to the fact that the primitive animals would be of delicate build, but it must also be remembered that the ancient rocks have been profoundly and repeatedly changed by pressure and heat, so that the traces which did exist would be very liable to obliteration." … (Thomson A. J., 1922, p. 91)

… "Only a minute fraction of the organisms living at any one time are preserved as fossils… During the formation of sedimentary rocks, dead organisms are sometimes washed down along with inorganic debris, such as mud or sand, and eventually reach the bottom of some pond, lake, or the ocean itself. Occasionally, dead organisms are covered by debris accumulated by wind. In exceptional circumstances, fossils may be preserved in an organic substance, such as tar … However, many organisms do not live in places where their remains are likely to be preserved in sedimentary rocks." … (Raven @ Johnson, 1992, p. 425)

Scientists are still looking for missing links (apes to human etc.). There is tremendous excitement when some scientists announce that they have found a previously unknown species or what they refer to as a possible missing link but often it is nothing more than just another peculiar creature created by God.

Edward Robinson

ON THE IMPERFECTION OF THE GEOLOGICAL RECORD

Darwin:

... "The main cause, however, of innumerable intermediate links not now occurring everywhere throughout nature, depends on the very process of natural selection, through which new varieties continually take the places of and supplant their parent-forms. But just in proportion as this process of extermination has acted on an enormous scale, so must the number of intermediate varieties, which have formerly existed, be truly enormous. Why then is not every geological formation and every stratum full of such intermediate links? Geology assuredly does not reveal any such finely-graduated organic chain; and this, perhaps, is the most obvious and serious objection which can be urged against the theory. The explanation lies, as I believe, in the extreme imperfection of the geological record. ...

... By the theory of natural selection all living species have been connected with the parent-species of each genus [type], by differences not greater than we see between the natural and domestic varieties of the same species at the present day; and these parent-species, now generally extinct, have in their turn been similarly connected with more ancient forms; and so on backwards, always converging to the common ancestor of each great class. So that the number of intermediate and transitional links, between all living and extinct species, must have been inconceivably great. But assuredly, if this theory be true, such have lived upon the earth. ...

Now let us turn to our richest geological museums, and what a paltry display we behold! That our collections are imperfect is admitted by every one. The remark of that admirable palaeontologist, Edward Forbes, should never be forgotten, namely, that very many fossil species are known and named from single and often broken specimens, or from a few specimens collected on some one spot. Only a small portion of the surface of the earth has been geologically explored, and no part with sufficient care, as the important discoveries made every year in Europe prove. No organism wholly soft can be preserved. Shells and bones decay and disappear when left on the bottom of the sea, where sediment is not accumulating. We probably take a quite erroneous view, when we assume that sediment is being deposited over nearly the whole bed of the sea, at a rate sufficiently quick to embed and preserve fossil remains. Throughout an enormously large proportion of the ocean, the bright blue tint of the water bespeaks its purity. The many cases on record of a formation conformably covered, after an immense interval of time, by another and later formation, without the underlying bed having suffered in the interval any wear and tear, seem explicable only on the view of the bottom of the sea not rarely lying for ages in an unaltered condition. The remains which do become embedded, if in sand or gravel, will, when the beds are upraised, generally be dissolved by the percolation of rain-water charged with carbonic acid. Some of the many kinds of animals which live on the beach between high and low water mark seem to be rarely preserved. For instance, the several species of the Chthamalinae (a sub-family of sessile cirripedes) coat the rocks all over the world in infinite numbers: they are all strictly littoral, with the exception of a single Mediterranean species, which inhabits deep water, and this has been found fossil in Sicily, whereas not one other species has hitherto been found in any tertiary formation: yet it is known that the genus Chthamalus existed during the Chalk period. Lastly, many great deposits requiring a vast length of time for their accumulation, are entirely destitute of organic remains, without our being able to assign any reason: one of the most striking instances is that of the Flysch formation, which consists of shale and sandstone, several thousand, occasionally even six thousand feet, in thickness, and extending for at least 300 miles from Vienna to Switzerland; and although this great mass has been most carefully searched, no fossils, except a few vegetable remains, have been found." … (Darwin C., 1872, pp. 264-271)

It is observable even from the meager fossil record that change takes place and change is still happening today. Varieties crossing with varieties create change. This type of change is never to the extent where one species develops into an entirely different species [kind]. Some examples are as follows:

Edward Robinson

Lions:

taken at Lion Safari Cambridge Canada

Today we have lions, tigers, and all kinds of domestic cats. It is obvious that over time the cat varieties have changed so drastically that some cannot even mate with other cat varieties.

A liger is a hybrid of a male lion and a female tiger. Many may classify the liger as a new species because they cannot interbreed with other cats, but the lion, tiger and liger are all the same "kind"- they are all cats. The consequence of this cross if repeated is very consistent in creating a liger every time. A liger can have characteristics from either or both parents, but one noticeable exception is that a liger is much larger than its parentage, and the male ligers are known to be sterile. The liger can be used as an example of a tremendous change, but not in a Darwinian step-by step fashion over time.

Example of extinction in lions and tigers are as follows: Cape Lion—Extinct since the 1860's, the Bali Tiger — 1930's or 1940's, the Caspian Tiger—1950's, the Javan Tiger—1970's etc.

Dogs:

All doges are believed to be decedent from wolves. With a wolf-dog combination, the more wolf in the mix, the more wild.

Pure-bread dogs can remain constant from generation to generation, but other dog breeds and varieties are created to fit the needs and whims of owners. An example of controlled breeding for a specific result is when Russian scientists creating a super sniffer dog to help in the fight against criminals and especially drug smugglers.

"The Sulimov dog … is a Russian jackal-dog hybrid originating from an initial hybrid between two Lapponian Herders and two Turkmen golden jackals." … (Sulimov dog)

The Sulimov dog is an example of selective breeding by crossing existing varieties to create a new novel variety. The Sulimov dog didn't come into existence by chance through Darwinian evolution. The creation of the Sulimov dog was designed. And if the original breeds are still in existence, a repeat in crossing the same varieties would reproduce the same result 'the Sulimov dog'. If any or all of the original varieties become extinct, then the process could not be repeated with the same outcome.

Some other examples of creation are *Affenhuahua*—a Chihuahua and Affenpinscher cross, *Aussie Siberian*—Siberian husky and Australian shepherd cross, Yorwich—Yorkshire terrier and Norwich Terrier cross etc. These are a few out of hundreds and non are created in a slow step by step Darwinian fashion over immense time. An example of a dog variety that went extinct because it was no longer used or desirable is the 'Turnspit Dog'.

Turnspit Dog:

… "The Turnspit Dog was a short-legged, long-bodied dog bred to run on a wheel, called a turnspit or dog wheel, to turn meat. The type is now extinct. It is mentioned in *Of English Dogs* in 1576 under the name *Turnespete*. Rev. W. Bingley's *Memoirs of British Quadrupeds (1809)* also talks of a dog employed to help chefs and cooks. It is also known as the Kitchen Dog, the Cooking Dog, the Underdog and the *Vernepator*." … (Wikipedia, 2012)

John George Wood:

"Just as the invention of the spinning jenny abolished the use of distaff and wheel, which were formerly the occupants of every well-ordained English cottage, so the invention of automaton roasting-jacks has destroyed the occupation of the Turnspit Dog, and by degrees has almost annihilated its very existence. Here and there a solitary Turnspit may be seen, just as a spinning-wheel or a distaff may be seen in a few isolated cottages; but both the Dog and the implement are exceptions to the general rule, and are only worthy of notice as being curious relics of a bygone time.

In former days, and even within the remembrance of the present generation, the task of roasting a joint of meat or a fowl was a comparatively serious one, and required the constant attendance of the cook, in order to prevent the meat from being spoiled by the unequal action of the fire. The smoke-jack, as it was rather improperly termed—inasmuch as it was turned, not by the smoke, but by the heated air that rushed up the chimney—was a great improvement, because the spit revolved at a rate that corresponded with the heat of the fire.

So complicated an apparatus, however, could not be applied to all chimneys, or in all localities, and therefore the services of the Turnspit Dog were brought into requisition. At one extremity of the spit was fastened a large circular box, or hollow wheel, something like the wire wheels which are so often appended to squirrel-cages; and in this wheel the Dog was accustomed to perform its daily task, by keeping it continually working. As the labor would be too great for a single Dog, it was usual to keep at least two animals for the purpose, and to make them relieve each other at regular intervals. The dogs were quite able to appreciate the lapse of time, and, if not relieved from their toils at the proper hour, would leap out of the wheel without orders, and force their companions to take their place, and complete their portion of the daily toil.

There are one or two varieties of this Dog, but the true turnspit breed is now nearly extinct in this country. On the continent, the spits are still turned by canine labor in some localities; but the owners of spit and Dog are not particular about the genealogy of the animal, and press into service any kind of Dog, provided that it is adequately small, and sufficiently amenable to authority." (Wood, 1853)

There are countless other dog breeds and varieties that are new existent. One example is the *Welsh Hillman*, an ancient Welsh breed or type of herding dog, used for herding and droving. The breed is thought to have become extinct around 1990.

As we all know, many current dog varieties can be the descendants of extinct varieties. Thus, many genetic traits of extinct dog varieties are present in today's breeds.

Bears:

A heading of a science article In the Los Angeles Times by Amina Khan, July 8, 2011 states. ""Polar bear's ancestor is Irish brown bear, study finds"—they base this conclusion on DNA. The findings were made by analyzing the mitochondrial DNA extracted from 242 bear lineages. Some of them were polar bears and some were brown bears. Some lived recently and others have been dead since the late Pleistocene, which ended nearly 12,000 years ago" … (kham, 2011)

The article also declares that scientists believed the polar bear' closest ancestry was the brown bear on islands off Alaska. Whether this claim is true or not does not negate the fact that all bears are related and hybridisation occurs both in the wild and in zoos. In addition, a number of bear species have gone extinct as well.

There are many examples of extinct bears. One of the most interesting is what is referred to as the 'cave bear', (so named because its fossils are found in caves). The cave bear lived in Europe over 27,500 years ago. Perhaps if the remains of the cave bear were not in caves, we may never know that this bear variety ever existed.

The polar grizzly hybrid bear is another perfect example of two varieties of the same species crossing creating something novel. The polar bear grizzly hybrids known as either "pizzly" or "grolar" are very rare.

"In 2006 Jim Mirtell, an American hunter, shot a polar bear grizzly hybrid in the Canadian Artic. David Kuptana shot another bear in 2010 which was a second-generation hybrid." (Wingrove, 2011)

If the polar bear ever becomes extinct because of climate change, and this polar/grizzly becomes the only existing bear, the polar bears genes would still exist in the polar/grizzly 'DNA'. This same process might explain the disappearance of creatures such as the woolly mammoth and the existence of the modern-day elephant.

None of the above indicates the creation of an entirely different creature or "kind "by means of Darwinian evolutionary.

Humans:

Modern humans come in all shapes and sizes. There is more diversity with modern humans compared to all the human fossils found. There are people who are born hydrocephalic- with very large skulls, or microcephaly- with very small heads. There are the very short and the very tall, such as pigmies and the Somalis. Modern giants are not linear descendants of extinct pigmies or vice versa, but if both were found in the fissile record, could they not falsely be believed that one descendent from the other?

Modern Humans – My Family: From left to right - Hannah, Letty, Rachel and Ed

Human races are so very dissimilar, and yet we are one big (not necessarily happy) family. As the world becomes more globalized, relationships will become further mixed. An example is my family - my wife is from the Philippines and my ancestry is Irish. I affectionately call my daughters two beautiful mixed up kids. I often told my oldest daughter (jokingly) that since I am taller than she is, "I am still 'the boss'". It is obvious from the picture of my family, that if height equates authority – I am in trouble. Both my daughters grew taller than I am – I am really in trouble.

Today with globalization, people seem to be moving from place to place with increased numbers. It is not unusual to find people from all over the world at any bus stop in a crowded city. Chances are that we or our ancestors are not native to where we are living today - thus it would be hypocritical to complain if the people living next door are immigrants.

From Statistics Canada:

"The proportion of mixed unions rises with time spent in Canada, from 12% among first-generation visible minority Canadians (immigrants) to 69% among the third generation. People in mixed unions are younger than those in other couples, and 10% had at least one child under two at home and no children older than five, comparedwww.statcan.gc.ca. with 5.6% of other couples" ... (www.statcan.gc.ca.)

It is obvious that people have and will change from generation to generation. And also, many peoples of the past can have the appearance of being extinct, yet they will live on through their genes in future generations.

An example of human extinction is the Beothuk who were an aboriginal people on the island of Newfoundland Canada. This small group of indigenous people is believed to be extinct since 1829 with the death of Shanawdithit, the last known individual of her tribe. Although considered extinct, the Beothuk's genes may still be carried in other people today.

"Beothuk, North American Indian tribe of hunters and gatherers that resided on the island of Newfoundland. ... The Beothuk were decimated by Europeans and by Mi'kmaq (Micmac) hunters crossing from Nova Scotia. A few survivors may have escaped to Labrador to intermarry with the Innu" ... (Encyclopedia Britannica)

"Oral histories asserted that a few Beothuk survived for some years around the region of the Exploits River, Twillingate, Newfoundland; and Labrador; and formed unions with European colonists, Inuit and Mi'kmaq. Their children carried Beothuk genes as well as those of other ancestors. Some families from Twillingate claim partial descent from Beothuk people of the early 19th century." ... (Wikipedia, 2012)

If one considers the linages of lions, dogs, bears and humans etc. as a typical sample of biological life, then explanations for change through time fits a Mendelian model of inheritance, and not Darwinian where evolution happens in a slow step-by-fashion and where the new replaces or annihilates the old.

Can it be that a Creator God created all creatures distinct with the capability to transform? As we have seen, we are not always a copy of our parents and also all life shares much in common, but there is no evidence that new creatures or 'kinds' were created from existing ones such as a human from an ape like creature, or a cat from a dog etc.

HUMAN ADVENT - CREATION OR EVOLUTION?

As we have seen, modern Homo sapiens come in all shapes and sizes. Therefore, there should not be any surprise that our ancestry was in all shapes and sizes as well. Ian Sample in The Guardian writes: "A haul of fossils found in Georgia suggests that half a dozen species of early human ancestor were actually all Homo erectus."

"David Lordkipanidze … said: "If you found the Dmanisi skulls at isolated sites in Africa, some people would give them different species names. But one population can have all this variation."" … (Sample, 2013)

… "The researchers who reported these findings concluded that there was only one lineage of genus *Homo* that spread from Africa to other continents; their findings suggested, in other words, that the early evolution of *Homo* (*H. habilis*, *H. erectus*, and others) was characterized not by distinct species but by different variations of the same species." … (Encyclopaedia Britannica, Last Updated 10-21-2013)

So much from so little! Scientists are looking to fossils for missing links in support of their world view that humankind and apes had a common ancestry. A Darwinian assessment of the decent of mankind hasn't changed much from the views of what follows

From "The Outline of Science":

"It may be urged that we are attaching too much importance to the arboreal apprenticeship, since many tree-loving animals remain to-day very innocent creatures. To this reasonable objection there are two answers, first that in its many acquisitions the arboreal evolution of the '*humanoid*' precursors of man prepared the way for the survival of a '*human*' type marked by a great step in brain-development; and second that the passage from the humanoid to the human was probably associated with *a return to mother earth.*

According to Professor Lull, to whose fine textbook, *Organic Evolution* (1917), we are much indebted, "climatic conditions in Asia in the Miocene or early Pliocene were such as to compel the descent of the pre-human ancestor from the trees, a step which was absolutely essential to further human development." Continental elevation and consequent aridity led to a dwindling of the forests, and forced the ape-man to come to earth. "And at the last arose the man."

According to Lull, the descent from the trees was associated with the assumption of a more erect posture, with increased liberation and plasticity of the hand, with becoming a hunter, with experiments towards clothing and shelter, with an exploring habit, and with the beginning of communal life.

It is a plausible view that the transition from the humanoid to the human was affected by a discontinuous variation of considerable magnitude, what is nowadays called a *mutation*, and that it had mainly to do with the brain and the vocal organs. But given the gains of the arboreal apprenticeship, the stimulus of an enforced descent to terra firma, and an evolving brain and voice, we can recognise accessory factors which helped success to succeed. Perhaps the absence of great physical strength prompted reliance on wits; the prolongation of infancy would help to educate the parents in gentleness; the strengthening of the feeling of kinship would favour the evolution of family and social life—of which there are many anticipations at lower levels. There is much truth in the saying: "Man did not make society, society made man." (Thomson J. A., The Outline of Science Vol. 1, 1922, p. 168)

Is it credible that necessity creates? Could necessity have transformed our ape-like so-called cousins to human? Could it be that humans needed bigger brains, bigger hip muscles for upright posture, and thumbs for grasping after coming down from the trees, and like magic, our brains grew larger and larger and by chance developed larger hip muscles and better thumb for grasping?

Where is the evidence that necessity created these or any other part of our body? We need two eyes for binocular vision, therefor we have two eyes. We need a knee caps for walking, therefore we have knee caps. Necessity cannot create. We cannot create hair on a bald man's head or bring back to life anyone when dead. Humans made wings on airplanes and wheels on automobiles; they did not arrive by themselves because they were needed. There is more truth in saying, "Man-made society, society did not make man".

With Darwinian evolution, species change from one to another in a slow step-by-step fashion as in a series of transformations; this involves creation and destruction with most if not all our inferior ancestries becoming extinct. (In with new, out with the old). To change from an ape like creature to human would necessitate a tremendous amount of positive mutations with the newer continuously replacing the older. Where is the evidence?

From "The Outline of Science":

"So far, the story has been that of the sifting out of a humanoid stock and of the transition to human kind, from the ancestors of apes and men to the man-ape, and from the man-ape to man. It looks as if the sifting-out process had proceeded further, for there were several human branches that did not lead on to the modern type of man. ...

The first of these is represented by the scanty fossil remains known as *Pithecanthropus erectus*, found in Java in fossiliferous beds which date from the end of the Pliocene or the beginning of the Pleistocene era. Perhaps this means half a million years ago, and the remains occurred along with those of some mammals which are now extinct. Unfortunately, the remains of Pithecanthropus the Erect consisted only of a skull-cap, a thigh-bone, and two back teeth, so it is not surprising that experts should differ considerably in their interpretation of what was found. Some have regarded the remains as those of a large gibbon, others as those of a pre-human ape-man, and others as those of a primitive man off the main line of ascent. According to Sir Arthur Keith, Pithecanthropus was "a being human in stature, human in gait, human in all its parts, save its brain." The thigh-bone indicates a height of about 5 feet 7 inches, one inch less than the average height of the men of to-day. The skull-cap indicates a low, flat forehead, beetling brows, and a capacity about two-thirds of the modern size. The remains were found by Dubois, in 1894, in Trinil in Central Java." ... (Ibid PP 167-168)

Java Man or *Pithecanthropus erectus* (Homo erectus) - is it human or ape or a combination of both? So much from so little:

From Wikipedia the Free encyclopedia: "Dubois was able to argue that he had found a creature intermediate in its evolutionary position between apes and humans. Dubois originally classified his find as Pithecanthropus erectus."

From, "The Outline of Science: "The next offshoot is represented by the Heidelberg man (*Homo heidelbergensis*), discovered near Heidelberg in 1907 by Dr. Schoetensack. But the remains consisted only of a lower jaw and its teeth. Along with this relic were bones of various mammals, including some long since extinct in Europe, such as elephant, rhinoceros, bison, and lion. The circumstances indicate an age of perhaps 300,000 years ago. There were also very crude flint implements (or eoliths). But the teeth are human teeth, and the jaw seems transitional between that of an anthropoid ape and that of man. Thus there was no chin. According to most authorities the lower jaw from the Heidelberg sand-pit must be regarded as a relic of a primitive type off the main line of human ascent." (Ibid 167)

THE NEANDERTHAL

From, "The Outline of Science":

"It was in all probability in the Pliocene that there took origin the Neanderthal species of man, *Homo neanderthalensis*, first known from remains found in 1856 in the Neanderthal ravine near Düsseldorf. According to some authorities, Neanderthal man was living in Europe a quarter of a million years ago. Other specimens were afterwards found elsewhere, e.g. in Belgium ("the men of Spy"), in France, in Croatia, and at Gibraltar, so that a good deal is known of Neanderthal man. He was a loose-limbed fellow, short of stature and of slouching gait, but a skilful artificer, fashioning beautifully worked flints with a characteristic style. He used fire; he buried his dead reverently and furnished them with an outfit for a long journey; and he had a big brain. But he had great beetling, ape-like eyebrow ridges and massive jaws, and he showed "simian characters swarming in the details of his structure." In most of the points in which he differs from modern man he approaches the anthropoid apes, and he must be regarded as a low type of man off the main line. Huxley regarded the Neanderthal man as a low form of the modern type, but expert opinion seems to agree rather with the view maintained in 1864 by Professor William King of Galway, that the Neanderthal man represents a distinct species off the main line of ascent. He disappeared with apparent suddenness (like some aboriginal races today) about the end of the Fourth Great Ice Age; but there is evidence that before he ceased to be there had emerged a successor rather than a descendant—the modern man." (Thomson J., 1922, pp. 169-170)

This image and the description of the Neanderthal is obviously evolutionary bias. Neanderthals remains were as the cave bear– found in caves. The belief that the Neanderthal were not intelligent and brutish is probably false. The Neanderthal buried their dead, made tools for hunting, used fire, made pigment for art, and wore jewelry.

The belief that the Neanderthals were completely annihilated by the more modern humans out of Africa is probably false as well. Where is the evidence for large battles of annihilation? The Neanderthals were in significant numbers spread out over a huge area. They hunted and killed large animals for food and could probably use these same tools as weapons if needed.

Many believe that at least some Neanderthals practiced cannibalism because of cut marks left on some Neanderthal bones made by stone tools. We may never know whether these marks demonstrate acts of love or violence. These marks may have another explanation. The Neanderthal may have had an extraordinary tradition similar to that practiced in an area of the Philippines where they scrap the bones of dead relatives clean for a ritual in what they call 'the celebration of the bones'.

Darwin's book "On the Origin of Species by Means of Natural Selection" was first published in 1859 and the first discovery of the Neanderthal in Germany was in 1856. The belief that modern man destroyed the inferior Neanderthals could be influenced by the Darwinian worldview. A more reasonable explanation for the disappearance of the Neanderthals is interbreeding with other races and perhaps also infectious diseases.

From the National Geography Daly News:

… "The researchers, under the direction of Svante Pääbo of the Max Planck Institute for Evolutionary Anthropology, found that 2.5 percent of the genome of an average human living outside Africa today is made up of Neanderthal DNA. The average modern African has none." …

… The even larger percentage of Neanderthal DNA found in Asians and South Americans, announced in *Science* in August, could indicate additional interbreeding in Asia long ago, or could mean that the percentage of Neanderthal DNA in Europeans was diluted by later encounters." … (Zielinski, 2012)

… "Neanderthals are classified alternatively as a subspecies of *Homo sapiens* (*Homo sapiens neanderthalensis*) or as a separate human species (*Homo neanderthalensis*) Genetic evidence suggests they are closer to non-African than African anatomically modern humans, which is probably due to interbreeding between Neanderthals and the ancestors of the Eurasians. This is thought to have occurred between 80,000 and 50,000 years ago, shortly after (or perhaps before) the proto-Eurasians emigrated from Africa, and while they were still one population. It resulted in 1–4% of the genome of people from Eurasia having been contributed by Neanderthals." … (Wikipedia, 2012)

PILTDOWN MAN

Piltdown man, or Eoanthropus Dawsoni, was an incredible hoax not substantiated for almost forty years. There have been many ideas for "whodunit" including Charles Darwin, but why this fraud was so readily accepted is obvious. The Piltdown man fitted what many scientists wanted to believe. Piltdown man was a perfect missing link from ape like creature to human…

Group portrait of the Piltdown skull being examined. Back row (from left): F. O. Barlow, G. Elliot Smith, Charles Dawson, Arthur Smith Woodward. Front row: A S Underwood, Arthur Keith, W. P. Pycraft, and Ray Lankester. Note the portrait of Charles Darwin on the wall. Painting by John Cooke. (Wikipedia, Piltdown Man, 1915)

What follows was written before the discovery that the Piltdown Man was a hoax. It also demonstrates the Darwinian world view of human origin.

From The Outline of Science (1922): "Another offshoot from the main line is probably represented by the Piltdown man, found in Sussex in 1912. The remains consisted of the walls of the skull, which indicate a large brain, and a high forehead without the beetling eyebrows of the Neanderthal man and Pithecanthropus. The "find" included a tooth and part of a lower jaw, but these perhaps belong to some ape, for they are very discrepant. The Piltdown skull represents the most ancient human remains as yet found in Britain, and Dr. Smith Woodward's establishment of a separate genus Eoanthropus expresses his conviction that the Piltdown man was off the line of the evolution of the modern type. If the tooth and piece of lower jaw belong to the Piltdown skull, then there was a remarkable combination of ape-like and human characters. As regards the brain, *inferred* from the skull-walls, Sir Arthur Keith says:

"There are some which must be regarded as primitive. There can be no doubt that it is built on exactly the same lines as our modern brains. A few minor alterations would make it in all respects a modern brain. ... Although our knowledge of the human brain is limited—there are large areas to which we can assign no definite function—we may rest assured that a brain which All the essential features of the brain of modern man are to be seen in the brain cast. was shaped in a mould so similar to our own was one which responded to the outside world as ours does. Piltdown man saw, heard, felt, thought, and dreamt much as we do still. And this was 150,000 years ago at a modern estimate, and some would say half a million. There is neither agreement nor certainty as to the antiquity of man, except that the modern type was distinguishable from its collaterals hundreds of thousands of years ago. The general impression left is very grand. In remote antiquity the Primate stem diverged from the other orders of mammals; it sent forth its tentative branches, and the result was a tangle of monkeys; ages passed and the monkeys were left behind, while the main stem, still probing its way, gave off the Anthropoid apes, both small and large. But they too were left behind, and the main line gave off other experiments—indications of which we know in Java, at Heidelberg, in the Neanderthal, and at Piltdown. None of these lasted or was made perfect. They represent *tentative* men who had their day and ceased to be, our predecessors rather than our ancestors. Still, the main stem goes on evolving, and who will be bold enough to say what fruit it has yet to bear!" (Thomson J., 1922, pp. 170-171)

In 1953, nearly forty years after it was first revealed, the hoax of Piltdown Man was exposed. The hoaxer or hoaxers are still a matter of conjecture.

"A team led by geologist Kenneth Oakley, anatomist Wilfrid Le Gros Clark and anthropologist Joseph Weiner took a closer look and in 1953 announced that Piltdown's big braincase belonged to a modern human being while the jawbone came from an orangutan or chimpanzee. Each piece had been stained to look as if they were from the same skull while the teeth had been flattened with a metal file and the "cricket bat" carved with a knife. As Bournemouth University archaeologist Miles Russell puts it: "The earliest Englishman was nothing more than a cheap fraud." ... ("Courtesy of Guardian News & Media Ltd".) (https://www.theguardian.com/international)

LUCY

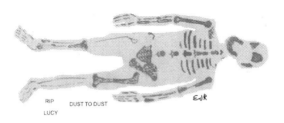

... ""Lucy," consisting of a <u>skeleton</u> forty percent complete, was discovered in Ethiopia by <u>Donald Johanson</u> in 1974, and was dated at 3.2 million years of age. ...

Everyone agrees that from the neck up, "Lucy" was gorilla-like. Her brain size was about one-fourth the size of a human brain; her jaw was "U"-<u>shaped</u>, typical of gorillas; her teeth were large, far larger than those in humans. ...

From the neck down, nearly every: feature was likewise non-human. *Australopithecus* fossils, the features which suggest <u>upright</u> posture to Johanson are primarily the hip and <u>knee joints</u>, but numerous studies on the hip have shown otherwise." ... (Wikapedia)

Lucy or Australopithecus afarensis was assembled as a patchwork of many parts, and not necessary of the same species. Whether Lucy walked more upright or on all fours is debateable, but either way, that would not discredit independent creation. Who and how Lucy fits in origins frequently depends on one's view of the world.

DEDUCTION

All life was and is in flux; modern species' varieties are very different one to another and also very different to their lineage as well; there are varieties and species that cannot propagate with their parentage while others are created sterile. Many species and varieties are also going extinct all the time. With the knowledge of Mendelian genetics, these changes have a predictable, logical, and accepted explanation.

For an animal to fossilize it has to be quickly covered with sediment, often in a swamp etc. therefore, most fossils are for obvious reasons marine organisms. Soft tissues are rare in the fossil record. There could have been at least some cataclysmic event in at least some of the areas where fossils are found. In areas of catastrophe, birds could fly away, swift moving animals could run away and intelligent species like humans may not even be in the area.

For Darwinian evolution to be plausible, it has to have had thousands of positive changes with the death of thousands of parental. Where is the evidence? Also, Darwinian evolution does not explain first causes [our beginning]. There is no proof that a Creator God in the beginning did not form individual species [kinds] distinct. We humans have much in common with all other primates, but are designed very distinct as well.

CHARLES DARWIN'S WORLD VIEW AND LACK OF FAITH

Darwin:

"Although I did not think much about the existence of a personal God until a considerably later period of my life, I will here give the vague conclusions to which I have been driven. The old argument from design in Nature, as given by Paley, which formerly seemed to me so conclusive, fails, now that the law of natural selection has been discovered. We can no longer argue that, for instance, the beautiful hinge of a bivalve shell must have been made by an intelligent being, like the hinge of a door by man. There seems to be no more design in the variability of organic beings, and in the action of natural selection, than in the course which the wind blows. But I have discussed this subject at the end of my book on the 'Variation of Domesticated Animals and Plants, and the argument there given has never, as far as I can see, been answered." (Darwin C., The life and letters of Charles Darwin, including an autobiographical chapter. London: John Murray. Volume 1., 1887, p. 309)

In a footnote to the above, Frances Darwin writes:

"My father asks whether we are to believe that the forms are preordained of the broken fragments of rock tumbled from a precipice which are fitted together by man to build his houses. If not, why should we believe that the variations of domestic animals or plants are preordained for the sake of the breeder? "But if we give up the principle in one case,... no shadow of reason can be assigned for the belief that variations, alike in nature and the result of the same general laws, which have been the groundwork through natural selection of the formation of the most perfectly adapted animals in the world, man included, were intentionally and specially guided."—('The Variation of Animals and Plants,' 1st Edit. vol. ii. p. 431. —F. D.)

If a complex stricter such as a stone house with walls, windows, doors, roof, rafters and beams all placed in proper order needs an organizer, how much more so a human body.

It would seem irrelevant which stones a builder chooses to build a stone house, but God knows all. This seem baffling to our human mind, but so does never ending space and time.

Isaiah 46:9-10:

9 Remember the former things of old, For I am God, and there is no other; I am God, and there is none like Me,

10 Declaring the end from the beginning, and from ancient times things that are not yet done, Saying, 'My counsel shall stand, And I will do all My pleasure,' (NKJV)

Charles Darwin's world view and lack of faith is evident in his writings. It is obvious that he has read the Christian Bible but dismisses it as untrustworthy.

CONSCIOUSNESS

There is much more to human life then our physical existence. As living beings, we have self-awareness. We have consciousness. From where did consciousness derive?

My daughter Rachel noticed a small crack on the passenger side of the windshield while driving in the family car. The next day, I took it to two repair shops that were recommended by my insurance company. When I arrived at the counter of the second shop the attendant cheerfully said, "I will check it out – myself." For some unknown reason to me he stressed the word, "myself".

I started to laugh and then stated what I found humorous in that "myself" reminded me of the statement, "I think, therefore I am". Then, I tapped my head and said, "If I hit myself and feel pain, then I will know that I exist, and if I tap you, then you will know we both exist; you are not dreaming. I am more than just a figment of your imagination."

We both had a good laugh for this was a fun and silly conversation. Still, in some way it explains consciousness. We are not just machines like computers. A computer can be developed with a very large brain (having all the memory and calculating power in the world), but it lacks consciousness. It will never have a soul – garbage in, garbage out. Also, a dead human body has all the cells and organization necessary for life, but just like a computer, it is dead. It has no consciousness - no self-awareness, no emotions, etc.

From an interview with J.P. Moreland in his book, "The Case for a Creator", Lee Strobel writes: "Perhaps Darwinists can explain how consciousness was shaped in a certain way over time, because the behaviour that consciousness caused had survival value. But it can't explain the *origin* of consciousness, because it can't explain how you can get something from nothing. ... Consciousness cannot be reduced merely to the physical brain. This means the atheist creation story is inadequate and false. And yet there is an alternative explanation that makes sense of all the evidence: our consciousness came from a greater Consciousness." ... (Strobel, p. 335)

Geneses 2:7 And the LORD God formed man of the dust of the ground, and breathed into his nostrils the breath of life; and man became a living soul.

EMOTIONS

The beginning and development of empathy for our dead ancestors would be hard if not impossible to explain by means of Darwinian evolution. It does not have any survival benefits.

Humans have buried their dead in different ways for millenniums. The picture with the many stacks of coffins was taken from a cave in Sagada in the Philippines. In this method of entombment, the wooden coffins survived a very long time in caves unless disturbed. In areas where there are no caves and where corpses have been buried in the ground, after time there would be no evidence that they ever existed except perhaps in the memory of a few relatives and friends. With time, even this fades away.

My wife Letty is from Banaue Ifugao, which is north of Manila in the Philippines. In this area, they treat their dead with great dignity and respect, but very, very differently than we do here in North America. What they do there would be considered criminal here. I learned this first-hand on our first family trip to the Philippians in 2000. At that time, our daughters were only five and three.

This is from a section of my notes of our trip which I called, "Grandpa Left Today".

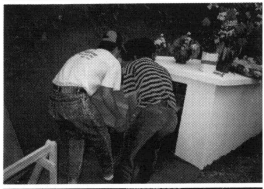

… "I always had a desire to meet Letty's father but unfortunately he died four years previous. Before he died, he was ill for some time and not expected to live. This prompted a trip home to the Philippines for my wife while I stayed back in Ottawa. When she arrived back in Canada, she told me that he died in her arms. She also told me that her family had a traditional ceremony in which they killed an ox and fed a study stream of relatives and villagers for several days. When the ceremony was over, they buried grandpa in a newly made crypt in back of her sister Flora's house.

Flash forward four years, and we are all visiting Letty's family in the Philippines. We were to stay at Flora's house, where the crypt with Letty's father was in the back yard. We had spent over seven hours on a bus from Manila, and when we arrived it was coming on evening. After settling inside for a while, I told my wife my desire to visit where they had put Grandpa. She pulled me to the landing underneath the stairs and said, "He is there. They put him there". I was astonished! Every time I went down or up the stairs, I realized that I was stepping over a senior member of Letty's family."[18]

Before we arrived, Grandpa had been removed from the crypt. His bones had been scraped clean, wrapped several times, and then put into a sack and placed underneath the landing of the stairs. Letty told me that they were following a very old tradition in which a dead relative's body would be exhumed and placed on a traditional garment. The bones then would be scraped clean, wrapped, and eventually placed underneath a native hut, on a board strung between pillars.

---

[18] pictures – Taken by author and others - used by permission

I asked Letty what then happens to the bones and she said that they eventually just rot away and disappear. Today with modern homes, the bones are often placed in a cupboard or hidden safe place inside the house.

The above is not Letty's family home, but similar structures can be found in the Philippines.

After about two weeks one of my wife's brothers removed Grandpa's bones from the landing and placed them on his motor bike between himself and the handle bars. He then took them away to another brother's house where they held a tradition which my wife calls 'the celebration of the bones'.

'The celebration of the bones' is like a very costly funeral all over again. They would kill a pig a day for five days and finally an ox to feed the continual stream of relatives, friends and locals. My wife has told me that many of these poor people often put themselves into debt to carry on these traditions.

Darwinism does not explain first cases [where did emotions come from in the first place]. It would be difficult to explain the evolution of Love which often entails giving without expecting anything in return. How can Darwinian evolution explain why a mother would, if needed, even die for her children? Feelings, such as empathy, compassion love, are they not of God?

The Illustrations that follow may not be the best examples of love but I hope the reader will find them as enchanting as I so.

This is from my daughter Rachel's school assignment when she was in sixth grade:

"I have a loving family that cares about me. I have a very unusual family as well. My mom's side of my family is petite and my dad's side is the opposite.

My mom comes from the Philippines. She's is from a family of nine children. Her country is very poor.

My grgrgreat grandfather (3 greats) from my dad's sides name is John James Muldoon he was the biggest man in Canada at that time he weighed 486 pounds.

My dad's mother's name was Margaret Muldoon before she was married to John James Robinson. They both died before I was born. They had 15 biological and 3 adopted children and are Irish. They lived on a farm in Quyon, Quebec. They owned at least 300 acres of land. They had 4 horses 2 baby horses and 2 adult horses named Minnie and Queen. They both pull hay and give wagon rides to people: haw to go left and gee to go right to control them. My grandfather and grandmother never had to go and buy food because they had food there already.

Including thirty to twenty milk cows and twenty-five chickens in the hen house and five roosters and they have their very own apple tree. They had a garden too they grew carrots, lettuce, tomatoes, potatoes and wheat and much more. My dad is the 6th kid out of 15. The oldest of the family jest turned 70. My aunt Maggie now owns my grandparents farm. My mom, dad, sister and I go to the farm once and a while and on the way there, there's this hill called ghost hill. Why is it called ghost hill might you ask? Well a long time ago a farmer was going home with his horses and wagon and on the hill, he believed to have seen a ghost. Ever since then this hill has been known as ghost hill.

The farthest back we can trace is James Wilson, who married Janet Somerville in 1650. They are my grgrgrgrgrgrgrgrgrgreat grandparents (9 greats) on my dad's side and are descendants of John, Third Lord of Somerville. As you can see my dad comes from Ireland and my mom comes from the Philippines there for I'm a mixed up kid. The End. "[19]

What follows is from my daughter Hannah's assignment when she was in grade eight:

"Four Years More:
English Reflection Assignment
Hannah Robinson

Almost every single year, maybe twice a year l would find two big cardboard boxes in our living room. Ever since l could remember, l would find them there. My mother, an immigrant from the Philippines has a ritual she does; she packs belongings, possessions into the big brown boxes until they are

---

[19] Used by permission

over packed with goodies, until they can't hold anymore. Goodies like candy and chocolate for those sweet toothed children. Toys and school supplies too, for those who don't have much. Practical items would too be included, for instance mugs, pots and pans mainly those every day appliances. She would pack items people would need or are too costly to buy. She often packed my hand me downs, as well as my sister's. Late into the night she could be found packing for her mother, brothers, sisters, cousins, aunts and uncles. She would pack for her family to have a taste of what she has now, for what they should have to at least live a better life. My mom knows how it's like to not have much, so she packs. I understood more about my family on the other side of the world from helping my mother pack. Whenever we would go shopping she would often say "oh, this would be good for so and so or such and such". It made me know more about a person I've met but can't remember for I was only about two years old when I first arrived there.

The second time we traveled to the Philippines I was around twelve. Since I was so young I didn't understand some of what was going on around me. Everything was different, the culture and surroundings was so new; it was mind blowing to experience. Right off the plane the climate of the Philippines came right at you, embracing you with its hot humidity. The atmosphere was extremely colorful; we were covered by tropical forests and vast areas where rice and a variety of exotic fruits grow.

I met my family who I didn't know before, some of them didn't know who I was but it was the same for them because I didn't know who they were either. I had no clue who I was meeting, who was who, and if they' re even related to me. I don't even speak their language so even striking up a conversation to get back the ten years we have missed has proved impossible.

My family was so loving and welcoming I felt it was like a second home there. But for my mom, Canada's her second home; she still calls the Philippines "home". Seeing her back in her own environment made me so happy because she was so happy. After ten years it was like she never left. She was doing what her sisters were, she was talking in her language 24/7 and she was spending time with her eighty-some years old mother who has Alzheimer's Unfortunately her mom is so sick she doesn't even remember her most of the time.

The third visit was for three weeks. It was this summer, the best summer of my life. I felt as though my family knew me a bit better even though we're kind of strangers but I love them just the same. My cousins I've met before are all grown up, it's weird, and it's like we've only met for a second and then when I turn my head then look back, they changed. It's like they're different people. It made me realize that four years is a long time. I know, because my baby cousin, Isaiah, was just only born and now he's four. When I first laid eyes on him, I couldn't even recognize who he was. It was like I was expecting him to still be a baby. it's crazy how much time flies.

When I was there living in my aunt's house, I noticed items from Canada, the things we shipped there. Our tea was there, our peanut butter and other various items so it was like I had Canada with me while I was in the Philippines. I've also noticed some of my family wearing the clothes we packed and shipped over. I liked seeing that I had some impact in their lives even if l wasn't with them. They at least have a part of us to remember us by, and recall our short stay with them in their home. When they're in their everyday lives, they have a piece of us with them. It always seems that we're constantly desperate to be in each other's memory. I came back with plenty of different knick-knacks that my numerous cousins gifted me with. I thought it was funny that my older cousin Miriam had dumped a whole lot of jewelry on a table and told us to pick what we want from it. She must have been a bit worried of not being recalled the next time we meet, another four years later.

When my family and I were leaving for the airport we all tried to soak in the feeling of being in that surrounding one last time. We were trying to get the last hug and laugh from our family members before we become 'different people'. Before I grow up and look different, maybe like different things, and become more mature. Before I become an adult, before my baby cousin turns eight. When my sister and I went shopping around the local small market she went looking for blouses, for job interviews. I thought it was funny so I jokingly called her 'old'. Funny, because the next time I go, l will be the one looking for blouses. Four years is a long time."[20]

---

[20] Used by permission

WHAT DID DARWIN SAY?

Much of what follows are selections from the sixth edition of Charles Darwin's book, "The Origin of Species by Means of Natural Selection or Preservation of Favoured Races in the Struggle for Life", also with numerous comments and comparisons to William Paley's, "Natural Theology or, Evidences of the Existence and Attributes of the Deity". Scientific knowledge has increased enormously in the last one hundred and fifty years since Charles Darwin, and many statements given as fact at that time are incorrect.

Darwin:

"I WILL here a give a brief sketch of the progress of opinion on the Origin of Species. Until recently the great majority of naturalists believed that species were immutable productions, and had been separately created. This view has been ably maintained by many authors. Some few naturalists, on the other hand, have believed that species undergo modification, and that the existing forms of life are the descendants by true generation of pre-existing forms. Passing over allusions to the subject in the classical writers, the first author who in modern times has treated it in a scientific spirit was Buffon. But as his opinions fluctuated greatly at different periods, and as he does not enter on the causes or means of the transformation of species, I need not here enter on details.

Lamarck was the first man whose conclusions on the subject excited must attention. This justly-celebrated naturalist first published his views in 1801; he much enlarged them in 1809 in his 'Philosophie Zoologique,' and subsequently, in 1815, in the Introduction to his 'Hist. Nat. des Animaux sans Vertébres.' In these works, he upholds the doctrine that all species, including man, are descended from other species. He first did the eminent service of arousing attention to the probability of all change in the organic, as well as in the inorganic world, being the result of law, and not of miraculous interposition. Lamarck seems to have been chiefly led to his conclusion on the gradual change of species, by the difficulty of distinguishing species and varieties, by the almost perfect gradation of forms in certain groups, and by the analogy of domestic productions. With respect to the means of modification, he attributed something to the direct action of the physical conditions of life, something to the crossing of already existing forms, and much to use and disuse, that is, to the effects of habit. To this latter agency, he seems to attribute all the beautiful adaptations in nature; —such as the long neck of the giraffe for browsing on the branches of trees. But he likewise believed in a law of progressive development; and as all the forms of life thus tend to progress, in order to account for the existence at the present day of simple productions, he maintains that such forms are now spontaneously generated. … (Darwin C., 1872, pp. xiii-xiv)

Darwin's beliefs did not exist in isolation. Do species including man come from other species through natural laws without God's involvement?

Without knowing genetics, Charles Darwin accepted Lamarck's concept of "use and disuse" as a viable means of evolutionary change. This was more apparent in the 6th edition of "The Origin of Species" published in 1872 than in earlier versions.

Lamarck's theory of "use and disuse" basically states that 'use' creates generational change. For example, as a giraffe reaches for its food on higher and higher branches, its neck will grow longer and longer, consequently this process leaves a gradation in length of the giraffe from what it used to be (short) to what it is today (long). A blacksmith for example, if he uses his muscles and increases strength will pass his larger muscles to his future offspring. Laziness can be acquired in the same way. – (Can a lazy child, avoiding his chores, fault his father?)

The Lamarckian theory of "use and disuse" was totally debunked by a German biologist. August Weismann, at the University of Freiburg in1813. Weismann cut or the tails of mice up to the twenty second generation. The offspring of these mice were still being born with tails, thus demonstrating that the theory of "use and disuse" is false.

Many believe that our appendix is a useless leftover remnant becoming smaller and smaller by disuse, however the appendix may have a greater use then what has been previously thought. The appendix may have use in a developing fetus, and or used to 'reboot' the stomach with 'good bacteria' following intestine problems. There is no more proof that the disuse of an organ over time would make it smaller and smaller any more than its use would make it get bigger and bigger. This is highly speculative. Genetics does not work this way.

During Darwin's time, there was some confusion in naming what is a variety and what constitutes a species. As we all know today, by crossing any two varieties, change takes place. Could this be why dissimilar varieties of species are found in diverse parts of the world? Varieties of a species might be transported to an island and the island varieties change through cross-breeding as well as those on the mainland. Thus, over time, varieties would become very dissimilar, (mainland to island), principally through genetic causes and not environmental. There could also be extinction in one or both locals as well and therefore through this process creating endemic species and varieties of species on an island or mainland or both.

Darwin:

"In 1813, Dr. W. C. Wells read before the Royal Society 'An Account of a White Female, part of whose skin resembles that of a Negro; but his paper was not published until his famous 'Two Essays upon Dew and Single Vision' appeared in 1818. In this paper he distinctly recognises the principle of natural selection, and this is the first recognition which has been indicated; but he applies it only to the races of man, and to certain characters alone. After remarking that negroes and mulattoes enjoy an immunity from certain tropical diseases, he observes, firstly, that all animals tend to vary in some degree, and, secondly, that agriculturists improve their domesticated animals by selection; and then, he adds, but what is done in this latter case "by art, seems to be done with equal efficacy, though more slowly, by nature, in the formation of varieties of mankind, fitted for the country which they inhabit. Of the accidental varieties of man, which would occur among the first few and scattered inhabitants of the middle regions of Africa, some one would be better fitted than the others to bear the diseases of the country. This race would consequently multiply, while the others would decrease; not only from their inability to sustain the attacks of disease, but from their incapacity of contending with their more vigorous neighbours. The colour of this vigorous race I take for granted, from what has been already said, would be dark. But the same disposition to form varieties still existing, a darker and a darker race would in the course of time occur: and as the darkest would be the best fitted for the climate, this would at length become the most prevalent, if not the only race, in the particular country in which it had originated." He then extends these same views to the white inhabitants of colder climates. I am indebted to Mr. Rowley, of the United States, for having called my attention, through Mr. Brace, to the above passage in Dr. Well's work. (Darwin C., 1872, pp. xv-xvi)

Climate or environment cannot change an organism; mutations and the creation of novel varieties can. However, there is no doubt that the best-fitted varieties for a climate have a better chance of survival. This process does not negate the existence of a God who created kinds [species] distinct in the first place.

Darwin:

"The Hon. and Rev. W. Herbert, afterwards Dean of Manchester, in the fourth volume of the 'Horticultural Transactions,' 1822, and in his work on the 'Amaryllidaceae' (1837, p. 19, 339), declares that "horticultural experiments have established, beyond the possibility of refutation, that botanical species are only a higher and more permanent class of varieties." He extends the same view to animals. The Dean believes that single species of each genus were created in an originally highly plastic condition, and that these have produced, chiefly by intercrossing, but likewise by variation, all our existing species." (Ibid 5-6)

Some of the above paragraph can be accepted as correct from a Christian biblical point of view. As we know, varieties crossing with varieties generate something different, but a species, in a contemporary definition of species, cannot cross with another species. This is genetically impossible.

Darwin:

"Professor Owen, in 1849 ('Nature of Limbs,' p. 86), wrote as follows: —"The archetypal [usual] idea was manifested in the flesh under diverse such modifications, upon this planet, long prior to the existence of those animal species that actually exemplify it. To what natural laws or secondary causes the orderly succession and progression of such organic phenomena may have been committed, we, as yet, are ignorant." In his Address to the British Association, in 1858, he speaks (p. li.) of "the axiom of the continuous operation of creative power, or of the ordained becoming of living things." Farther on (p. xc.), after referring to geographical distribution, he adds, "These phenomena shake our confidence in the conclusion that the Apteryx of New Zealand and the Red Grouse of England were distinct creations in and for those islands respectively. Always, also, it may be well to bear in mind that by the word 'creation' the zoologist means 'a process he knows not what.'" He amplifies this idea by adding, that when such cases as that of the Red Grouse are "enumerated by the zoologist as evidence of distinct creation of the bird in and for such islands, he chiefly expresses that he knows not how the Red Grouse came to be there, and there exclusively; signifying also, by this mode of expressing such ignorance, his belief that both the bird and the islands owed their origin to a great first Creative Cause." If we interpret these sentences given in the same Address, one by the other, it appears that this eminent philosopher felt in 1858 his confidence shaken that the Apteryx and the Red-Grouse first appeared in their respective homes, "he knew not how," or by some process "he knew not what." … (Ibid pp xviii-xix)

Notice the deduction of the above – "He knows not how the Apteryx (flightless bird) and the Red Grouse could be created distinct in their respective homes." Today, with our knowledge of Mendel's genetics, we can understand how varieties are scattered all over the world.

GEOGRAPHICAL DISTRIBUTION

Darwin:

… "In the case of those species, which have undergone during whole geological periods little modification, there is not much difficulty in believing that they have migrated from the same region; for during the vast geographical and climatal changes which have supervened [appeared] since ancient times, almost any amount of migration is possible. But in many other cases, in which we have reason to believe that the species of a genus have been produced within comparatively recent times, there is great difficulty on this head. It is also obvious that the individuals of the same species, though now inhabiting distant and isolated regions, must have proceeded from one spot, where their parents were first produced: for, as has been explained, it is incredible that individuals identically the same should have been produced from parents specifically distinct.

… If the existence of the same species at distant and isolated points of the earth's surface, can in many instances be explained on the view of each species having migrated from a single birthplace; then, considering our ignorance with respect to former climatal and geographical changes and to the various occasional means of transport, the belief that a single birthplace is the law, seems to me incomparably the safest.

In discussing this subject, we shall be enabled at the same time to consider a point equally important for us, namely, whether the several species of a genus, which must on our theory all be descended from a common progenitor, can have migrated, undergoing modification during their migration, from some one area. If, when most of the species inhabiting one region are different from those of another region, though closely allied to them, it can be shown that migration from the one region to the other has probably occurred at some former period, our general view will be much strengthened; for the explanation is obvious on the principle of descent with modification? [Heredity with revision] A volcanic island, for instance, upheaved and formed at the distance of a few hundreds of miles from a continent, would probably receive from it in the course of time a few colonists, and their descendants, though modified, would still be related by inheritance to the inhabitants of that continent. Cases of this nature are common, and are, as we shall hereafter see, inexplicable on the theory of independent creation." … (Darwin C., 1872, pp. 320-323)

Different varieties found in diverse regions of the world are not incompatible with creation. "Independent creation" here could be creatures and varieties created where we now find them. This is neither a Darwinian nor a Biblical Christian belief. The Christian bible does not state that plants and animals were created where we find them currently. The Christian view is that Life was created and expected to fill the earth. It is common knowledge that variety crossed with variety creates additional variety. (The obvious Darwinian evolutionary inference here could be that new varieties evolved from a common stock, and thus new species can evolve as well).

Spaces were created and expected to fill the earth.

Genesis:

20. Then God said, "Let the waters abound with an abundance of living creatures, and let birds fly above the earth across the face of the firmament of the heavens."

21. So God created great sea creatures and every living thing that moves, with which the waters abounded, according to their kind, and every winged bird according to its kind. And God saw that it was good.

22. And God blessed them, saying, be fruitful and multiply, and fill the waters in the seas, and let birds multiply on the earth." (Scripture taken from the New King James Version. Copyright © 1982 by Thomas Nelson, Inc. Used by permission. All rights reserved.)

With varieties crossing with varieties and other varieties created, there should be no puzzle of how one can find different varieties of the same species in different parts of the world: Not all varieties of one area of the world would travel to another area, but if only one or a few varieties of a species make it to a new home, and then if each group would continue to mix and change independently of the other, then eventually each group would become very dissimilar, one from the other. There would then be different varieties of the same species located in different parts of the world. This does not negate the fact that God initially created distinct species ['kinds'].

Darwin:

"In this same year, 1853, Dr. Schaaffhausen published an excellent pamphlet ('Verhand. des Naturhist. Vereins der Preuss. Rheinlands,' &c.), in which he maintains the progressive development of organic forms on the earth. He infers that many species have kept true for long periods, whereas a few have become modified. The distinction of species he explains by the destruction of intermediate graduated forms. "Thus, living plants and animals are not separated from the extinct by new creations, but are to be regarded as their descendants through continued reproduction." ...

... The 'Philosophy of Creation' has been treated in a masterly manner by the Rev. Baden Powell, in his 'Essays on the Unity of Worlds,' 1855.

Nothing can be more striking than the manner in which he shows that the introduction of new species is "a regular, not a casual phenomenon," or, as Sir John Herschel expresses it, "a natural in contradistinction [marked differences] to a miraculous process."" (Ibid page xx-xxi)

With a belief in a Creator, what we might refer to as miraculous or natural are all under His control.

From the book of Job 38:1-6

1. Then the Lord answered Job "out of the whirlwind, and said:

2. "Who" is this who darkens counsel by words without knowledge?

3. "Now prepare yourself like a man; I will question you, and you shall answer Me,

4. "Where" were you when I laid the foundations of the earth? Tell Me, if you have understanding.

5 Who determined its measurements? Surely you know! Or who stretched the line upon it?

6. To what were its foundations fastened. Or who laid its cornerstone. (Scripture taken from the New King James Version. Copyright © 1982 by Thor Nelson, Inc. Used by permission. All rights reserved.)

Darwin:

… "In June, 1859, Professor Huxley gave a lecture before the Royal Institution on the 'Persistent Types of Animal life.' Referring to such cases, he remarks, "It is difficult to comprehend the meaning of such facts as these, if we suppose that each species of animal and plant, or each great type of organisation, was formed and placed upon the surface of the globe at long intervals by a distinct act of creative power; and it is well to recollect that such an assumption is as unsupported by tradition or revelation as it is opposed to the general analogy of nature. If, on the other hand, we view 'Persistent Types' in relation to that hypothesis which supposes the species living at any time to be the result of the gradual modification of pre-existing species—a hypothesis which, though unproven, and sadly damaged by some of its supporters, is yet the only one to which physiology lends any countenance; their existence would seem to show that the amount of modification which living beings have undergone during geological time is but very small in relation to the whole series of changes which they have suffered."" (Darwin C., p. xxii)

We know that the hypothesis that all existing species are the result of the gradual modification of pre-existing species is unproven. The number of fluctuations needed for gradual change from one species to another would be enormous. Change on the physical, and instinctive levels, and all this in a gradational positive process is problematic, and especially problematic when we consider in the Darwinian theory that the new is continually replacing most, if not all, the old or parental.

The above is only a selection of a few authors named by Darwin in his Historical Sketch. Darwin and others could see organic change, but not knowing genetics, he gives incorrect speculative reasons why change takes place. As we currently know, Varieties were and are dissimilar in different local which does not negate the biblical account of creation.

FACTS AND THEORIES

Darwin:

"WHEN on board H.M.S. 'Beagle,' as naturalist, I was much struck with certain facts in the distribution of the organic beings inhabiting South America, and in the geological relations of the present to the past inhabitants of that continent. These facts, as will be seen in the latter chapters of this volume, seemed to throw some light on the origin of species—that mystery of mysteries, as it has been called by one of our greatest philosophers. On my return home, it occurred to me, in 1837, that something might perhaps be made out on this question by patiently accumulating and reflecting on all sorts of facts which could possibly have any bearing on it. After five years' work I allowed myself to speculate on the subject, and drew up some short notes; these I enlarged in 1844 into a sketch of the conclusions, which then seemed to me probable: from that period to the present day, I have steadily pursued the same object. I hope that I may be excused for entering on these personal details, as I give them to show that I have not been hasty in coming to a decision. ...

... No one can feel more sensible than I do of the necessity of hereafter publishing in detail all the facts, with references, on which my conclusions have been grounded; and I hope in a future work to do this. For I am well aware that scarcely a single point is discussed in this volume on which facts cannot be adduced, often apparently leading to conclusions directly opposite to those at which I have arrived. A fair result can be obtained only by fully stating and balancing the facts and arguments on both sides of each question; and this is here impossible." ... (Ibid page 1-2)

Drawing on Darwin's many facts does not lead us all to the same conclusion.

The origin of species — that mystery of mysteries — why doesn't God reveal Himself? The answer could be that free will would not be free will if God revealed Himself as many would like.

Luke 11:29-30

[29] while the crowds were thickly gathered together, He began to say, "This is an evil generation. It seeks a sign, and no sign will be given to it except the sign of Jonah the prophet.

[30] "For as Jonah became a sign to the Ninevites, so also the Son of Man will be to this generation. (NKJV)

Darwin:

... "In considering the Origin of Species, it is quite conceivable that a naturalist, reflecting on the mutual affinities of organic beings, on their embryological relations, their geographical distribution, geological succession, and other such facts, might come to the conclusion that species had not been independently created, but had descended, like varieties, from other species. Nevertheless, such a conclusion, even if well founded, would be unsatisfactory, until it could be shown how the innumerable species inhabiting this world have been modified, so as to acquire that perfection of structure and coadaptation which justly excites our admiration. Naturalists continually refer to external conditions, such as climate, food, &c., as the only possible cause of variation. In one limited sense, as we shall hereafter see, this may be true; but it is preposterous to attribute to mere external conditions, the structure, for instance, of the woodpecker, with its feet, tail, beak, and tongue, so admirably adapted to catch insects under the bark of trees. In the case of the mistletoe, which draws its nourishment from certain trees, which has seeds that must be transported by certain birds, and which has flowers with separate sexes absolutely requiring the agency of certain insects to bring pollen from one flower to the other, it is equally preposterous to account for the structure of this parasite, with its relations to several distinct organic beings, by the effects of external conditions, or of habit, or of the volition [wish]of the plant itself.

... Although much remains obscure, and will long remain obscure, I can entertain no doubt, after the most deliberate study and dispassionate judgment of which I am capable, that the view which most naturalists until recently entertained, and which I formerly entertained—namely, that each species has been independently created—is erroneous. I am fully convinced that species are not immutable [unchangeable]; but that those belonging to what are called the same genera are lineal descendants of some other and generally extinct species, in the same manner as the acknowledged varieties of any one species are the descendants of that species. Furthermore, I am convinced that Natural Selection has been the most important, but not the exclusive, means of modification." ... (Darwin C., 1872, pp. 2-3)

In the above, there is no consideration for the participation of a creator God. There is only supposition to natural causes, such as Natural Selection, climate, food, habit etc.

The bible teaches that God created Homo sapiens autonomously. It does not teach that Humans have to be carbon copies of the original. It is a misconception that Christians and their bible reject the obvious – There are mutations and variety change. We are not identical to our ancestors, but we still remain human.

Genesis 2:7

"And the Lord God formed man of dust from the ground, and breathed into his nostrils the breath of life; and man became a living being." (NKJV)

VARIATION UNDER DOMESTICATION

Darwin:

"WHEN we compare the individuals of the same variety or sub-variety of our older cultivated plants and animals, one of the first points which strikes us is, that they generally differ more from each other than do the individuals of any one species or variety in a state of nature. And if we reflect on the vast diversity of the plants and animals which have been cultivated, and which have varied during all ages under the most different climates and treatment, we are driven to conclude that this great variability is due to our domestic productions having been raised under conditions of life not so uniform as, and somewhat different from, those to which the parent-species had been exposed under nature. There is, also, some probability in the view propounded by Andrew Knight, that this variability may be partly connected with excess of food. It seems clear that organic beings must be exposed during several generations to new conditions to cause any great amount of variation; and that, when the organisation has once begun to vary, it generally continues varying for many generations. No case is on record of a variable organism ceasing to vary under cultivation. Our oldest cultivated plants, such as wheat, still yield new varieties: our oldest domesticated animals are still capable of rapid improvement or modification." ... (Darwin C., The Origin of Species by Means of Natural Selection. 6th ed., 1872, p. 5)

Once a variety is created from crossing dissimilar varieties of a species, this change would not continue to vary for many generations. Climate does not alter a species, however, a new hybrid created by the crosses of existing varieties creates change and this new hybrid may have an advantage in a changing climate while older varieties may perish. Today, many varieties and whole species are either being threatened or going extinct in various parts of the world. A surprising example of extinction is the disappearance of the 'Passenger Pigeon' of North America. It was one of the most abundant varieties of pigeon during the nineteenth century that went to extinction in the twentieth. Two main reasons for this bird's demise was over-kill and destruction of habitat.

Today, there is no mystery for the causes of change which are Mendelian Genetics, mutations, and extinction. This change does not change one kind of creature created by God into another. Darwin's lack of knowledge of genetics is clearly evident in what follows.

Darwin:

"As far as I am able to judge, after long attending to the subject, the conditions of life appear to act in two ways, —directly on the whole organisation or on certain parts alone, and indirectly by affecting the reproductive system. With respect to the direct action, we must bear in mind that in every case, as Professor Weismann has lately insisted, and as I have incidentally shown in my work on 'Variation under Domestication,' there are two factors: namely, the nature of the organism, and the nature of the conditions. The former seems to be much the more important; for nearly similar variations sometimes arise under, as far as we can judge, dissimilar conditions; and, on the other hand, dissimilar variations arise under conditions which appear to be nearly uniform. The effects on the offspring are either definite or indefinite. They may be considered as definite when all or nearly all the offspring of individuals exposed to certain conditions during several generations are modified in the same manner. It is extremely difficult to come to any conclusion in regard to the extent of the changes which have been thus definitely induced. There can, however, be little doubt about many slight changes, —such as size from the amount of food, colour from the nature of the food, thickness of the skin and hair from climate, &c. Each of the endless variations which we see in the plumage of our fowls must have had some efficient cause; and if the same cause were to act uniformly during a long series of generations on many individuals, all probably would be modified in the same manner. Such facts as the complex and extraordinary out-growths which invariably follow from the insertion of a minute drop of poison by a gall-producing insect show us what singular modifications might result in the case of plants from a chemical change in the nature of the sap." (Ibid pp 5-6)

How can hereditary change be induced by changes in conditions such as food or climate? Charles Darwin seems to be groping in the dark for possible causes of change. An obvious blunder was using the theory of 'use and disuse of parts'. Why are our legs so much bigger than our arms, could it be that we have larger legs because our ancestors used their legs more and their arms less? (It is all in our genes.)

EFFECTS OF HABIT AND OF THE USE OR DISUSE OF PARTS

Darwin:

"Changed habits produce an inherited effect, as in the period of the flowering of plants when transported from one climate to another. With animals the increased use or disuse of parts has had a more marked influence; thus I find in the domestic duck that the bones of the wing weigh less and the bones of the leg more, in proportion to the whole skeleton, than do the same bones in the wild-duck; and this change may be safely attributed to the domestic duck flying much less, and walking more, than its wild parents. The great and inherited development of the udders in cows and goats in countries where they are habitually milked, in comparison with these organs in other countries, is probably another instance of the effects of use. Not one of our domestic animals can be named which has not in some country drooping ears; and the view which has been suggested that the drooping is due to the disuse of the muscles of the ear, from the animals being seldom much alarmed, seems probable." ... (Darwin C., 1872, p. 8)

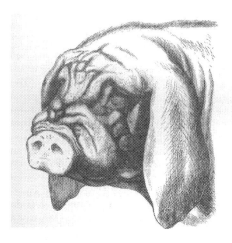

Changed habits do not produce an inherited effect. As any gardener knows, an annual plant never becomes perennial because of colder climate. In my wife's garden, her perennials grow from year to year while she always has to purchase her annuals.

Drooping ears through lack of use and the pull of gravity; if this happens, we should all have drooping ears and everything else that gravity affects would be closer to the ground.

LAWS REGULATE VARIATION

Darwin:

"Many laws regulate variation, some few of which can be dimly seen, and will hereafter be briefly discussed. I will here only allude to what may be called correlated variation. Important changes in the embryo or larva will probably entail changes in the mature animal. In monstrosities, the correlations between quite distinct parts are very curious; and many instances are given in Isidore Geoffroy St. Hilaire's great work on this subject. Breeders believe that long limbs are almost always accompanied by an elongated head. Some instances of correlation are quite whimsical: thus cats which are entirely white and have blue eyes are generally deaf; but it has been lately stated by Mr. Tait that this is confined to the males. Colour and constitutional peculiarities go together, of which many remarkable cases could be given amongst animals and plants. From facts collected by Heusinger, it appears that white sheep and pigs are injured by certain plants, whilst dark-coloured individuals escape: Professor Wyman has recently communicated to me a good illustration of this fact; on asking some farmers in Virginia how it was that all their pigs were black, they informed him that the pigs ate the paint-root (Lachnanthes), which coloured their bones pink, and which caused the hoofs of all but the black varieties to drop off; and one of the "crackers" (*i. e.* Virginia squatters) added, "we select the black members of a litter for raising, as they alone have a good chance of living." Hairless dogs have imperfect teeth: long-haired and coarse-haire animals are apt to have, as is asserted, long or many horns; pigeons with feathered feet have skin between their outer toes; pigeons with short beaks have small feet, and those with long beaks large feet. Hence if man goes on selecting, and thus augmenting, any peculiarity, he will almost certainly modify unintentionally other parts of the structure, owing to the mysterious laws of correlation.

The results of the various, unknown, or but dimly understood laws of variation are infinitely complex and diversified. It is well worth while carefully to study the several treatises on some of our old cultivated plants, as on the hyacinth [lily], potato, even the dahlia, &c.; and it is really surprising to note the endless points of structure and constitution in which the varieties and sub-varieties differ slightly from each other. The whole organisation seems to have become plastic, and departs in a slight degree from that of the parental type." (Darwin C., 1872, pp. 8-9)

What a species is to become is largely determined at conception, and the laws that regulate variation and correlation are currently understood through Mendelian genetics. With today's commercial farming, many of our fruits, grains and vegetables are the chosen varieties that fit best our usage, while other varieties may go extinct because they are not cultivated. It is interesting that the lowly potato was stated in the above. The potato has become such a staple in our diet and yet many of its varieties are in danger of extinction.

Varieties of plants and animals are shaped by genetics. Farmers have been selective breeding their plants and animals for eons. An early example is

Edward Robinson

in Genesis of the Christian bible concerning wages between Jacob and his father-in-law Laban.

Genesis 30:26-34:

26 Give me my wives and my children for whom I have served you, and let me go; for you know my service which I have done for you."

31 So he said, "What shall I give you?" And Jacob said, "You shall not give me anything. If you will do this thing for me, I will again feed and keep your flocks:

32 Let me pass through all your flock today, removing from there all the speckled and spotted sheep, and all the brown ones among the lambs, and the spotted and speckled among the goats; and these shall be my wages.

33 So my righteousness will answer for me in time to come, when the subject of my wages comes before you: every one that is not speckled and spotted among the goats, and brown among the lambs, will be considered stolen, if it is with me."

34 And Laban said, "Oh, that it was according to your word!"

Darwin did not know genetics, but he knew of its effects.

Darwin:

… "When any deviation of structure often appears, and we see it in the father and child, we cannot tell whether it may not be due to the same cause having acted on both; but when amongst individuals, apparently exposed to the same conditions, any very rare deviation, due to some extraordinary combination of circumstances, appears in the parent—say, once amongst several million individuals—and it reappears in the child, the mere doctrine of chances almost compels us to attribute its reappearance to inheritance. Every one must have heard of cases of albinism, prickly skin, hairy bodies, &c., appearing in several members of the same family. If strange and rare deviations of structure are really inherited, less strange and commoner deviations may be freely admitted to be inheritable. Perhaps the correct way of viewing the whole subject would be, to look at the inheritance of every character whatever as the rule, and non-inheritance as the anomaly.

The laws governing inheritance are for the most part unknown. No one can say why the same peculiarity in different individuals of the same species, or in different species, is sometimes inherited and sometimes not so." ... (Ibid 9-11)

"The laws governing inheritance are for the mast part unknown" is a self-explanatory statement by Charles Darwin. He did not understand the many causes of inheritance. One of his apparent unusual concepts seems to be that inheritance can be age-related. For example, if a calf were conceived from young hornless parents (before they grew horns) the result would be hornless offspring. On the other hand, if a bull were older when it grew horns and then reproduced, its male offspring would grow horns later in life as well.

CHARACTER OF DOMESTIC VARIETIES

Darwin:

"In attempting to estimate the amount of structural difference between allied domestic races, we are soon involved in doubt, from not knowing whether they are descended from one or several parent species. This point, if it could be cleared up, would be interesting; if, for instance, it could be shown that the greyhound, bloodhound, terrier, spaniel, and bull-dog, which we all know propagate their kind truly, were the offspring of any single species, then such facts would have great weight in making us doubt about the immutability [not changing] of the many closely allied natural species—for instance, of the many foxes—inhabiting different quarters of the world. I do not believe, as we shall presently see, that the whole amount of difference between the several breeds of the dog has been produced under domestication; I believe that a small part of the difference is due to their being descended from distinct species. In the case of strongly marked races of some other domesticated species, there is presumptive or even strong evidence, that all are descended from a single wild stock.

It has often been assumed that man has chosen for domestication animals and plants having an extraordinary inherent tendency to vary, and likewise to withstand diverse climates. I do not dispute that these capacities have added largely to the value of most of our domesticated productions; but how could a savage possibly know, when he first tamed an animal, whether it would vary in succeeding generations, and whether it would endure other climates? Has the little variability of the ass and goose, or the small power of endurance of warmth by the reindeer, or of cold by the common camel, prevented their domestication? I cannot doubt that if other animals and plants, equal in number to our domesticated productions, and belonging to equally diverse classes and countries, were taken from a state of nature, and could be made to breed for an equal number of generations under domestication, they would on an average vary as largely as the parent species of our existing domesticated productions have varied.".... (Darwin C., 1872, pp. 12-13)

As already been stated, the Russian Sulimov dogs were created to control drug smuggling at airports. They were produced primarily by crossing two already existing varieties as the Siberian husky "domesticated dogs" and the "wild" Turkmen Jackals. These new Sulimov dogs were made from what already existed to make something novel and useful. Also, these Russian dogs were not created through changes in its environment, such as climate or food etc.

A fact that all domestic dog varieties are offspring of wild animals, does not deny that a Creator God made the canine as an autonomous entity.

Darwin:

... "So it is in India. Even in the case of the breeds of the domestic dog throughout the world, which I admit are descended from several wild species, it cannot be doubted that there has been an immense amount of inherited variation; for who will believe that animals closely resembling the Italian greyhound, the bloodhound, the bull-dog, pug-dog, or Blenheim spaniel, &c.—so unlike all wild Canidae—ever existed in a state of nature? It has often been loosely said that all our races of dogs have been produced by the crossing of a few aboriginal species; but by crossing we can only get forms in some degree intermediate between their parents; and if we account for our several domestic races by this process, we must admit the former existence of the most extreme forms, as the Italian greyhound, bloodhound, bull-dog, &c., in the wild state. Moreover, the possibility of making distinct races by crossing has been greatly exaggerated. Many cases are on record, showing that a race may be modified by occasional crosses, if aided by the careful selection of the individuals which present the desired character; but to obtain a race intermediate between two quite distinct races, would be very difficult. Sir J. Sebright expressly experimented with this object, and failed. The offspring from the first cross between two pure breeds is tolerably and sometimes (as I have found with pigeons) quite uniform in character, and everything seems simple enough; but when these mongrels are crossed one with another for several generations, hardly two of them are alike, and then the difficulty of the task becomes manifest." (Darwin C., 1872, p. 15)

As stated above, "Many cases are on record, showing that a race may be modified by occasional crosses". As we already know through Mendelian genetics, a hybrid is created by crossing two varieties of the same species. Darwin also indicates that domesticated dogs are believed to be offspring from wild dogs.

The Russia Sulimov breed of dog is not intermediate between the domestic husky and the wild jackal, and neither is the liger intermediate between the lion and tiger. Furthermore, neither was created by Darwinian evolution in a slow step-by-step fashion through time.

Blending is not a good concept, because with Mendelian genetics, traits are carried forward from generation to generation either in a dominant or recessive state.

Darwin:

Breeds of the Domestic Pigeon, their Differences and Origin

"Believing even that it is always best to study some special group, I have, after deliberation, taken up domestic pigeons. I have kept every breed which I could purchase or obtain, and have been most kindly favored with skins from several quarters of the world, more especially by the Hon. W. Elliot from India, and by the Hon. C. Murray from Persia. Many treatises in different languages have been published on pigeons, and some of them are very important, as being of considerable antiquity. I have associated with several eminent fanciers, and have been permitted to join two of the London Pigeon Clubs. The diversity of the breeds is something astonishing …

… Great as are the differences between the breeds of the pigeon, I am fully convinced that the common opinion of naturalists is correct, namely, that all are descended from the rock-pigeon (Columba Livia), including under this term several geographical races or sub-species, which differ from each other in the most trifling respects. As several of the reasons which have led me to this belief are in some degree applicable in other cases, I will here briefly give them. If the several breeds are not varieties, and have not proceeded from the rock-pigeon, they must have descended from at least seven or eight aboriginal stocks; for it is impossible to make the present domestic breeds by the crossing of any lesser number. …

… An argument of great weight, and applicable in several other cases, is, that the above-specified breeds, though agreeing generally with the wild rock-pigeon in constitution, habits, voice, colouring, and in most parts of their structure, yet are certainly highly abnormal in other parts; we may look in vain through the whole great family of Columbidæ for a beak like that of the English carrier, or that of the short-faced tumbler, or barb; for reversed feathers like those of the Jacobin; for a crop like that of the pouter; for tail-feathers like those of the fantail. Hence it must be assumed not only that half-civilised man succeeded in thoroughly domesticating several species, but that he intentionally or by chance picked out extraordinarily abnormal species; and further, that these very species have since all become extinct or unknown. So many strange contingencies are improbable in the highest degree." (Darwin C., 1872, pp. 15-19)

Darwin observations of pigeons led to this conclusion that they vary but are all allied to the rock-pigeon. Darwin's observation of pigeons could be used as a model for Mendelian genetics where varieties cross to obtain other and dissimilar varieties and even with a mutation, a new variety could arise that would not be able to cross with its parentage. Nevertheless, they are all the same 'kind' since they all came from the same origin. They are all pigeons, no more and no less.

Darwin:

"I have discussed the probable origin of domestic pigeons at some, yet quite insufficient, length; because when I first kept pigeons and watched the several kinds, well knowing how truly they breed, I felt fully as much difficulty in believing that since they had been domesticated they had all proceeded from a common parent, as any naturalist could in coming to a similar conclusion in regard to the many species of finches, or other groups of birds, in nature.

One circumstance has struck me much; namely, that nearly all the breeders of the various domestic animals and the cultivators of plants, with whom I have conversed, or whose treatises I have read, are firmly convinced that the several breeds to which each has attended, are descended from so many aboriginally distinct species."… (Darwin C., 1872, p. 21)

Varieties can be linear descendants of other varieties, but to state that all species [kinds] are lineal descendants of other species would contradict the teaching of the Christian Bible which declares that 'kinds' were separately created.

A zebra and horse hybrid is usually called a zorse, and also by crossing a male donkey and a female horse creates a mule. The zebra, horse, zorse, donkey and mule all have the same origin; they are all descendants from the horse family. They are one of a "kind" originally created by God.

Darwin:

Principles of Selection anciently followed, and their Effects

"Let us now briefly consider the steps by which domestic races have been produced, either from one or from several allied species. Some effect may be attributed to the direct and definite action of the external conditions of life, and some to habit; but he would be a bold man who would account by such agencies for the differences between a dray and race horse, a greyhound and bloodhound, a carrier and tumbler pigeon. One of the most remarkable features in our domesticated races is that we see in them adaptation, not indeed to the animal's or plant's own good, but to man's use or fancy. Some variations useful to him have probably arisen suddenly, or by one step; many botanists, for instance, believe that the fuller's teasel, with its hooks, which cannot be rivalled by any mechanical contrivance, is only a variety of the wild Dipsacus; and this amount of change may have suddenly arisen in a seedling. So, it has probably been with the turnspit dog; and this is known to have been the case with the ancon sheep. But when we compare the dray-horse and race-horse, the dromedary and camel, the various breeds of sheep fitted either for cultivated land or mountain pasture, with the wool of one breed good for one purpose, and that of another breed for another purpose; when we compare the many breeds of dogs, each good for man in different ways; when we compare the game-cock, so pertinacious in battle, with other breeds so little quarrelsome, with "everlasting layers" which never desire to sit, and with the bantam so small and elegant; when we compare the host of agricultural, culinary, orchard, and flower-garden races of plants, most useful to man at different seasons and for different purposes, or so beautiful in his eyes, we must, I think, look further than to mere variability. We cannot suppose that all the breeds were suddenly produced as perfect and as useful as we now see them; indeed, in many cases, we know that this has not been their history. The key is man's power of accumulative selection: nature gives successive variations; man adds them up in certain directions useful to him. In this sense he may be said to have made for himself useful breeds. ...

The great power of this principle of selection is not hypothetical. It is certain that several of our eminent breeders have, even within a single lifetime, modified to a large extent their breeds of cattle and sheep. In order fully to realise what they have done, it is almost necessary to read several of the many treatises devoted to this subject, and to inspect the animals. Breeders habitually speak of an animal's organisation as something plastic, which they can model almost as they please." ... (Darwin C., 1872, pp. 22-23)

In a sense, man makes breeds useful to him, but in reality, he picks out what he has already been given. For example, the best vegetables for the dinner table were already in the garden. He did not create them. These chosen vegetables could very well have arrived as hybrids from the crosses of other varieties, and some varieties may also transmit mutations. Likewise, some of the seeds of this chosen variety would have to be saved for the next year's crop. Again, an example of selection and change is the Russian Sulimov dogs (previously stated) created by crossing already existing varieties of dogs as the Siberian husky and the Turkmen jackal, creating something novel.

My father was a farmer and within our farming district the Holstein was the favoured variety of cattle. We kept about twenty milking cows and only one very fortunate bull for the whole herd. Our bull was always selected as a calf, and the rest of the males were castrated and raised as beef. Selecting a bull in this way kept the herd in its highest standard possible, and yet the herd from year to year were never better or dissimilar from our neighbor's Holstein cattle.

Darwin:

"It may be objected that the principle of selection has been reduced to methodical practice for scarcely more than three-quarters of a century; it has certainly been more attended to of late years, and many treatises have been published on the subject; and the result has been, in a corresponding degree, rapid and important. But it is very far from true that the principle is a modern discovery. I could give several references to works of high antiquity, in which the full importance of the principle is acknowledged. In rude and barbarous periods of English history choice animals were often imported, and laws were passed to prevent their exportation: the destruction of horses under a certain size was ordered, and this may be compared to the "roguing" of plants by nurserymen. The principle of selection I find distinctly given in an ancient Chinese encyclopedia. Explicit rules are laid down by some of the Roman classical writers. From passages in Genesis, it is clear that the colour of domestic animals was at that early period attended to. Savages[21] now sometimes cross their dogs with wild canine animals, to improve the breed, and they formerly did so, as is attested by passages in Pliny. The savages in South Africa match their draught cattle by colour, as do some of the Esquimaux their teams of dogs. Livingstone states that good domestic breeds are highly valued by the negroes in the interior of Africa who have not associated with Europeans. Some of these facts do not show actual selection, but they show that the breeding of domestic animals was carefully attended to in ancient times, and is now attended to by the lowest savages. It would, indeed, have been a strange fact, had attention not been paid to breeding, for the inheritance of good and bad qualities is so obvious." (Darwin C., 1872, p. 25)

Same species but changed; Stirring the pot does not change the overall contents. The cross of a wild pig and a barnyard variety does not change the fact that they are all pigs. --- (You would have to be a pig to call your brother a pig and be telling the truth.)

---

[21] ('Savages' etc.) – Rightfully construed as bigoted language.

Edward Robinson

UNCONSCIOUS SELECTION

Darwin:

"At the present time, eminent breeders try by methodical selection, with a distinct object in view, to make a new strain or sub-breed, superior to anything of the kind in the country. But, for our purpose, a form of Selection, which may be called Unconscious, and which results from every one trying to possess and breed from the best individual animals, is more important. Thus, a man who intends keeping pointers naturally tries to get as good dogs as he can, and afterwards breeds from his own best dogs, but he has no wish or expectation of permanently altering the breed.

… Some highly competent authorities are convinced that the setter is directly derived from the spaniel, and has probably been slowly altered from it. It is known that the English pointer has been greatly changed within the last century, and in this case the change has, it is believed, been chiefly effected by crosses with the foxhound; but what concerns us is, that the change has been effected unconsciously and gradually, and yet so effectually, that, though the old Spanish pointer certainly came from Spain, Mr. Borrow has not seen, as I am informed by him, any native dog in Spain like our pointer." (Darwin C., 1872, pp. 25-26)

The fastest racehorse will only run so fast and no faster, and the best milking cow has a limit on its production (unless hormonally injected). Alteration of any species is determined by the fixed laws of genetics.

Darwin:

…" If there exist savages so barbarous as never to think of the inherited character of the offspring of their domestic animals, yet any one animal particularly useful to them, for any special purpose, would be carefully preserved during famines and other accidents, to which savages are so liable, and such choice animals would thus generally leave more offspring than the inferior ones; so that in this case there would be a kind of unconscious selection going on. We see the value set on animals even by the barbarians of Tierra del Fuego, by their killing and devouring their old women, in times of dearth, as of less value than their dogs.

In plants the same gradual process of improvement, through the occasional preservation of the best individuals, whether or not sufficiently distinct to be ranked at their first appearance as distinct varieties, and whether or not two or more species or races have become blended together by crossing, may plainly be recognised in the increased size and beauty which we now compared with the older varieties or with their parent-stocks. ...

No one would expect to raise a first-rate melting pear from the seed of the wild pear, though he might succeed from a poor seedling growing wild, if it had come from a garden-stock. The pear, though cultivated in classical times, appears, from Pliny's description, to have been a fruit of very inferior quality. I have seen great surprise expressed in horticultural works at the wonderful skill of gardeners, in having produced such splendid results from such poor materials; but the art has been simple, and, as far as the final result is concerned, has been followed almost unconsciously. It has consisted in always cultivating the best-known variety, sowing its seeds, and, when a slightly better variety chanced to appear, selecting it, and so onwards. But the gardeners of the classical period, who cultivated the best pears which they could procure, never thought what splendid fruit we should eat; though we owe our excellent fruit, in some small degree, to their having naturally chosen and preserved the best varieties they could anywhere find.

A large amount of change, thus slowly and unconsciously accumulated, explains, as I believe, the well-known fact, that in a number of cases we cannot recognise, and therefore do not know, the wild parent-stocks of the plants which have been longest cultivated in our flower and kitchen gardens. If it has taken centuries or thousands of years to improve or modify most of our plants up to their present standard of usefulness to man, we can understand how it is that neither Australia, the Cape of Good Hope, nor any other region inhabited by quite uncivilised man, has afforded us a single plant worth culture. It is not that these countries, so rich in species, do not by a strange chance possess the aboriginal stocks of any useful plants, but that the native plants have not been by continued selection up to a standard of perfection comparable with that acquired by the plants in countries anciently civilised" ... (Darwin C., 1872, pp. 26-27)

Whether unconscious or planned, all of the above change can be explained through Mendelian genetics. Changes in racehorses, dogs and plants are variety change, and not one species [kind] changing into another. Man's power of selection is no greater than what nature provides.

Charles Darwin lived during the time of slavery and colonization. He was against slavery but a reflection of his possible prejudice is obvious in the above paragraphs. Slavery officially ended in the United States in 1863.

Darwin:

"To sum up on the origin of our domestic races of animals and plants. Changed conditions of life are of the highest importance in causing variability, both by acting directly on the organisation, and indirectly by affecting the reproductive system. It is not probable that variability is an inherent and necessary contingent, under all circumstances. The greater or less force of inheritance and reversion determine whether variations shall endure. Variability is governed by many unknown laws, of which correlated growth is probably the most important. Something, but how much we do not know, may be attributed to the definite action of the conditions of life. Some, perhaps a great, effect may be attributed to the increased use or disuse of parts. The final result is thus rendered infinitely complex. In some cases, the intercrossing of aboriginally distinct species appears to have played an important part in the origin of our breeds. When several breeds have once been formed in any country, their occasional intercrossing, with the aid of selection, has, no doubt, largely aided in the formation of new sub-breeds; but the importance of crossing has been much exaggerated, both in regard to animals and to those plants which are propagated by seed. With plants which are temporarily propagated by cuttings, buds, &c., the importance of crossing is immense; for the cultivator may here disregard the extreme variability both of hybrids and of mongrels, and the sterility of hybrids; but plants not propagated by seed are of little importance to us, for their endurance is only temporary. Over all these causes of Change, the accumulative action of Selection, whether applied methodically and quickly, or unconsciously and slowly but more efficiently, seems to have been the predominant Power". (Darwin C., 1872, pp. 31-32)

Charles Darwin's lack of understanding of Mendelian genetics and the causes of inheritance is very evident in his summation for chapter one. He states that, "Variability is governed by many unknown laws". Darwin notes the importance of crossing, but dismisses it as much exaggerated. Today with Mendelian genetics, these laws are understood. For instance, we know that changed conditions do not create variation unless it causes a mutation; reversion can be recessive gene expression. Correlation is often traits inherited simultaneously, perhaps even on the same chromosome. Some varieties have changed through hybridization sometimes to the extent that they cannot cross with their original lineage, and some varieties are completely sterile - for example, the liger and the mule. Greater numbers are not necessarily beneficial for change because a cross of only two dissimilar varieties can lead to change and this change can be sudden repeated and predictable; a barn full of one variety of beef-cattle can hold true but if mixed with other varieties would create change. Charles Darwin's 'facts' does not prove that species are linear decedents of other species, such as dogs from cats or humans from ape like creatures etc. nor disproves the existence of a Creator God who created species or "kinds" distinct. Variety change is not species change such as a cat becoming a dog etc. (stirring the pot does not change its contents). Many of Charles Darwin's observations are correct but his conclusions wrong.

Currently, genetic engineering takes what is available, and alters it creating a permanent and sudden change. This sudden change is not in a slow Darwinian step-by-step fashion, but a deliberate change by an intelligent creature (Man).

Darwin clearly shows the confusion in labeling at the time of his writings. Today, we have a clearer understating of species and their many varieties. The changes and slight changes that Darwin ranked as the most important are often no more than other varieties.

VARIATION UNDER NATURE

Darwin:

"Before applying the principles arrived at in the last chapter to organic beings in a state of nature, we must briefly discuss whether these latter are subject to any variation. To treat this subject properly, a long catalogue of dry facts ought to be given; but these I shall reserve for a future work. Nor shall I here discuss the various definitions which have been given of the term species. No one definition has satisfied all naturalists; yet every naturalist knows vaguely what he means when he speaks of a species. …

The forms which possess in some considerable degree the character of species, but which are so closely similar to other forms, or are so closely linked to them by intermediate gradations, that naturalists do not like to rank them as distinct species, are in several respects the most important for us. We have every reason to believe that many of these doubtful and closely allied forms have permanently retained their characters for a long time; for as long, as far as we know, as have good and true species. Practically, when a naturalist can unite by means of intermediate links any two forms, he treats the one as a variety of the other; ranking the most common, but sometimes the one first described, as the species, and the other as the variety. But cases of great difficulty, which I will not here enumerate, sometimes arise in deciding whether or not to rank one form as a variety of another, even when they are closely connected by intermediate links; nor will the commonly-assumed hybrid nature of by intermediate links; nor will the commonly-assumed hybrid nature of the intermediate forms always remove the difficulty. In very many cases, however, one form is ranked as a variety of another, not because the intermediate links have actually been found, but because analogy leads the observer to suppose either that they do now somewhere exist, or may formerly have existed; and here a wide door for the entry of doubt and conjecture is opened. Nevertheless, no certain criterion can possibly be given by which variable forms, local forms, sub-species, and representative species can be recognised.

Many years ago, when comparing, and seeing others compare, the birds from the closely neighbouring islands of the Galapagos archipelago, one with another, and with those from the American mainland, I was much struck how entirely vague and arbitrary is the distinction between species and varieties. On the islets of the little Madeira group there are many insects which are characterized as varieties in Mr. Wollaston's admirable work but which would certainly be ranked as distinct species by many entomologists. Even Ireland has a few animals, now generally regarded as varieties, but which have been ranked as species by some zoologists. Several experienced ornithologists consider our British red grouse as only a strongly-marked race of a Norwegian species, whereas the greater number ranks it as an undoubted species peculiar to Great Britain. A wide distance between the homes of two doubtful forms leads many naturalists to rank them as distinct species; but what distance, it has been well asked, will suffice; if that between America and Europe is ample, will that between Europe and the Azores, or Madeira, or the Canaries, or between the several islets of these small archipelagos, be sufficient?

… But to discuss whether they ought to be called species or varieties, before any definition of these terms has been generally accepted, is vainly to beat the air. Certainly no clear line of demarcation has as yet been drawn between species and sub-species—that is, the forms which in the opinion of some naturalists come very near to, but do not quite arrive at, the rank of species: or, again, between sub-species and well-marked varieties, or between lesser varieties and individual differences. These differences blend into each other by an insensible series; and a series impresses the mind with the idea of an actual passage.

Hence I look at individual differences, though of small interest to the systematist, as of the highest importance for us, as being the first steps towards such slight varieties as are barely thought worth recording in works on natural history. And I look at varieties which are in any degree more distinct and permanent, as steps towards more strongly-marked and permanent varieties; and at the latter, as leading to sub-species, and then to species. The passage from one stage of difference to another may, in many cases, be the simple result of the nature of the organism and of the different physical conditions to which it has long been exposed; but with respect to the more important and adaptive characters, the passage from one stage of difference to another, may be safely attributed to the cumulative action of natural selection, hereafter to be explained, and to the effects of the increased use or disuse of parts. A well-marked variety may therefore be called an incipient species; but whether this belief is justifiable must be judged by the weight of the various facts and considerations to be given throughout this work; but whether this belief is justifiable must be judged by the weight of the various facts and considerations to be given throughout this work." (Ibid PP 43)

Much of what Darwin expresses as change is Mendelian variation and not species change. And what has already been stated, 'physical conditions', unless inducing a mutation, don't create a species or a variety, and neither can 'use and disuse of parts'.

For one kind of animal to change into another is highly theoretical. Humankind shares much in common with all primates which seems to indicate that the modern ape and humankind had a common ancestry, but we are vastly different as well. Statically, there should be as many or even more negative deviations as functionally positive. There would have to be countless changes or steps in a positive direction for an ape like creature to become human. For many bible-believing Christians, what all primates have in common are that they were independent created by the same Maker.

William Paley believed that we observe the existence of a benevolent God through his creation. An example is in his description of muscles, which follows.

Paley:

… "The great mechanical variety in the figure of the muscles may be thus stated. It appears to be a fixed law, that the contraction of a muscle shall be towards its centre Therefore, the subject for mechanism on each occasion is, so to modify the figure, and adjust the position of the muscle, as to produce the motion required, agreeably with this law. This can only be done by giving to different muscles a diversity of configuration, suited to their several offices [workplace], and to their situation with respect to the work which they have to perform. On which account we find them under a multiplicity of forms and attitudes; sometimes with double, sometimes with treble tendons, sometimes with none: sometimes one tendon to several muscles, at other times one muscle to several tendons. The shape of the organ is susceptible of an incalculable variety, whilst the original property of the muscle, the law and line of its contraction, remains the same, and is simple. Herein the muscular system may be said to bear a perfect resemblance to our works of art. An artist does not alter the native quality of his materials, or their laws of action." … (Paley W., Natural Theology or Evidences of the Existence and Attributes of the Deity, 1829, pp. 78-79)

What follows is an interesting footnote from the same page:

"The convenience and beauty of the tendons seem only an ulterior object, their necessity and utility principally claim our attention. The forcee [force] which a muscle possesses is as the number of the muscular fibres, but a limited number of fibres only can be fixed to any certain point of bone destined to be moved, therefore the contrivance is, to attach them to a cord, called a sinew or tendon, which can be conveniently conducted and fixed to the bone. If we are desirous of moving a heavy weight, we tie a strong cord to it, that a greater number of men may apply their strength. Thus a similar effect is produced — the muscular fibres are the moving powers, the tendons are the cords attached to the point to be moved." (Paxton)

Our fingers and heart muscles are quite different in size, shape; function etc. and both are optimal sized and placed to function for the purpose for which they were made. Does this not likewise indicate the existence of a Creator?

Darwin:

"Species of the Larger Genera [types or group] in each Country vary more frequently than the Species of the Smaller Genera.

… These facts are of plain signification on the view that species are only strongly-marked and permanent varieties; for wherever many species of the same genus have been formed, or where, if we may use the expression, the manufactory of species has been active, we ought generally to find the manufactory still in action, more especially as we have every reason to believe the process of manufacturing new species to be a slow one. And this certainly holds true, if varieties be looked at as incipient species; for my tables clearly show as a general rule that, wherever many species of a genus [type] have been formed, the species of that genus present a number of varieties, that is of incipient [budding] species, beyond the average. It is not that all varying large genera are now much, and are thus increasing in the number of their species, or that no small genera are now varying and increasing; for if this had been so, it would have been fatal to my theory; inasmuch as geology plainly tells us that small genera have in the lapse of time often increased greatly in size; and that large genera have often come to their maxima, declined, and disappeared. All that we want to show is, that, where many species of a genus have been formed, on an average many are still forming; and this certainly holds good." (Darwin C., 1958, p. 44)

The above is obvious: species of larger genera [plural for genus or type] vary more than smaller but only if an area has more varieties to interbreed in the first place. If the greater numbers are purebred and kept isolated from other varieties of the same species, they would remain purebred from generation to generation unless there is a mutation. For example, many dog varieties wandering the streets of a large city would create variety change while purebred dogs in a small kennel would remain true.

STRUGGLE FOR EXISTENCE AND NATURAL SELECTION

Darwin:

"Again, it may be asked, how is it that varieties, which I have called incipient species, become ultimately converted into good and distinct species, which in most cases obviously differ from each other far more than do the varieties of the same species? How do those groups of species, which constitute what are called distinct genera, and which differ from each other more than do the species of the same genus, arise? All these results, as we shall more fully see in the next chapter, follow from the struggle for life. Owing to this struggle, variations, however slight, and from whatever cause proceeding, if they be in any degree profitable to the individuals of a species, in their infinitely complex relations to other organic beings and to their physical conditions of life, will tend to the preservation of such individuals, and will generally be inherited by the offspring. The offspring, also, will thus have a better chance of surviving, for, of the many individuals of any species which are periodically born, but a small number can survive. I have called this principle, by which each slight variation, if useful, is preserved, by the term Natural Selection. ... (Ibid 48-49)

... The elder De Candolle and Lyell have largely and philosophically shown that all organic beings are exposed to severe competition. In regard to plants, no one has treated this subject with more spirit and ability than W. Herbert, Dean of Manchester, evidently the result of his great horticultural knowledge. Nothing is easier than to admit in words the truth of the universal struggle for life, or more difficult—at least I have found it so—than constantly to bear this conclusion in mind. Yet unless it be thoroughly engrained in the mind, the whole economy of nature, with every fact on distribution, rarity, abundance, extinction, and variation, will be dimly seen or quite misunderstood. We behold the face of nature bright with gladness, we often see superabundance of food; we do not see or we forget, that the birds which are idly singing round us mostly live on insects or seeds, and are thus constantly destroying life; or we forget how largely these songsters, or their eggs, or their nestlings, are destroyed by birds and beasts of prey; we do not always bear in mind, that, though food may be now superabundant, it is not so at all seasons of each recurring year." (Ibid 48-49)

Paley:

… "In domesticated animals, we find the effect of their fecundity [fertility] to be, that we can always command numbers; we can always have as many of any particular species as we please, or as we can support. Nor do we complain of its excess; it being much more easy to regulate abundance, than to supply scarcity. But then this super fecundity, though of great occasional use and importance, exceeds the ordinary capacity of nature to receive or support its progeny [offspring]. All superabundance supposes destruction, or must destroy itself. Perhaps there is no species of terrestrial animals whatever, which would not overrun the earth, if it were permitted to multiply in perfect safety; or of fish, which would not fill the ocean: at least, if any single species were left to their natural increase without disturbance or restraint, the food of other species would be exhausted by their maintenance. It is necessary, therefore, that the effects of such prolific faculties be curtailed." … (Paley W., Natural Theology or Evidences of the Existence and Attributes of the Deity, 1829, p. 240)

GEOMETRICAL RATIO OF INCREASE

Darwin:

"A struggle for existence inevitably follows from the high rate at which all organic beings tend to increase. Every being, which during its natural lifetime produces several eggs or seeds, must suffer destruction during some period of its life, and during some season or occasional year, otherwise, on the principle of geometrical increase, its numbers would quickly become so inordinately great that no country could support the product. Hence, as more individuals are produced than can possibly survive, there must in every case be a struggle for existence, either one individual with another of the same species, or with the individuals of distinct species, or with the physical conditions of life. It is the doctrine of Malthus applied with manifold force to the whole animal and vegetable kingdoms; for in this case there can be no artificial increase of food, and no prudential restraint from marriage. Although some species may be now increasing, more or less rapidly, in numbers, all cannot do so, for the world would not hold them.

There is no exception to the rule that every organic being naturally increases at so high a rate, that, if not destroyed, the earth would soon be covered by the progeny of a single pair. Even slow-breeding man has doubled in twenty-five years, and at this rate, in less than a thousand years, there would literally not be standing-room for his progeny. Linnaeus has calculated that if an annual plant produced only two seeds—and there is no plant so unproductive as this—and their seedlings next year produced two, and so on, then in twenty years there would be a million plants. The elephant is reckoned the slowest breeder of all known animals, and I have taken some pains to estimate its probable minimum rate of natural increase; it will be safest to assume that it begins breeding when thirty years old, and goes on breeding till ninety years old, bringing forth six young in the interval, and surviving till one hundred years old; if this be so, after a period of from 740 to 750 years there would be nearly nineteen million elephants alive, descended from the first pair." ... (Darwin C., 1872, pp. 50-51)

NATURE OF THE CHECKS TO INCREASE

Darwin:

"In the case of every species, many different checks, acting at different periods of life, and during different seasons or years, probably come into play; some one check or some few being generally the most potent; but all will concur in determining the average number or even the existence of the species. In some cases it can be shown that widely-different checks act on the same species in different districts. When we look at the plants and bushes clothing an entangled bank, we are tempted to attribute their proportional numbers and kinds to what we call chance. But how false a view is this! Every one has heard that when an American forest is cut down, a very different vegetation springs up; but it has been observed that ancient Indian ruins in the Southern United States, which must formerly have been cleared of trees, now display the same beautiful diversity and proportion of kinds as in the surrounding virgin forest. What a struggle must have gone on during long centuries between the several kinds of trees, each annually scattering its seeds by the thousand; what war between insect and insect—between insects, snails, and other animals with birds and beasts of prey—all striving to increase, all feeding on each other, or on the trees, their seeds and seedlings, or on the other plants which first clothed the ground and thus checked the growth of the trees! Throw up a handful of feathers, and all fall to the ground according to definite laws: but how simple is the problem where each shall fall compared to that of the action and reaction of the innumerable plants and animals which have determined, in the course of centuries, the proportional numbers and kinds of trees now growing on the old Indian ruins!" ... (Darwin C., 1872, p. 58)

Paley: [note the similarity and differences - Darwin to Paley]

... What we call blights [diseases], are oftentimes legions [many] of animated beings, claiming their portion in the bounty of nature. What corrupts the produce of the earth to us, prepares it for them. And it is by means of their rapid multiplication, that they take possession of their pasture; a slow propagation would not meet the opportunity. But in conjunction with the occasional use of this fruitfulness, we observe, also, that it allows the proportion between the several species of animals, to be differently modified, as different purposes of utility may require. When the forests of America come to be cleared, and the swamps drained, our gnats will give place to other inhabitants. If the population of Europe should spread to the north and the east, the mice will retire before the husbandman and the shepherd, and yield their station to herds and 'locks. If, what concerns the human species, it may be a part of the scheme of Providence, that the earth should be inhabited by a shifting, or perhaps a circulating population. In this economy, it is possible that there may be the following advantages: When old countries are become exceedingly corrupt, simpler modes of life, purer morals, and better institutions, may rise up in new ones, whilst fresh soils reward the cultivator with more plentiful returns. Thus the different portions of the globe come into use in succession as the residence of man; and, in his absence, entertain other guests, which, by their sudden multiplication, fill the chasm." ... (Paley W., 1829, pp. 245-246)

Edward Robinson

Darwin:

"The dependency of one organic being on another, as of a parasite on its prey, lies generally between beings remote in the scale of nature. This is likewise sometimes the case with those which may be strictly said to struggle with each other for existence, as in the case of locusts and grass-feeding quadrupeds. But the struggle will almost invariably be most severe between the individuals of the same species, for they frequent the same food, and are exposed to the same dangers. ...

... All that we can do, is to keep steadily in mind that each organic being is striving to increase in a geometrical ratio; that each at some period of its life, during some season of the year, during each generation or at intervals, has to struggle for life and to suffer great destruction. When we reflect on this struggle, we may console ourselves with the full belief, that the war of nature is not incessant [continuous], that no fear is felt, that death is generally prompt, and that the vigorous, the healthy, and the happy survive and multiply." (Darwin C., 1872, pp. 58-61)

Paley:

... "Immortality upon this earth is out of the question. Without death there could be no generation, no sexes, no parental relation, i. e. as things are constituted, no animal happiness. The particular duration of life, assigned to different animals, can form no part of the objection; because, whatever that duration be, whilst it remains finite and limited, it may always be asked, why it is no longer. The natural age of different animals varies, from a single day to a century of years. No account can be given of this; nor could any be given, whatever other proportion of life had obtained amongst them.

The term then of life in different animals being the same as it is, the question is, what mode of taking it away is the best even for the animal itself?

Now, according to the established order of nature, (which we must supposed to prevail, or we cannot reason at all upon the subject,) the three methods by which life is usually put an end to, are acute diseases, decay, and violence." ... (Paley W., Natural Theology or Evidences of the Existence and Attributes of the Deity, 1829, p. 265)

Nature needs its checks and balances. Both William Paley's and Charles Darwin's accounts of the checks and balances in nature are extremely similar even to the inclusion of the slow breeding elephant, but their deductions vastly differ. Paley envisioned nature as mostly blissful, and perhaps the balance of nature as another indicator of design conveying the existence of a Creator God. In Darwin's view, it was a means of the removal of the less suited in favour of the more adapted. This process he called, 'Natural Selection'. Darwin sees the world in a continual struggle for existence leading to change; change even to the extent of new species replacing parental; survival of the fittest, thus evolution. It is obvious that in his worldview there is no heaven on earth. In this view, would the more brutal and not the meek inherit the earth?

(Genesis 3:17) Humankind is to struggle with thistles and thrones for food.

NATURAL SELECTION - THE SURVIVAL OF THE FITTEST

Darwin:

"As man can produce, and certainly has produced, a great result by his methodical and unconscious means of selection, what may not natural selection effect? Man can act only on external and visible characters: Nature, if I may be allowed to personify the natural preservation or survival of the fittest, cares nothing for appearances, except in so far as they are useful to any being. She can act on every internal organ, on every shade of constitutional difference, on the whole machinery of life. Man selects only for his own good: Nature only for that of the being which she tends …

We see nothing of these slow changes in progress, until the hand of time has marked the lapse of ages, and then so imperfect is our view into long-past geological ages, that we see only that the forms of life are now different from what they formerly were in order that any great amount of modification should be effected in a species, a variety when once formed must again, perhaps after a long interval of time, vary or present individual differences of the same favourable nature as before; and these must be again preserved, and so onwards step by step. Seeing that individual differences of the same kind perpetually recur, this can hardly be considered as an unwarrantable assumption. But whether it is true, we can judge only by seeing how far the hypothesis accords with and explains the general phenomena of nature. On the other hand, the ordinary belief that the amount of possible variation is a strictly limited quantity is likewise a simple assumption." ...

"In looking at many small points of difference between species, which, as far as our ignorance permits us to judge, seem quite unimportant, we must not forget that climate, food, &c., have no doubt produced some direct effect. It is also necessary to bear in mind that, owing natural selection, other modifications, often of the most unexpected nature, will ensue." ... (Darwin C., 1872, pp. 62-67)

Charles Darwin's Natural selection and survival of the fittest is not a complicated concept. In fact, it is rather simple. Species change and the best suited for the environments in which they find themselves survive — most if not all of the rest perish, and thus, there is change in a step-by-step or gradated fashion.

For ape-like creatures to evolve into humans by means of Darwinian evolution is problematic. With Darwinian evolution, each forward step has to be a favourable mutation and the new is to replace the former. Statistically there should be as many or more negative or harmful mutations as positive. (Keep in mind that with Darwinian evolution, an irreducibly complex ape like creature first has to be in existence to become human.) With Mendelian genetics, varieties change, not species and not in a gradated step by step fashion.

Charles Darwin's assessment for change is wrong. As already indicated, hybrids are created by varieties of the same species crossing. Climate and food do not cause genetic change unless it induces a mutation. Darwin did not know genetics, or how co-related inheritance functioned. Correlation is traits inherited together and one does not impact the other. With genetics, change is only as far as nature allows (necessity does not create change). Darwin also states that, "She can act on every internal organ, on every shade of constitutional difference, on the whole machinery of life." Darwin does not indicate where the internal organisms originate in the first place. Darwin's theory is also problematic because each internal organ is very irreducibly complex; each organ works independently for the function of the whole entity; take away any essential internal organ and the entire creature doesn't exist.

(A human body needs its internal organs functioning for existence. Just ask anyone who is waiting on a kidney or heart transplant. Who survives without a heart of kidney or any other vital organ?)

There would have to be an enormous number of steps in the right direction with Darwinian evolution for one species to change into another. An organism is made up of many independent parts functioning for the purpose of the whole. For one species to evolve into another would entail changes in the heart, lungs, stomach, eyes, ears etc., and also the muscles and nervous system which controls these parts would have to change as well. With Darwinian evolution, there is a slow step by step change over immense time. There should be as many steps forward as backward Darwinian evolution is highly problematic.

Darwin:

"As we see that those variations which, under domestication appear at any particular period of life, tend to reappear in the offspring at the same period;— for instance, in the shape, size, and flavour of the seeds of the many varieties of our culinary and agricultural plants; in the caterpillar and cocoon stages of the varieties of the silkworm; in the eggs of poultry, and in the colour of the down of their chickens; in the horns of our sheep and cattle when nearly adult;—so in a state of nature, natural selection will be enabled to act on than in the cotton-planter increasing and improving by selection the down in the pods on his cotton-trees. Natural selection may modify and adapt the larva of an insect to a score of contingencies, wholly different from those which concern the mature insect; and these modifications may affect, through correlation, the structure of the adult. So, conversely, modifications in the adult may affect the structure of the larva; but in all cases natural selection will ensure that they shall not be injurious: for if they were so, the species would become extinct." (Darwin C., 1872, p. 67)

What a creature is to become is determined at conception. Natural-selection does not modify and adapt the larva of an insect to a score of contingencies [possibilities] unless there is a somatic [body] mutations which would not be passed onto future generations. For any permanent hereditary change caused by a mutation, it has to occur in the sex-cells produced through meiosis; thus, modification in the adult would not change the larva. Natural selection or survival of the fittest cannot create. It can only select from what already exists, therefore, for seeds to improve in their ability to be carried by the wind through natural selection in a step-by-step fashion is highly speculative.

Darwin:

... "Natural selection will modify the structure of the young in relation to the parent, and of the parent in relation to the young. In social animals it will adapt the structure of each individual for the benefit of the whole community; if the community profits by the selected change. What natural selection cannot do, is to modify the structure of one species, without giving it any advantage, for the good of another species; and though statements to this effect may be found in works of natural history, I cannot find one case which will bear investigation. A structure used only once in an animal's life, if of high importance to it, might be modified to any extent by natural selection; for instance, the great jaws possessed by certain insects, used exclusively for opening the cocoon—or the hard tip to the beak of unhatched birds, used for breaking the egg. It has been asserted, that of the best short-beaked tumbler-pigeons a greater number perish in the egg than are able to get out of it; so that fanciers assist in the act of hatching. Now if nature had to make the beak of a full-grown pigeon very short for the bird's own advantage, the process of modification would be very slow, and there would be simultaneously the most rigorous selection of all the young birds within the egg, which had the most powerful and hardest beaks, for all with weak beaks would inevitably perish; or, more delicate and more easily broken shells might be selected, the thickness of the shell being known to vary like every other structure." (Darwin C., 1872, pp. 67-68)

If hard beaks of a chick are necessary for hatching, where did they come from in the first place? Also, what derived first - the chicken or egg?

SEXUAL SELECTION?

Darwin:

"Inasmuch as peculiarities often appear under domestication in one sex and become hereditarily attached to that sex, so no doubt it will be under nature.

Thus it is rendered possible for the two sexes to be modified through natural selection in relation to different habits of life, as is sometimes the case; or for one sex to be modified in relation to the other sex, as commonly occurs. This leads me to say a few words on what I have called Sexual Selection. This form of selection depends, not on a struggle for existence in relation to other organic beings or to external conditions, but on a struggle between the individuals of one sex, generally the males, for the possession of the other sex. The result is not death to the unsuccessful competitor, but few or no offspring …

… Thus it is, as I believe, that when the males and females of any animal have the same general habits of life, but differ in structure, colour, or ornament, such differences have been mainly caused by sexual selection: that is, by individual males having had, in successive generations, some slight advantage over other males, in their weapons, means of defence, or charms, which they have transmitted to their male offspring alone. Yet, I would not wish to attribute all sexual differences to this agency: for we see in our domestic animals' peculiarities arising and becoming attached to the male sex, which apparently have not been augmented through selection by man. The tuft of hair on the breast of the wild turkey-cock cannot be or any use, and it is doubtful whether it can be ornamental in the eyes of the female bird; indeed, had the tuft appeared under domestication, it would have been called a monstrosity." (Darwin C., 1872, pp. 67-68)

Paley:

"The covering of birds cannot escape the most vulgar observation. Its lightness, its smoothness, its warmth; the disposition of the feathers all inclined backward, the down about their stem, the overlapping of their tips, their different configuration in different parts, not to mention the variety of their colors, constitute a vestment for the body ; so beautiful, and so appropriate to the life which the animal is to lead, as that, I think, we should have had no conception of anything equally perfect, if we had never seen it, or can now imagine anything more so. Let us suppose (what is possible only in supposition) a person who had never seen a bird, to be presented with a plucked pheasant, and bid to set his wits to work, how to contrive for it a covering which shall unite the qualities of warmth, levity [lightness], and least resistance to the air, and the highest degree of each; giving it also as much of beauty and ornament as he could afford. He is the person to behold the work of the Deity, in this part of his creation, with the sentiments which are due to it. The commendation, which the general aspect of the feathered world seldom fails of exciting, will be increased by farther examination. It is one of those cases in which the philosopher has more to admire than the common observer. Every feather is a mechanical wonder. If we look at the quill, we find properties not easily brought together, — strength and lightness. I know few things more remarkable than the strength and lightness of the very pen with which I am writing. If we cast our eye to the upper part of the stem, we see a material, made for the purpose, used in no other class of animals, and in no other part of birds; tough, light, pliant, elastic. The pith, also, which feeds the feathers, is, amongst animal substances, *sui generis*: neither bone, flesh, membrane, nor tendon. But the artificia part of a feather is the beard, or, as it is sometimes, I believe, called, the vane. By the beards are meant, what are fastened on each side of the stem, and what constitute the breadth of the feather; what we usually strip off, from one side or both, when we make a pen. The separate pieces of laminae, of which the beard is composed, are called threads, sometimes filaments, or rays. Now the first thing which an attentive observer will remark is, how much stronger the beard of the feather shows itself to be, when pressed in a direction perpendicular to its plane, than when rubbed, either up or down, in the line of the stem; and he will soon discover the structure which occasions this difference, viz. that the laminae, whereof these beards are composed, are flat, and placed with their flat sides towards each other; by which means, whilst they easily tend for the approaching of each other, as any one may perceive by drawing his finger ever so lightly upwards, they are much harder to bend out of their plane, which is the direction in which they have to encounter the impulse and pressure of the air, and in which their strength is wanted and put to the trial. This is one particularity in the structure of a feather; a second is still more extraordinary. Whoever examines a feather, cannot help taking notice, that the threads or laminae, of which we have been speaking, in their natural state unite; that their union is something more than the mere apposition of loose surfaces; that they are not parted asunder without some degree of force; that nevertheless there in no glutinous [sticky] cohesion between them-, that, therefore, by some mechanical means or other, they catch or clasp among themselves, thereby giving to the beard or vane its closeness and compactness of texture. Nor is this all: when two laminae, which have been separated by accident or force, are brought together again, they immediately reclasp; the connexion, whatever it was, is perfectly recovered, and the beard of the feather becomes as smooth and firm as if nothing had happened to it. Draw your finger down the feather, which is against the grain, and you break probably the junction of some of the contiguous threads; draw your finger up the feather, and you restore all things to their former state. This is no common contrivance: and now for the mechanism by which it is affected. The threads or laminae above mentioned, are interlaced with one another; and the interlacing is performed by means of a vast number of fibres, or teeth, which the laminae shoot forth on each side, and which hook and grapple together. A friend of mine counted fifty of these fibres in one twentieth of an inch. These fibres are crooked ; but curved after a different manner: for those which proceed from the thread on the side towards the extremity if the feather, are longer, more flexible, and bent down ward; whereas those which proceed from the side towards the beginning, or quill-end of the feather, are shorter, firmer, and turn upwards. The process then which takes place is as follows: When two laminae are pressed together, so that these long fibres are forced far enough over the short ones, their crooked parts fall into the cavity made by the crooked parts of the others; just as the latch that is fastened to a door enters into the cavity of the catch fixed to the door-post, and there hooking itself, fastens the door" … (Paley W., Natural Theology or Evidences of the Existence and Attributes of the Deity, 1829, pp. 124-127)

I often picked up a discarded feather from the ground and marveled how the sides or laminae could be pulled apparent and restored. A single feather is a very irreducibly complex structure. The obvious conclusion which William Paley would make, is that this is additional reason to believe in a Creator God. If a solitary feather is so irreducible complex, how much more is an entire bird in flight!

Sexual selection did not create the essential differences between males and females since sex is essential for reproduction, and sexual selection did not create a single bird or their feathers. But, if female birds choose a more colorful variety and reject all other varieties, this variety may gain an advantage.

I remember when I was a boy on our family farm that our mares would be very hostile towards a stallion until the time when they were ready to mate. In the animal kingdom, female ovulation is often at the same time as their desire for sexual intercourse. If the female does not have a desire or arousal in response to the male's display, then all the efforts of the male with his many charms are in vain. This could be why many potential partners are rejected. In addition, sexual behavior is inherited and species specific. Other bird species and animals would be uninterested in an elaborate peacock courtship display.

Instincts and sexual traits are also gender specific. The ability for a bird to lay eggs is one thing, but the instinct to incubate them to maturity is quite another. It is safe to assume that a bird dose not reason that her choice of a particular mate would change anything, or that when she sits on her eggs that she has any preconceived idea of what her chicks would even look like after hatching. If her eggs were replaced by other eggs or even with stones, she would still nurture as if they were her own.

SURVIVAL OF THE FITTEST

Darwin:

"In order to make it clear how, as I believe, natural selection acts, I must beg permission to give one or two imaginary illustrations. Let us take the case of a wolf, which preys on various animals, securing some by craft, some by strength, and some by fleetness; and let us suppose that the fleetest prey, a deer for instance, had from any change in the country increased in numbers, or that other prey had decreased in numbers, during that season of the year when the wolf was hardest pressed for food. Under such circumstances the swiftest and slimmest wolves would have the best chance of surviving, and so be preserved or selected, —provided always that they retained strength to master their prey at this or some other period of the year, when they were compelled to prey on other animals. I can see no more reason to doubt that this would be the result, than that man should be able to improve the fleetness of his greyhounds by careful and methodical selection, or by that kind of unconscious selection which follows from each man trying to keep the best dogs without any thought of modifying the breed. …

It should not, however, be overlooked that certain rather strongly marked variations, which no one would rank as mere individual differences, frequently recur owing to a similar organisation being similarly acted on,—of which fact numerous instances could be given with our domestic productions. In such cases, if the varying individual did not actually transmit to its offspring its newly-acquired character, it would undoubtedly transmit to them, as long as the existing conditions remained the same, a still stronger tendency to vary in the same manner. There can also be little doubt that the tendency to vary in the same manner has often been so strong that all the individuals of the same species have been similarly modified without the aid of any form of selection …. Or only a third, fifth, or tenth part of the individuals may have been thus affected, of which fact several instances could be given. Thus Graba estimates that about one-fifth of the guillemots in the Faroe Islands consist of a variety so well marked, that it was formerly ranked as a distinct species under the name of Uria lacrymans. In cases of this kind, if the variation were of a beneficial nature, the original form would soon be supplanted by the modified form, through the survival of the fittest.

To the effects of intercrossing in eliminating variations of all kinds, I shall have to recur; but it may be here remarked that most animals and plants keep to their proper homes, and do not needlessly wander about; we see this even with migratory birds, which almost always return to the same spot. Consequently, each newly-formed variety would generally be at first local, as seems to be the common rule with varieties in a state of nature; so that similarly modified individuals would soon exist in a small body together, and would often breed together. If the new variety were successful in its battle for life, it would slowly spread from a central district, competing with and conquering the unchanged individuals on the margins of an ever-increasing circle." (Darwin C., 1872, pp. 70-73)

Darwin's 'natural selection' or 'the survival of the fittest' has merit, but it has to follow the laws of nature as well: Hybrids could be born with advantages over existing varieties such as Darwin's examples of the swiftest and slimmest wolves and birds with better-suited beaks for gathering food, and these would have the best chance of surviving. Also, if the new hybrids of a species could breed or cross with the original or common variety then the whole species could change over time. However, new hybrids do not have a still stronger tendency to vary in the same manner. Conditions don't create hybrids, but as stated, new hybrids of a species could be better suited for the conditions in which they find themselves in. These changes do not negate the fact that God created each "kind" distinct, because hybrid species are direct descendants of a mutual stock.

"Walking home I passed a woman talking to her cat. When I got home, I told my dog all about it and we both had a great laugh". – "Some people think that animals are human." (From my wife Letty).

Darwin:

Circumstances favourable for the production of new forms through Natural Selection.

"Isolation, also, is an important element in the modification of species through natural selection. In a confined or isolated area, if not very large, the organic and inorganic conditions of life will generally be almost uniform; so that natural selection will tend to modify all the varying individuals of the same species in the same manner. Intercrossing with the inhabitants of the surrounding districts will, also, be thus prevented …

… Lastly, isolation will give time for a new variety to be improved at a slow rate; and this may sometimes be of much importance. If, however, an isolated area be very small, either from being surrounded by barriers, or from having very peculiar physical conditions, the total number of the inhabitants will be small; and this will retard the production of new species through natural selection, by decreasing the chances of favorable variations arising.

… Finally, I conclude that, although small isolated areas have been in some respects highly favourable for the production of new species, yet that the course of modification will generally have been more rapid on large areas; and what is more important, that the new forms produced on large areas, which already have been victorious over many competitors, will be those that will spread most widely, and will give rise to the greatest number of new varieties and species. They will thus play a more important part in the changing history of the organic world." (Darwin C., 1872, pp. 80-83)

As has already been stated, varieties are frequently changing in different local. We have already seen that variety crosses cause changes. If a number of varieties are split, some remaining on a mainland and other varieties which are in some way different removed to an island, then through time, both groups would remain the same species, but become quite different in variety one to the other.

ON THE INHABITANTS OF OCEANIC ISLANDS

Darwin:

"Oceanic islands are sometimes deficient in animals of certain whole classes, and their places are occupied by other classes: thus in the Galapagos Islands reptiles, and in New Zealand gigantic wingless birds, take, or recently took, the place of mammals. Although New Zealand is here spoken of as an oceanic island, it is in some degree doubtful whether it should be so ranked; it is of large size, and is not separated from Australia by a profoundly deep sea; from its geological character and the direction of its mountain-ranges, the Rev. W.

B. Clarke has lately maintained that this island, as well as New Caledonia, should be considered as appurtenances [part] of Australia. Turning to plants, Dr. Hooker has shown that in the Galapagos Islands the proportional numbers of the different orders are very different from what they are elsewhere. All such differences in number, and the absence of certain whole groups of animals and plants, are generally accounted for by supposed differences in the physical conditions of the islands; but this explanation is not a little doubtful. Facility of immigration seems to have been fully as important as the nature of the conditions.

Many remarkable little facts could be given with respect to the inhabitants of oceanic islands. For instance, in certain islands not tenanted [occupied] by a single mammal, some of the endemic plants have beautifully hooked seeds; yet few relations are more manifest than that hooks serve for the transportal of seeds in the wool or fur of quadrupeds. But a hooked seed might be carried to an island by other means; and the plant then becoming modified would form an endemic species, still retaining its hooks, which would form a useless appendage like the shrivelled wings under the soldered wing-covers of many insular beetles. Again, islands often possess trees or bushes belonging to orders which elsewhere include only herbaceous species; now trees, as Alph. de Candolle has shown, generally have, whatever the cause may be, confined ranges. Hence trees would be little likely to reach distant oceanic islands; and an herbaceous plant, which had no chance of successfully competing with the many fully developed trees growing on a continent, might, when established on an island, gain an advantage over other herbaceous plants by growing taller and taller and overtopping them. In this case, natural selection would tend to add to the stature of the plant, to whatever order it belonged, and thus first convert it into a bush and then into a tree." (Darwin C., 1872, pp. 349-350)

Why would a plant convert, like magic, into a bush and then into a tree? All this can be explained through Mendelian genetics.

ABSENCE OF BATRACHIANS AND TERRESTRIAL MAMMALS ON OCEANIC ISLANDS

Darwin:

"With respect to the absence of whole orders of animals on oceanic islands, Bory de St. Vincent long ago remarked that Batrachians (frogs, toads, newts) are never found on any of the many islands with which the great oceans are studded. I have taken pains to verify this assertion, and have found it true, with the exception of New Zealand, New Caledonia, the Andaman Islands, and perhaps the Salomon Islands and the Seychelles." ...

"Mammals offer another and similar case. I have carefully searched the oldest voyages, and have not found a single instance, free from doubt, of a terrestrial mammal (excluding domesticated animals kept by the natives) inhabiting an island situated above 300 miles from a continent or great continental island. ...

... Although terrestrial mammals do not occur on oceanic islands, aerial mammals do occur on almost every island. New Zealand possesses two bats found nowhere else in the world: Norfolk Island, the Viti Archipelago, the Bonin Islands, the Caroline and Marianne Archipelagoes, and Mauritius, all possess their peculiar bats. Why, it may be asked, has the supposed creative force produced bats and no other mammals on remote islands? On my view this question can easily be answered; for no terrestrial mammal can be transported across a wide space of sea, but bats can fly across. Bats have been seen wandering by day far over the Atlantic Ocean; and two North American species either regularly or occasionally visit Bermuda, at the distance of 600 miles from the mainland. I hear from Mr. Tomes, who has specially studied this family, that many species have enormous ranges, and are found on continents and on far distant islands. Hence we have only to suppose that such wandering species have been modified in their new homes in relation to their new position, and we can understand the presence of endemic bats on oceanic islands, with the absence of all other terrestrial mammals.

Another interesting relation exists, namely between the depth of the sea separating islands from each other or from the nearest continent, and the degree of affinity of their mammalian inhabitants. ...

… we can understand how it is that a relation exists between the depth of the sea separating two mammalian faunas, and the degree of their affinity [kinship], —a relation which is quite inexplicable on the theory of independent acts of creation. … (Ibid. 350- 352)

The existence of the many varieties of species throughout the world is explainable through Mendelian Genetics and therefore Charles Darwin is wrong in his statement that this is inexplicable on independent acts of creation.

Darwin:

"The most striking and important fact for us is the affinity [similarity in structure] of the species which inhabit islands to those of the nearest mainland, without being actually the same. Numerous instances could be given. The Galapagos Archipelago, situated under the equator, lies at the distance of between 500 and 600 miles from the shores of South America. Here almost every product of the land and of the water bears the unmistakeable stamp of the American continent." … (ibid.353)

These birds are often referred to as 'Darwin's finches'.[22] The most striking difference between these birds is the shape and size of their beaks which are used for different food sources.

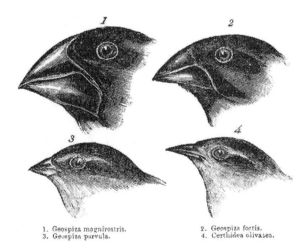

1. Geospiza magnirostris.
3. Geospiza parvula.
2. Geospiza fortis.
4. Certhidea olivacea.

---

[22] 'Darwin's finches' image is in public domain.

The differences between these Galapagos' birds are no more radical then modern-day dogs or cats created by the crossing of existing varieties.

Darwin:

"There are twenty-six land-birds; of these, twenty-one or perhaps twenty-three are ranked as distinct species, and would commonly be assumed to have been here created; yet the close affinity of most of these birds to American species is manifest in every character, in their habits, gestures, and tones of voice. So it is with the other animals, and with a large proportion of the plants, as shown by Dr. Hooker in his admirable Flora of this archipelago. The naturalist, looking at the inhabitants of these volcanic islands in the Pacific, distant several hundred miles from the continent, feels that he is standing on American land. Why should this be so? Why should the species which are supposed to have been created in the Galapagos Archipelago, and nowhere else, bear so plainly the stamp of affinity to those created in America? The inhabitants of the Cape Verde Islands are related to those of Africa, like those of the Galapagos to America. Facts such as these, admit of no sort of explanation on the ordinary view of independent creation; whereas on the view here maintained, it is obvious that the Galapagos Islands would be likely to receive colonists from America, whether by occasional means of transport or (though I do not believe in this doctrine) by formerly continuous land, and the Cape Verde Islands from Africa; such colonists would be liable to modification,—the principle of inheritance still betraying their original birthplace.

Many analogous facts could be given: indeed it is an almost universal rule that the endemic [native?] productions of islands are related to those of the nearest continent, or of the nearest large island." ...

"The same law which has determined the relationship between the inhabitants of islands and the nearest mainland, is sometimes displayed on a small scale, but in a most interesting manner, within the limits of the same archipelago. Thus each separate island of the Galapagos Archipelago is tenanted, and the fact is a marvellous one, by many distinct species: but these species are related to each other in a very much closer manner than to the inhabitants of the American continent, or of any other quarter of the world. This is what might have been expected, for islands situated so near to each other would almost necessarily receive immigrants from the same original source, and from each other. But how is it that many of the immigrants have been differently modified, though only in a small degree, in islands situated within sight of each other, having the same geological nature, the same height, climate, &c.? This long appeared to me a great difficulty: but it arises in chief part from the deeply-seated error of considering the physical conditions of a country as the most important; whereas it cannot be disputed that the nature of the other species with which each has to compete, is at least as important, and generally a far more important element of success. Now if we look to the species which inhabit the Galapagos Archipelago and are likewise found in other parts of the world, we find that they differ considerably in the several islands. This difference might indeed have been expected if the islands have been stocked by occasional means of transport—a seed, for instance, of one plant having been brought to one island, and that of another plant to another island, though all proceeding from the same general source. Hence, when in former times an immigrant first settled on one of the islands, or when it subsequently spread from one to another, it would undoubtedly be exposed to different conditions in the different islands, for it would have to compete with a different set of organisms; a plant for instance, would find the ground best fitted for it occupied by somewhat different species in the different islands, and would be exposed to the attacks of somewhat different enemies. If then it varied, natural selection would probably favour different varieties in the different islands. Some species, however, might spread and yet retain the same character throughout the group, just as we see some species spreading widely throughout a continent and remaining the same.

The really surprising fact in this case of the Galapagos Archipelago, and in a lesser degree in some analogous cases, is that each new species after being formed in any one island, did not spread quickly to the other islands. But the islands, though in sight of each other, are separated by deep arms of the sea, in most cases wider than the British Channel, and there is no reason to suppose that they have at any former period been continuously united. The currents of the sea are rapid and sweep between the islands, and gales of wind are extraordinarily rare; so that the islands are far more effectually separated from each other than they appear on a map. Nevertheless some of the species, both of those found in other parts of their world and of those confined to the archipelago, are common to the several islands; and we may infer from their present manner of distribution, that they have spread from one island to the others." ... (Ibid. 354-356)

If there is only one variety present in isolation, it would be the indigenous species variety, and if there is no mutation, the variety would hold true. If, however, there are two or more varieties of a species on an isolated island, there would be a tendency to crossbreed, and thus there would be change. If we had several varieties of a species intermingling and crossing, the original varieties would mix and would no longer be a distinct variety. Similarly, if one race of humans existed on an isolated island for a long time, the race would hold true. If two races of humans mixed over many centuries, they would conceivably become one race — it is all in the genes.

Not all species or varieties of species make it to an isolated island from a mainland because they would have to endure the ocean that lies between. An analogy could be a sieve effect. For example, at our home, we have screens on our back-patio door to keep flies out, but small fruit flies occasionally got through the screen. Thus, there are flies on both sides of the screen but different varieties. An island and a mainland would have many of the same species but different varieties. The water between an island and a mainland would be as the sieve stopping some whole species and while allowing only the varieties of others which are suitable for the journey to cross. This could explain the large turtles of the Galapagos and also why there are different varieties of finches (Darwin's finches) on different island, etc.

None of the proceeding denies that species were initially autonomously created. Today, species are continually being modified on main lands as well as islands. For example, new dog breeds and cat breads are created all the time. There are bat varieties on mainland and bats on islands found nowhere else in the world, but they are all still – "bats". There is also the mingling of human races creating other peoples. With Mendelian Genetics, these occurrences are explainable through variety change and not species or kinds changing into other species over time. Change depends on the availability of varieties to propagate, and the creation of a hybrid is not a slow step-by-step process. As always, the limit to the amount of change possible is fixed by the rules of genetics.

Another possible analogy of these changes could be languages. Today, languages are very different from any languages of their source. For example, the English language is a combination of many languages. A language of an isolated native tribe would endure until this tribe encounters other peoples and then their language would mix creating change. Language has been very fluid in the past and for any society trying to maintain a language as part of their culture seems futile.

EXTINCTION CAUSED BY NATURAL SELECTION

Darwin:

"I think it inevitably follows, that as new species in the course of time are formed through natural selection, others will become rarer and rarer, and finally extinct. The forms which stand in closest competition with those undergoing modification and improvement, will naturally suffer most. And we have seen in the chapter on the Struggle for Existence that it is the most closely-allied forms,—varieties of the same species, and species of the same genus or of related genera,—which, from having nearly the same structure, constitution, and habits, generally come into the severest competition with each other; consequently, each new variety or species, during the progress of its formation, will generally press hardest on its nearest kindred, and tend to exterminate them. We see the same process of extermination amongst our domesticated productions, through the selection of improved forms by man. Many curious instances could be given showing how quickly new breeds of cattle, sheep, and other animals, and varieties of flowers, take the place of older and inferior kinds. In Yorkshire, it is historically known that the ancient black cattle were displaced by the long-horns, and that these "were swept away by the short- horns" (I quote the words of an agricultural writer) "as if by some murderous pestilence."… (Darwin C., 1872, pp. 85-86)

Variety change is not species change. There would be a tendency for varieties to interbreed and not compete (making love not war). Novel varieties are plentiful.

Scientists are still looking for missing links. There would have to be countless missing links for one species "kind" to change into another. For example, a fish into a bird!

Darwin:

Divergence of Character

"The principle, which I have designated by this term, is of high importance, and explains, as I believe, several important facts. In the first place, varieties, even strongly-marked ones, though having somewhat of the character of species—as is shown by the hopeless doubts in many cases how to rank them—yet certainly differ far less from each other than do good and distinct species. Nevertheless, according to my view, varieties are species in the process offormationn, (sic) [of formation] or are, as I have called them, incipient [just beginning] species. How, then, does the lesser difference between varieties become augmented into the greater difference between species? That this does habitually happen, we must infer from most of the innumerable species throughout nature presenting well-marked differences; whereas varieties, the supposed prototypes and parents of future well-marked species, present slight and ill-defined differences. Mere chance, as we may call it, might cause one variety to differ in some character from its parents, and the offspring of this variety again to differ from its parent in the very same character and in a greater degree; but this alone would never account for so habitual and large a degree of difference as that between the species of the same genus

… Again, we may suppose that at an early period of history, the men of one nation or district required swifter horses, whilst those of another required stronger and bulkier horses. The early differences would be very slight; but, in the course of time, from the continued selection of swifter horses in the one case, and of stronger ones in the other, the differences would become greater, and would be noted as forming two sub-breeds. Ultimately, after the lapse of centuries, these sub-breeds would become converted into two well-established and distinct breeds. As the differences became greater, the inferior animals with intermediate characters, being neither very swift nor very strong, would not have been used for breeding, and will thus have tended to disappear. Here, then, we see in man's productions the action of what may be called the principle of divergence [deviation], causing differences, at first barely appreciable, steadily to increase, and the breeds to diverge in character, both from each other and from their common parent.

But how, it may be asked, can any analogous principle apply in nature? I believe it can and does apply most efficiently (though it was a long time before I saw how), from the simple circumstance that the more diversified the descendants from any one species become in structure, constitution, and habits, by so much will they be better enabled to seize on many and widely diversified places in the polity of nature, and so be enabled to increase in numbers." ... (Darwin C., 1872, pp. 86-87)

With Mendelian genetic, change is structured. Crossing two varieties routinely does not create a distinctive new species. A farmer cannot create a smaller horse or a better milking cow than what he is given in nature through crossing available varieties. A variety crossed with a variety of the same species creates a new variety, and this newer variety may be better suited to the environment in which it inhabits, however this is not a slow linear change to a new and very different species. A variety crossed with a variety is in a sense stirring the mix of what already exists, thus traits of two parents are passed on to hybrids. As has already been stated, an example of this change is the Russian Sulimov dogs created for detecting drugs on aircraft. The process of creating similar hybrids dog breeds can be repeated if the parent varieties are still in existence. Where there are no varieties, there will not be hybrids. Another possible analogy for genetics change could be a comparison with a deck of playing cards with a limited number of combinations. For example, when anyone is dealt seven cards from a deck of fifty-two, the resulting hand is limited to what the deck contains; with a deck of fifty-two cards there are only four aces, and never five or more. As has already been stated, a farmer who wishes to have the smallest or largest horse, or the strongest, is limited to what is genetically possible.

Today, with selective breeding and also genetic engineering we are altering our domestic plants and animals to an extent that would never happen naturally. We also are choosing a small number of varieties to meet our domestic needs and not cultivating others. Without cultivation, the non-selected varieties may go extinct leading to less diversity. Without variety, there may never be another Eureka moment of creation. For example - the possibility of crossing two shrivelled-up potato varieties and obtaining surprising results in a hybrid that is less disease prone, bigger, and hardier and more delicious then we have in our grocery shelves today.

DARWIN'S TREE

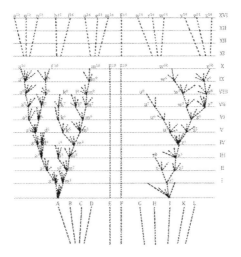

This illustration (similar to the original) is often referred to as Charles Darwin's — Tree of Life. This diagram seems self-explanatory, therefore, I left out Darwin's extensive account for a shortened summery that follows.

Darwin:

"The affinities of all the beings of the same class have sometimes been represented by a great tree. I believe this simile largely speaks the truth. The green and budding twigs may represent existing species; and those produced during former years may represent the long succession of extinct species. At each period of growth all the growing twigs have tried to branch out on all sides, and to overtop and kill the surrounding twigs and branches, in the same manner as species and groups of species have at all times overmastered other species in the great battle for life. The limbs divided into great branches, and these into lesser and lesser branches, were themselves once, when the tree was young, budding twigs; and this connection of the former and present buds by ramifying branches may well represent the classification of all extinct and living species in groups subordinate to groups. Of the many twigs which flourished when the tree was a mere bush, only two or three, now grown into great branches, yet survive and bear the other branches; so, with the species which lived during long-past geological periods, very few have left living and modified descendants. From the first growth of the tree, many a limb and branch has decayed and dropped off; and these fallen branches of various sizes may represent those whole orders, families, and genera which have now no living representatives, and which are known to us only in a fossil state. As we here and there see a thin straggling branch springing from a fork low down in a tree, and which by some chance has been favoured and is still alive on its summit, so we occasionally see an animal like the Ornithorhynchus [platypus] or Lepidosiren, which in some small degree connects by its affinities two large branches of life, and which has apparently been saved from fatal competition by having inhabited a protected station. As buds give rise by growth to fresh buds, and these, if vigorous, branch out and overtop on all sides many a feebler branch, so by generation I believe it has been with the great Tree of Life, which fills with its dead and broken branches the crust of the earth, and covers the surface with its ever-branching and beautiful ramifications." (Darwin C., 1872, pp. 104-105)

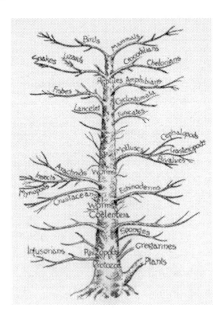

Darwin's tree of life is a theme depicting the relationships of all life through time.

This tree representation is prevailing even today. The illustration that follows is from 1922:

"Showing in order of evolution the general relations of the chief classes into which the world of living things is divided. This scheme represents the present stage of our knowledge, but is admittedly provisional". (Thomson A. J., 1922, p. 55)

Charles Darwin knew that his 'tree of life' illustration did not fit the reality of the geological record, but with time and added fossil discoveries, he expected to be vindicated.

Darwin:

"There is another and allied difficulty, which is much more serious. I allude to the manner in which species belonging to several of the main divisions of the animal kingdom suddenly appear in the lowest known fossiliferous rocks. Most of the arguments which have convinced me that all the existing species of the same group are descended from a single progenitor, apply with equal force to the earliest known species. For instance, it cannot be doubted that all the Cambrian and Silurian trilobites are descended from some one crustacean, which must have lived long before the Cambrian age, and which probably differed greatly from any known animal. Some of the most ancient animals, as the Nautilus, Lingula, &c., do not differ much from living species; and it cannot on our theory be supposed, that these old species were the progenitors of all the species belonging to the same groups which have subsequently appeared, for they are not in any degree intermediate in character.

Consequently, if the theory be true, it is indisputable that before the lowest Cambrian stratum was deposited, long periods elapsed, as long as, or probably far longer than, the whole interval from the Cambrian age to the present day; and that during these vast periods the world swarmed with living creatures. Here we encounter a formidable objection; for it seems doubtful whether the earth, in a fit state for the habitation of living creatures, has lasted long enough" ... "To the question why we do not find rich fossiliferous deposits belonging to these assumed earliest periods prior to the Cambrian system, I can give no satisfactory answer." ... (Darwin C., 1872, pp. 285-286)

"The abrupt manner in which whole groups of species suddenly appear in certain formations, has been urged by several palaeontologists—for instance, by Agassiz, Pictet, and Sedgwick—as a fatal objection to the belief in the transmutation [change] of species. If numerous species, belonging to the same genera or families, have really started into life at once, the fact would be fatal to the theory of evolution through natural selection." ... (Ibid 282)

This abrupt presence of species and varieties of species within the Cambrian layer is often referred to as 'The Cambrian Explosion'. Scientists place the Cambrian layer at about 530 million years ago. The fossil record shows that, within the Cambrian layer, virtually every phyla or body type and varieties of each, coexisted simultaneously. Today, about ninety-eight percent of species that existed at the Cambrian era are new extinct. All of this refutes Darwinism, which expected the slow, gradual increase in diversity over time. Darwin believed that with the passage of time the geological record would be filled in to align with his tree of life depiction, but it has not happened.

A biblical version of life's origin could be likened to a forest, or equated to a beautiful garden, where a Great Gardner established all kinds of plants and animals and not just a singular tree.

ON THE DEGREE TO WHICH ORGANISATION TENDS TO ADVANCE

Darwin:

"Natural Selection acts exclusively by the preservation and accumulation of variations, which are beneficial under the organic and inorganic conditions to which each creature is exposed at all periods of life. The ultimate result is that each creature tends to become more and more improved in relation to its conditions. This improvement inevitably leads to the gradual advancement of the organisation of the greater number of living beings throughout the world."

... of differentiation and specialisation of the several organs in each being when adult (and this will include the advancement of the brain for intellectual purposes), natural selection clearly leads towards this standard: for all physiologists admit that the specialisation of organs, inasmuch as in this state they perform their functions better, is an advantage to each being; and hence the accumulation of variations tending towards specialisation is within the scope of natural selection." (Ibid PP 97-98)

The above is clearly conjecture: Mendelian genetics could have a tendency to maintain what already exists. Also, the human body as a whole is very irreducibly complex. How can we explain human origins if all our organs are needed for our very existence in the first place?

Can we accurately say that children today are more intelligent than their ancestors? Technology has advanced tremendously, but who is to say that our hunter gatherer ancestors were less off then we are today. As long as they had plenty of food, water, and a good social life, they were probably more comfortable. Abundance does not always generate happiness. I know firsthand that many of the poorest people in the Philippines are happier than many of the affluent.

If we were to compare modern humans to the Neanderthal as an example, many Neanderthals had large cranium and probably bigger brains then we have. They also had a social existence, and as long as there was plenty of food, water, and a place to sleep - they would not have nor need a large house with a mortgage or rent as we do today. They also lived without schools or government taxes (how pleasant!). Our world is changing but not everything is progressing.

INCREDIBLE ORGANIZATION NEEDS AN ORGANIZER

Intelligent Design or Darwinism! How can the source of wax in our ears, tears in our eyes, or the arrangement of our eyelashes and hear on our heads be explained through Darwinism?

Even the arrangement of the lowly earthworm is very organized.

Edward Robinson

(Schroeder, 2014) Retrieved from: https://commons.wikimedia.org/wiki/
File:Annelid_redone_w_white_background.svg

Anyone wishing to use this image on a different web site or publication is asked to provide the following details along with the image:

- Author: K.D. Schroeder
- *Annelid redone w white background.svg* from Wikimedia Commons
- License: CC-BY-SA 3.0

Darwin:

… "Finally, I believe that many lowly organised forms now exist throughout the world, from various causes. In some cases variations or individual differences of a favourable nature may never have arisen for natural selection to act on and accumulate. In no case, probably, has time sufficed for the utmost possible amount of development. In some few cases there has been what we must call retrogression [decline] of organisation. But the main cause lies in the fact that under very simple conditions of life a high organisation would be of no service, —possibly would be of actual disservice, as being of a more delicate nature, and more liable to be put out of order and injured.

Looking to the first dawn of life, when all organic beings, as we may believe, presented the simplest structure, how, it has been asked, could the first steps in the advancement or differentiation of parts have arisen? Mr. Herbert Spencer would probably answer that, as soon as simple unicellular organism came by growth or division to be compounded of several cells, or became attached to any supporting surface, his law "that homologous units of any order become differentiated in proportion as their relations to incident forces become different" would come into action. But as we have no facts to guide us, speculation on the subject is almost useless. It is, however, an error to suppose that there would be no struggle for existence, and, consequently, no natural selection, until many forms had been produced: variations in a single species inhabiting an isolated station might be beneficial, and thus the whole mass of individuals might be modified, or two distinct forms might arise. But, as I remarked towards the close of the Introduction, no one ought to feel surprise at much remaining as yet unexplained on the origin of species, if we make due allowance for our profound ignorance on the mutual relations of the inhabitants of the world at the present time, and still more so during past ages." (Darwin C., 1872, p. 100)

It is pure speculation that organisms would advance from simple creatures to highly complex forms - from a one-celled creature to a highly developed human. Today, with added knowledge of Mendelian genetics, we know a great deal more than what Charles Darwin ever did in understanding the mutual relations of the inhabitants of the world.

Since something cannot come from nothing, where did organic life derive from in the first place?

Necessity cannot create; an organism does not exist just because it is needed. The human body is also very organized and irreducibly complex, needing all its essential and independent units functioning for the existence of the whole. Darwin's Natural Selection does not explain our beginnings - it only infers that we derived from ape like creatures. What are the origins of apes, etc.? Darwin's Natural Selection does not create and only selects what has already been given. These facts are highly problematic for Darwinism.

There are parallels but vastly different deductions with Darwin's "spontaneous generation and natural selection" in Origin of Species 1872 to William Paley's account regarding "appetencies" published in Natural Theology 1829. [Referred to earlier]

Paley:

"Another system, which has lately been brought forward, and with much ingenuity, is that of *appetencies*. The principle, and the short account of the theory, is this: Pieces of soft, ductile matter, being endued with propensities [tendencies] or appetencies [desire] for particular actions, would, by continual endeavours, carried on through a long series of generations, work themselves gradually into suitable forms; and at length acquire, though perhaps by obscure and almost imperceptible improvements, an organization fitted to the action which their respective propensities led them to exert ...

... In one important respect, however, the theory before us coincides with atheistic systems, viz. in that, in the formation of plants and animals, in the structure and use of their parts, it does away final causes [purpose]. Instead of the parts of a plant or animal, or the particular structure of the parts, having been intended for the action or the use to which we see them applied, according to this theory, they have themselves grown out of that action, sprung from that use. The theory therefore dispenses with that which we insist upon, the necessity, in each particular case, of an intelligent, designing mind, for the contriving and determining of the form which organized bodies bear. Give our philosopher these appetencies; give him a portion of living irritable matter (a nerve, or the clipping of a nerve) to work upon; give also to his incipient [beginning] or progressive forms, the power, in every stage of their alteration, of propagating their like; and, if he is to be believed, he could replenish the world with all the vegetable and animal productions which we at present see in it. ...

... The scheme under consideration is open to the same objection with other conjectures of a similar tendency, viz. a total defect of evidence. No changes, like those which the theory requires, have ever been observed. All the changes in Ovid's Metamorphoses might have been affected by these appetencies, if the theory were true: yet not an example, nor the pretence of an example, is offered of a single change being known to have taken place. Nor is the order of generation obedient to the principle upon which this theory is built. The mammae [23]* of the male have not vanished by inusitation; [non-use] nee cur tor um, per multa scecula Judceorum propagini deest prceputium. It is easy to say, and it has been said, that the alterative process is too slow to be perceived; that it has been carried on through tracts of immeasurable time; and that the present order of things is the result of a gradation, of which no human records can trace the steps. It is easy to say this; and yet it is still true, that the hypothesis remains destitute of evidence. Through the analogies which have been alleged are of the following kind. The bunch of a camel is said to be no other than the effect of carrying burthens; a service in which the species has been employed from the most ancient times of the world The first race, by the daily loading of the back, would probably find a small grumous tumour to be

---

[23] * I confess myself totally at a loss to guess at the reason, either final or efficient, for this part of the animal frame, unless there be some foundation for an opinion, of which I draw the hint from a paper of Sir Everard Home's, (Phil. Transac. 1799, p. 2,) viz. that the mammae of the foetus may be formed before the sex is determined. [This footnote is from the original and has merit. Both sexes are born with teats, and with hormones, females' breasts develop to produce milk.]

formed in the flesh of that part. The next progeny would bring this tumour into the world with them. The life to which they were destined would increase it. The cause which first generated the tubercle being continued, it would go on, through every succession, to augment its size, till it attained the form and the bulk under which it now appears this may serve for one instance. Another, and that also of the passive sort, is taken from certain species of birds. Birds of the crane kind, as the crane itself, the heron, bittern, stork, have, in general, their thighs bare of feathers. This privation is accounted for from the habit of wading in water, and from the effect of that element to check the growth of feathers upon these parts; in consequence of which, the health and vegetation of the feathers declined through each generation of the animal; the tender down, exposed to cold and wetness, became weak, and thin, and rare, till the deterioration ended in the result which we see, of absolute nakedness. I will mention a third instance, because it is drawn from an active habit, as the two last were from passive habits; and that is the *pouch* of the pelican. The description, which naturalists give of this organ, is as follows:

"From the lower edges of the under chap hangs a bag, reaching from the whole length of the bill to the neck, which is said to be capable of containing fifteen quarts of water. This bag the bird has a power of wrinkling up into the hollow of the under chap. When the bag is empty, it is not seen; but when the bird has fished with success, it is incredible to what an extent it is often dilated. The first thing the pelican does in fishing is to fill the bag; and then it returns to digest its burden at leisure. The bird preys upon large fishes, and hides them by dozens in its pouch. When the bill is opened to its widest extent, a person may run his head into the bird's mouth, and conceal it in this monstrous pouch, thus adapted for very singular purposes."[24] Now this extraordinary conformation is nothing more, say our philosophers, than the result of habit; not of the habit or effort of a single pelican, or of a single race of pelicans, but of a habit perpetuated through a long series of generations. The pelican soon found the conveniency of reserving in its mouth, when its appetite was glutted the remainder of its prey, which is fish. The fullness produced by this attempt, of course stretched the skin which lies between the under chaps, as being the most yielding part of the mouth. Every distension [enlargement] increased the cavity. The original bird, and many generations which succeeded him, might find difficulty enough in making the pouch answer this purpose: but future

---

[24] Goldsmith, vol. vi. P.52

pelicans, entering upon life with a pouch derived from their progenitors, of considerable capacity, would more readily accelerate its advance to perfection, by frequently pressing down the sack with the weight of fish which it might now be made to contain.

These, or of this kind, are the analogies relied upon. Now, in the first place, the instances themselves are unauthenticated by testimony; and, in theory, to say the least of them, open to great objections. Who ever read of camels without bunches, or with bunches less than those with which they are at present usually formed? A bunch, not unlike the camel's, is found between the shoulders of the buffalo; of the origin of which it is impossible to give the account which is here given. In the second example; why should the application of water, which appears to promote and thicken the growth of feathers upon the bodies and breasts of geese and swans, and other water-fowls, have divested of this covering the thighs of cranes? The third instance, which appears to me as plausible as any that can be produced, has this against it, that it is a singularity restricted to the species; whereas, if it had its commencement in the cause and manner which have been assigned, the like conformation might be expected to take place in other birds which feed upon fish. How comes it to pass, that the pelican alone was the inventress, and her descendants the only inheritors, of this curious resource?

But it is the less necessary to controvert the instances themselves, as it is a straining of analogy beyond all limits of reason and credibility, to assert that birds, and beasts, and fish, with all their variety and complexity of organization, have been brought into their forms, and distinguished into their several kinds and natures, by the same process (even if that process could be demonstrated, or had it ever been actually noticed) as might seem to serve for the gradual generation of a camel's bunch, or a pelican's pouch.

The solution, when applied to the works of nature *generally*, is contradicted by many of the phenomena, and totally inadequate to others. The *ligaments* or strictures, by which the tendons are tied down at the angles of the joints, could by no possibility, be formed by the motion or exercise of the tendons themselves; by any appetency [desire] exciting these parts into action; or by any tendency arising therefrom. The tendency is all the other way; the conatus [effort] in constant opposition to them. Length of time does not help the case at all, but the reverse. The valves also in the blood vessels could never be formed in the manner which our theorist proposes. The blood, in its right and natural course, has no tendency to form them. When obstructed or refluent [flowing back], it has the contrary. These parts could not grow out of their use, though they had eternity to grow in.

The senses of animals appear to me altogether incapable of receiving the explanation of their origin which this theory affords. Including under the word "sense" the organ and the perception, we have no account of either. How will our philosopher get at vision, or make an eye? How should the blind animal effect sight, of which blind animals, we know, have neither conception nor desire? Affecting it, by what operation of its will, by what endeavour to see, could it so determine the fluids of its body, as to inchoate [develop] the formation of an eye; or suppose the eye formed, would the perception follow? The same of the other senses And this objection holds its force, ascribe [credit] what you will to the hand of time, to the power of habit, to changes too slow to be observed by man, or brought within any comparison which he is able to make of past things with the present: concede what you please to these arbitrary and unattested suppositions, how will they help you? Here is no inception [beginning]. No laws, no course, no powers of nature which prevail at present, nor any analogous to these, could give commencement to a new sense. And it is in vain to inquire how that might proceed, which could never begin.

I think the senses to be the most inconsistent with the hypothesis before us, of any part of the animal frame. But other parts are sufficiently so. The solution does not apply to the parts of animals which have little in them of motion. If we could suppose joints and muscles to be gradually formed by action and exercise, what action or exercise could form a skull, or fill it with brains? No effort of the animal could determine the clothing of its skin. What *conatus* [impulse] could give prickles to the porcupine or hedgehog or to the sheep its fleece?

In the last place: What do these appetencies mean when applied to plants? I am not able to give a signification to the term, which can be transferred from animals to plants, or which is common to both Yet a no less successful organization is found in plants, than what obtains in animals A solution is wanted for one as well as the other. Upon the whole; after all the schemes and struggles of a reluctant "Philosophy, the necessary resort is to a Deity.

The marks of design are too strong to be gotten over Design must have had a designer. That designer must have been a person. That person is God." (Paley W., Natural Theology or Evidences of the Existence and Attributes of the Deity, 1829, pp. 241-246)

We smell by breathing air through our nose where smell receptors are located and our sense of taste is acquired through our taste buds on our tongue located inside our mouth where we chew our food. These senses are ideally located to send signals to our brain where they are processed. Can the origin of our senses which are all highly organized and irreducibly complex be explained by Darwinian evolution in a slow step-by-step process?

CONVERGENCE OF CHARACTER

Darwin:

"But geology shows us, that from an early part of the tertiary period the number of species of shells, and that from the middle part of this same period the number of mammals, has not greatly or at all increased. What then checks an indefinite increase in the number of species? The amount of life (I do not mean the number of specific forms) supported on an area must have a limit, depending so largely as it does on physical conditions; ... therefore, if an area be inhabited by very many species, each or nearly each species will be represented by few individuals; and such species will be liable to extermination from accidental fluctuations in the nature of the seasons or in the number of their enemies. The process of extermination in such cases would be rapid, whereas the production of new species must always be slow. Imagine the extreme case of as many species as individuals in England, and the first severe winter or very dry summer would exterminate thousands on thousands of species. Rare species, and each species will become rare if the number of species in any country becomes indefinitely increased, will, on the principle often explained, present within a given period few favourable variations; consequently, the process of giving birth to new specific forms would thus be retarded. When any species becomes very rare, close interbreeding will help to exterminate it; authors have thought that this comes into play in accounting for the deterioration of the Aurochs in Lithuania, of Red Deer in Scotland, and of Bears in Norway,

&c. Lastly, and this I am inclined to think is the most important element, a dominant species, which has already beaten many competitors in its own home, will tend to spread and supplant many others. Alph. de Candolle has shown that those species which spread widely, tend generally to spread *very* widely; consequently, they will tend to supplant and exterminate several species in several areas, and thus check the inordinate increase of specific forms throughout the world. Dr. Hooker has recently shown that in the S.E. corner of Australia, where, apparently, there are many invaders from different quarters of the globe, the endemic Australian species have been greatly reduced in number. How much weight to attribute to these several considerations I will not pretend to say; but conjointly they must limit in each country the tendency to an indefinite augmentation [increase] of specific forms. (Darwin C., 1872, pp. 101-102)

Interbreeding does not necessarily eliminate a species or variety. Interbreeding of small numbers however will have a greater chance of recessive genes treats being expressed. Hemophilia in the royal families of Europe is an example. Hemophilia is a rare bleeding disorder in which the blood does not clot normally.

Notice the similarity and differences to the above!

Paley:

… "In conjunction with other checks and limits, all subservient to the same purpose, are the thinnings which take place among animals, by their action upon one another. In some instances we ourselves experience, very directly, the use of these hostilities. One species of insects rids us of another species; or reduces their ranks. A third species, perhaps, keeps the second within bounds; and birds or lizards are a fence against the inordinate increase by which even these last might infest us. In other more numerous, and possibly more important instances, this disposition of things, although less necessary or useful to us, and of course less observed by us, may be necessary and useful to certain other species; or even for the preventing of the loss of certain species from the universe: a misfortune which seems to be studiously guarded against. Though there may be the appearance of failure in some of the details of Nature's works, in her great purposes there never are. His species never fail. The provision which was originally made for continuing the replenishment of the world has proved itself to be effectual through a long succession of ages.

What farther shows, that the system of destruction amongst animals holds an express relation to the system of fecundity [fertility]; that they are parts indeed of one compensatory scheme; is, that in each species the fecundity bears a proportion to the smallness of the animal, to the weakness, to the shortness of its natural term of life, and to the dangers and enemies by which it is surrounded. An elephant produces but one calf: a butterfly lays six hundred eggs. Birds of prey seldom produce more than two eggs: the sparrow tribe, and the duck tribe, frequently sit upon a dozen. In the rivers, we meet with a thousand minnows for one pike; in the sea, a million of herrings for a single shark. Compensation obtains throughout. Defencelessness and devastation are repaired by fecundity [fertility]. We have dwelt the longer upon these considerations, because the subject to which they apply, namely, that of animals devouring one another, forms the chief, if not the only instance, in the works of the Deity, of an economy, stamped by marks of design, in which the character of utility can be called in question ...

... Our first proposition, and that which we have hitherto been defending, was, "that, in a vast plurality of instances in which contrivance is perceived, the design of the contrivance is beneficial." ... (Paley W., Natural Theology or Evidences of the Existence and Attributes of the Deity, 1829, pp. 264-265)

LAWS OF VARIATION

Darwin:

...When a variation is of the slightest use to any being, we cannot tell how much to attribute to the accumulative action of natural selection, and how much to the definite action of the conditions of life. Thus, it is well known to furriers that animals of the same species have thicker and better fur the further north they live; but who can tell how much of this difference may be due to the warmest-clad individuals having been favoured and preserved during many generations, and how much to the action of the severe climate? For it would appear that climate has some direct action on the hair of our domestic quadrupeds.

Instances could be given of similar varieties being produced from the same species under external conditions of life as different as can well be conceived;

and, on the other hand, of dissimilar varieties being produced under apparently the same external conditions. Again, innumerable instances are known to every naturalist, of species keeping true, or not varying at all, although living under the most opposite climates. Such considerations as these incline me to less weight on the direct lay action of the surrounding conditions, than on a tendency to vary, due to causes of which we are quite ignorant. (Darwin C., 1872, pp. 106-108)

Climate does not change one species into another species. I remember that on our family farm every spring our milking cows would lose clumps of hair from their fur. In addition, the rabbits in the forest change their snow-white winter coat for summer colors of gray and brown etc. This cyclic change is triggered by the environment and it is also inherited and species specific. A species does not automatically change to fit a changing environment; however climate and the environment can separate which species or varieties of species survive in a given local. A polar bear is well suited for its northern environment, and does not change when brought to a warmer location (often in zoos). We humans inhabit the world, and climate has never changed our bodies; we still need clothing. Mankind is a unique species where clothing has allowed us to live in every region of the world for thousands of years.

Darwin does not explain first-causes. [Where did life originate from in the first place?] Darwin's main inferences for organic changes were based on species that already exist and they cannot exist unless they existent as a functional unit from the beginning. For example, a bird cannot fly without feathers, wings, muscles, eyes and a brain to coordinate all these external and internal parts.

Environment cannot create; habitat change does not change a species unless it induces a mutation. Mutations are often harmful not helpful and for any species to change, there would have to be a tremendous series of changes in a positive direction which makes Darwinian evolution problematic.

We have through the ages lost countless varieties and whole species. An example is The Passenger Pigeon [stated earlier] which didn't change to fit its' environment, instead it became extinct. Two main reasons for this bird's demise was over-kill and destruction of habitat. The Passenger Pigeon is now extinct but who is to say that some of their genetic markup is not within our barnyard varieties today.

EFFECTS OF THE INCREASED USE AND DISUSE OF PARTS

Lamarck's theory of 'use and disuse' has been disproved, but Darwin used it as a means for change.

Effects of the increased Use and Disuse of Parts, as controlled by Natural Selection:

Darwin:

… "I think there can be no doubt that use in our domestic animals has strengthened and enlarged certain parts, and disuse diminished them; and that such modifications are inherited. Under free nature, we have no standard of comparison, by which to judge of the effects of long- continued use or disuse, for we know not the parent-forms; but many animals possess structures which can be best explained by the effects of disuse. As Professor Owen has remarked, there is no greater anomaly in nature than a bird that cannot fly; yet there are several in this state. The logger-headed duck of South America can only flap along the surface of the water, and has its wings in nearly the same condition as the domestic Aylesbury duck: it is a remarkable fact that the young birds, according to Mr. Cunningham, can fly, while the adults have lost this power. As the larger ground-feeding birds seldom take flight except to escape danger, it is probable that the nearly wingless condition of several birds, now inhabiting or which lately inhabited several oceanic islands, tenanted by no beast of prey, has been caused by disuse. The ostrich indeed inhabits continents, and is exposed to danger from which it cannot escape by flight, but it can defend itself by kicking its enemies, as efficiently as many quadrupeds. We may believe that the progenitor of the ostrich genus had habits like those of the bustard, and that, as the size and weight of its body were increased during successive generations, its legs were used more, and its wings less, until they became incapable of flight" … (Darwin C., 1872, p. 108)

Just as the Lager is so much different from its progenitor or ancestry, flightless birds could have been hybrids of flight birds, or flight birds from flightless, but this is also conjecture.

Here again, Darwin gives 'use and disuse' as best to explain evolutionary change According to the theory of *'use and disuse of parts'*, with right-handed people, our right arms should be so much bigger than the left but, right-handed babies are born with the right and left arms surprisingly similar. A basketball player's height is caused by inheritance, not use and disuse. It is inheritance—it is hybridization—it is all genetic—not *'use and disuse of parts'*.

Even today, *'use and disuse of parts'* have been assumed as causes for human change. Some examples are the almost disappearance of the human tail, and the increase of our buttocks for upright walking. Also, with use, our humanoid heads and brains have gotten bigger than our ape-like cousins and our appendix became smaller since we no longer eat leaves. Did the once-necessary appendix change to be the appendix we have today? Where is the proof for these and other changes through use and disuse other than speculation?

Many scientists today believe that our appendix may have function in developing babies, or used to kick-start the necessary bacteria in the stomach after a disease.

Darwin:

"In some cases, we might easily put down to disuse modifications of structure which are wholly, or mainly, due to natural selection. Mr. Wollaston has discovered the remarkable fact that 200 beetles, out of the 550 species (but more are now known) inhabiting Madeira, are so far deficient in wings that they cannot fly; and that, of the twenty-nine endemic genera, no less than twenty-three have all their species in this condition! Several facts,—namely, that beetles in many parts of the world are frequently blown to sea and perish; that the beetles in Madeira, as observed by Mr. Wollaston, lie much concealed, until the wind lulls and the sun shines; that the proportion of wingless beetles is larger on the exposed Desertas than in Madeira itself; and especially the extra- ordinary fact, so strongly insisted on by Mr. Wollaston, that certain large groups of beetles, elsewhere excessively numerous, which absolutely require the use of their wings, are here almost entirely absent;— these several considerations make me believe that the wingless condition of so many Madeira beetles is mainly due to the action of natural selection, combined probably with disuse. For during many successive generations each individual beetle which flew least, either from its wings having been ever so little less perfectly developed or from indolent [lethargic or alzy] habit, will have had the best chance of surviving from not being blown out to sea; and, on the other hand, those beetles which most readily took to flight would oftenest have been blown to sea, and thus destroyed.

The insects in Madeira which are not ground-feeders, and which, as certain flower-feeding coleoptera and lepidoptera, must habitually use their wings to gain their subsistence, have, as Mr. Wollaston suspects, their wings not at all reduced, but even enlarged. This is quite compatible with the action of natural selection. For when a new insect first arrived on the island, the tendency of natural selection to enlarge or to reduce the wings, would depend on whether a greater number of individuals were saved by successfully battling with the winds, or by giving up the attempt and rarely or never flying. As with mariners shipwrecked near a coast, it would have been better for the good swimmers if they had been able to swim still further, whereas it would have been better for the bad swimmers if they had not been able to swim at all and had stuck to the wreck." ... (Darwin C., 1872, pp. 109-110)

In the above, Darwin gives the example of the winged beetles swiped out to sea leaving more of the wingless on land, and thus there is a change. Natural selection does not create winged and wingless beetle varieties. This is an example where there was no species change but variety ratio in a specific area.

The following has often been used in student text-books as an example of natural selection at work: Before the industrial revelation in England, the peppered moths were predominantly light-coloured. During the industrial revolution a darker-coloured moth became more prevalent because they were camouflaged by pollution and the lighter were more easily seen by predators on a darkened background. With the introduction of pollution controls, the white coloured moths once again became predominant.

This is a good example of change, but not species change where one species becomes a linear descendent of another. The black and white peppered moths were in the population in lesser or greater numbers all the time. They were no more than varieties of the same species.

CORRELATED VARIATION

Darwin:

... "We shall presently see that simple inheritance often gives the false appearance of correlation. One of the most obvious real cases is, that variations of structure arising in the young or larvae naturally tend to affect the structure of the mature animal. The several parts of the body which are homologous [similar stricter], and which, at an early embryonic period, are identical in structure, and which are necessarily exposed to similar conditions, seem eminently liable to vary in a like manner: we see this in the right and left sides of the body varying in the same manner; in the front and hind legs, and even in the jaws and limbs, varying together, for the lower jaw is believed by some anatomists to be homologous with the limbs. These tendencies, I do not doubt may be mastered more or less completely by natural selection: thus a family of stags once existed with an antler only on one side; and if this had been of any great use to the breed, it might probably have been rendered permanent by selection.

Homologous parts, as has been remarked by some authors, tend to cohere; this is often seen in monstrous plants: and nothing is more common than the union of homologous parts in normal structures, as in the union of the petals into a tube. Hard parts seem to affect the form of adjoining soft parts; it is believed by some authors that with birds the diversity in the shape of the pelvis causes the remarkable diversity in the shape of their kidneys. Others believe that the shape of the pelvis in the human mother influences by pressure the shape of the head of the child. In snakes, according to Schlegel, the form of the body and the manner of swallowing determine the position and form of several of the most important viscera [internal organs]. ...

... We may often falsely attribute to correlated variation structures which are common to whole groups of species, and which in truth are simply due to inheritance; for an ancient progenitor may have acquired through natural selection some one modification in structure, and, after thousands of generations, some other and independent modification; and these two modifications, having been transmitted to a whole group of descendants with diverse habits, would naturally be thought to be in some necessary manner correlated. Some other correlations are apparently due to the manner in which natural selection can alone act. For instance, Alph. de Candolle has remarked that winged seeds are never found in fruits which do not open: I should explain this rule by the impossibility of seeds gradually becoming winged through natural selection, unless the capsules were open; for in this case alone could the seeds, which were a little better adapted to be wafted by the wind, gain an advantage over others less well fitted for wide dispersal." (Darwin C., 1872, pp. 114-118)

Inheritance is not the cause for antlers on one side of a stag's head. A missing antler on one side of a stag's head can be explained by natural cases such as a broken bone during development.

Correlated Variation can be simply explained through genetics in which correlated traits are inherited at the same time, and perhaps even on the same chromosome. It is in the genes at conception. Many evolutionists believe that we came down from the trees, stood upright and developed heavier brains, thus upright stature is correlated with brain size. Hair on a man's chin and going bald at the age of forty can be construed as co-related but a change in one trait does not necessarily affect the other. Shaving one's chin does not affect baldness!

Correlated is explainable through genetics. During meiosis, alleles of one trait separate independently from the alleles of another This is Mendel's law of independent assortment.

OF THE ANIMAL STRUCTURE
REGARDED AS A MASS

Paley:

"Contemplating *an animal body* in its collective capacity, we cannot forget to notice, what a number of instruments are brought together, and often within how small a compass. It is a cluster of contrivances. In a Canary bird, for instance, and in the single ounce of matter which composes its body, (but which seems to be all employed,) we have instruments for eating, for digesting, for nourishment, for breathing, for generation, for running, for flying, for seeing, for hearing, for smelling, each appropriate, each entirely different from all the rest.

The human, or indeed the animal frame, considered as a mass or assemblage, exhibits in its composition three properties, which have long struck my mind as indubitable evidences, not only of design, but of a great deal of attention and accuracy in prosecuting the design.

The first is, the exact correspondence of the two sides of the same animal; the right hand answering to the left, leg to leg, eye to eye, one side of the countenance to the other; and with a precision, to imitate which in any tolerable degree, forms one of the difficulties of statuary, and requires, on the part of the artist, a constant attention to this property of his work, distinct from every other.

… Of ten thousand eyes, I do not know that it would be possible to match one, except with its own fellow; or to distribute them into suitable pairs by any other selection than that which obtains. This regularity of the animal structure is rendered more remarkable by the three following considerations: —First, the limbs, separately taken, have not this correlation of parts; but the contrary of it. A knife drawn down the chine cuts the human body into two parts, externally equal and alike; you cannot draw a straight line which will divide a hand, a foot, the leg, the thigh, the cheek, the eye, the ear, into two parts equal and alike. Those parts which are placed upon the middle or partition line of the body, or which traverse that line, as the nose, the tongue, the lips, may be so divided, or, more properly speaking, are double organs; but other parts cannot. This shows that the correspondence which we have been describing, does not arise by any necessity in the nature of the subject: for, if necessary, it would be universal; whereas it is observed only in the system or assemblage: it is not true of the separate parts; that is to say, it is found where it conduces to beauty or utility; it is not found where it would subsist at the expense of both. The two wings of a bird always correspond: the two sides of a feather frequently do not. In centipedes, millipedes, and that whole tribe of insects, no two legs on the same side are alike; yet there is the most exact parity between the legs opposite to one another.

2. The next circumstance to be remarked is, that whilst the cavities of the body are so configured, as externally to exhibit the most exact correspondence of the opposite sides, the contents of these cavities have no such correspondence. A line drawn down the middle of the breast, divides the thorax into two sides exactly similar; yet these two sides enclose very different contents. The heart lies on the left side; a lobe of the lungs on the right; balancing each other neither in size nor shape. The same thing holds of the abdomen. The liver lies on the right side, without any similar viscus opposed to it on the left. The spleen indeed is situated over against the liver; but agreeing with the liver neither in bulk nor form. There is no equipollency between these. The stomach is a vessel both irregular in its shape, and oblique in its position. The foldings and doublings of the intestines do not present a parity of sides. let that symmetry which depends upon the correlation of the sides, is externally preserved throughout the whole trunk; and is the more remarkable in the lower parts of it, as the integuments are soft; and the shape, consequently, is not, as the thorax is by its ribs, reduced by natural stays. It is evident, therefore, that the external proportion does not arise from any equality in the shape or pressure of the internal contents. What is it indeed but a correction of inequalities? An adjustment, by mutual compensation, of anomalous forms into a regular congeries? The effect, in a word, of artful, and, if we might be permitted so to speak, of studied collocation?

3. Similar also to this, is the third observation; that at, internal inequality in the feeding vessels is so managed, as to produce no inequality in parts which were intended to correspond. The right arm answers accurately to the left, both in size and shape; but the arterial branches, which supply the two arms, do not go off from their trunk, in a pair, in the same manner, at the same

place, or at the same angle. Under which want of similitude, it is very difficult to conceive how the same quantity of blood should be pushed through each artery: yet the result is right; the two limbs, which are nourished by them, perceive no difference of supply, no effects of excess or deficiency." … (Paley W., Natural Theology or Evidences of the Existence and Attributes of the Deity, 1829, pp. 110-112)

Complex organization necessities an Organizer: it is extremely thought-provoking that the extremities of our body are so balanced, or homogenous left to right, and yet many of our internal organs are not. Could this happen by chance? When we consider the brain for example, it is divided into a right and left hemisphere that in appearance are very similar, and yet many areas are so different in function. In addition, our tongue is very rough on top but smooth underneath, and our upper and lower teeth grind together in unison. How can this be without an Intelligent Designer?

Paley:

… "What distinguishes the skull from every other cavity is, that the bony covering completely surrounds its contents, and is calculated, not for motion, but solely for defence. Those hollows, likewise, and inequalities, which we observe in the inside of the skull, and which exactly fit the folds of the brain, answer the important design of keeping the substance of the brain steady, and of guarding it against concussions. [Injury]" (Paley W., Natural Theology or Evidences of the Existence and Attributes of the Deity, 1829, p. 123)

COMPENSATION AND ECONOMY OF GROWTH

Darwin:

... "I suspect, also, that some of the cases of compensation which have been advanced, and likewise some other facts, may be merged under a more general principle, namely, that natural selection is continually trying to economise every part of the organisation. If under changed conditions of life, a structure, before useful, becomes less useful, its diminution will be favoured, for it will profit the individual not to have its nutriment wasted in building up a useless structure. ...

... Now the saving of a large and complex structure, when rendered superfluous [not needed], would be a decided advantage to each successive individual of the species; for in the struggle for life to which every animal is exposed, each would have a better chance of supporting itself, by less nutriment being wasted.

Thus, as I believe, natural selection will tend in the long run to reduce any part of the organisation, as soon as it becomes, through changed habits, superfluous [needless], without by any means causing some other part to be largely developed in a corresponding degree. And, conversely, that natural selection may perfectly well succeed in largely developing an organ without requiring as a necessary compensation the reduction of some adjoining part." (Darwin C., 1872, pp. 117-118)

Natural selection cannot think; how can a complex structure in itself be reduced by chance when not needed?

Necessity cannot create or reduce anything. Interesting speculation: why would large and complex structures when not needed just disappear, or become more efficient when needed? Also, we have already seen that co-relationship can be due to traits inherited together. This relationship becomes guesswork for Charles Darwin, because he didn't know genetics. Mendelian genetics is more scientific and factual.

On our farm we had two very large female horses. When my dad or any other farmer in the area wanted their mares to have foals, they would telephone another neighbor and for a fee, he would bring his stallion. There was a story told of one farmer who did not like the colour of this stallion so he would cover his mares' eyes, believing that if his mares did not see the stallion, the stallion color would not be passed on to their ponies. If these ponies were born hybrids with unique color and without the knowledge of Mendelian genetics, who is to say that his erroneous idea would not be correct?

Another possible misconception that some people have is that people are getting generationally taller. The tallness of Egyptian mummies might tend to discredit this idea. As we know, different races of people are either taller or shorter due to genetics and nutrition, and also that the height of elderly people can become shorter before their death.

RUDIMENTARY, ATROPHIED [WITHERED], AND ABORTED ORGANS

Darwin:

"Organs or parts in this strange condition, bearing the plain stamp of inutility [useless], are extremely common, or even general, throughout nature. It would be impossible to name one of the higher animals in which some part or other is not in a rudimentary condition. In the Mammalia, for instance, the males possess rudimentary mammae in snakes one lobe of the lungs is rudimentary; in birds the "bastard-wing" may safely be considered as a rudimentary digit, and in some species the whole wing is so far rudimentary that it cannot be used for flight. What can be more curious than the presence of teeth in foetal whales, which when grown up have not a tooth in their heads; or the teeth, which never cut through the gums, in the upper jaws of unborn calves? …

Useful organs, however little they may be developed, unless we have reason to suppose that they were formerly more highly developed, ought not to be considered as rudimentary. They may be in a nascent [emerging] condition, and in progress towards further development. Rudimentary organs, on the other hand, are either quite useless, such as teeth which never cut through the gums, or almost useless, such as the wings of an ostrich, which serve merely as sails. As organs in this condition would formerly, when still less developed, have been of even less use than at present, they cannot formerly have been produced through variation and natural selection, which acts solely by the preservation of useful modifications. They have been partially retained by the power of inheritance, and relate to a former state of things." …

"On the view of descent with modification, the origin of rudimentary organs is comparatively simple; and we can understand to a large extent the laws governing their imperfect development. We have plenty of cases of rudimentary organs in our domestic productions,—as the stump of a tail in tailless breeds,—the vestige of an ear in earless breeds of sheep,—the reappearance of minute dangling horns in hornless breeds of cattle, more especially, according to Youatt, in young animals,—and the state of the whole flower in the cauliflower. We often see rudiments of various parts in monsters; but I doubt whether any of these cases throw light on the origin of rudimentary organs in a state of nature, further than by showing that rudiments can be produced; for the balance of evidence clearly indicates that species under nature do not undergo great and abrupt changes. But we learn from the study of our domestic productions that the disuse of parts leads to their reduced size; and that the result is inherited.

It appears probable that disuse has been the main agent in rendering organs rudimentary. It would at first lead by slow steps to the more and more complete reduction of a part, until at last it became rudimentary,—as in the case of the eyes of animals inhabiting dark caverns, and of the wings of birds inhabiting oceanic islands, which have seldom been forced by beasts of prey to take flight, and have ultimately lost the power of flying. … (Ibid 387-401)

Mendelian genetics creates change. As already stated, flightless birds could have been the result of hybridization. The same could explain for the existence of animals that lack vision inhibiting dark caves. Disuse of an organ never renders it rudimentary. Genetics just does not work this way.

Darwin:

"A Part developed in any Species in an extraordinary degree or manner, in comparison with the same Part in allied Species, tends to be highly variable."

… "When we see any part or organ developed in a remarkable degree or manner in a species, the fair presumption is that it is of high importance to that species; nevertheless it is in this case eminently liable to variation. Why should this be so? On the view that each species has been independently created, with all its parts as we now see them, I can see no explanation. But on the view that groups of species are descended from some other species have, and been modified through natural selection.

I think we can obtain some light. First let me make some preliminary remarks. If, in our domestic animals, any part or the whole animal be neglected, and no selection be applied, that part (for instance, the comb in the Dorking fowl) or the whole breed will cease to have a uniform character; and the breed may be said to be degenerating. In rudimentary organs, and in those which have been but little specialised for any particular purpose, and perhaps in polymorphic [different forms] groups, we see a nearly parallel case; for in such cases natural selection either has not or cannot have come into full play, and thus the organisation is left in a fluctuating condition. But what here more particularly concerns us is, that those points in our domestic animals, which at the present time are undergoing rapid change by continued selection, are also eminently liable to variation. Look at the individuals of the same breed of the pigeon, and see what a prodigious [impressive] amount of difference there is in the beaks of tumblers, in the beaks and wattle of carriers, in the carriage and tail of fantails, &c., these being the points now mainly attended to by English fanciers. Even in the same sub-breed, as in that of the short-faced tumbler, it is notoriously difficult to breed nearly perfect birds, many departing widely from the standard. There may truly be said to be a constant struggle going on between, on the one hand, the tendency to reversion to a less perfect state, as well as an innate tendency to new variations, and, on the other hand, the power of steady selection to keep the breed true. In the long run selection gains the day, and we do not expect to fail so completely as to breed bird as coarse as a common tumbler pigeon from a good short-faced strain. But as long as selection is rapidly going on, much variability in the parts undergoing modification may always be expected.

Now let us turn to nature. When a part has been developed in an extraordinary manner in any one species, compared with the other species of the same genus [type], we may conclude that this part has undergone an extraordinary amount of modification since the period when the several species branched off from the common progenitor of the genus." ... (Darwin C., 1872, pp. 119-121)

None of the above negates independent creation. The above can all be explained through Mendelian genetics. As Darwin states, "There may truly be said to be a constant struggle going on between, on the one hand, the tendency to reversion to a less perfect state, as well as an innate tendency to new variations, and, on the other hand, the power of steady selection to keep the breed true." The amount of variation observed in pigeons probably is no more than what we observe in dog breeds or numerous other species. (A selection of an unusual characteristic in any species will only vary to the extent given by nature). For example, the arrival of the largest snout or tongue in a dog would not give rise to larger and larger tongues or snout in future generations. Charles Darwin is wrong in his belief that a part developed in an extraordinary degree or manner in comparison with the same part in allied species tends to be highly variable. Mendelian genetics and mutations just do not work this way. Size is controlled by the fixed laws of inheritances. With Mendelian genetics, hybrid animals do not continue to change in a step-by-step linear direction and then at some point in time stop changing. For example, a dog's snout does not continually grow from generation to generation in a systematic manner such as from short to long and longer or from short to shorter, and then become fixed. With Mendel's pea plants, they had fixed traits, for example, the peas were either smooth or wrinkled. The wrinkled did not tend to become more and more wrinkled etc. In addition, with Mendelian genetics, recessive genes are expressed or concealed. This would explain Darwin's reversion to an earlier form. Likewise, a mutation can be a permanent change that would not continue to vary. (It is all genetic like boldness on a man's head while growing a beard). Thus, Charles Darwin is wrong in his assessment of change in what follows.

Darwin:

… "An extraordinary amount of modification implies an unusually large and long-continued amount of variability, which has continually been accumulated by natural selection for the benefit of the species. But as the variability of the extraordinarily developed part or organ has been so great and long-continued within a period not excessively remote, we might, as a general rule, still expect to find more variability in such parts than in other parts of the organisation which have remained for a much longer period nearly constant. And this, I am convinced, is the case. That the struggle between natural selection on the one hand, and the tendency to reversion and variability on the other hand, will in the course of time cease; and that the most abnormally developed organs may be made constant, I see no reason to doubt. Hence, when an organ, however abnormal it may be, has been transmitted in approximately the same condition to many modified descendants, as in the case of the wing of the bat, it must have existed, according to our theory, for an immense period in nearly the same state; and thus it has come not to be more variable than any other structure. It is only in those cases in which the modification has been comparatively recent and extraordinarily great that we ought to find the *generative variability,* as it may be called, still present in a high degree. For in this case the variability will seldom as yet have been fixed by the continued selection of the individuals varying in the required manner and degree, and by the continued rejection of those tending to revert to a former and less-modified condition." ... (Darwin C., 1872, pp. 121-122)

The above is sheer guesswork and Darwin's lack of understanding as to how genetics works is evident here. If hybrids varieties are crossed, their offspring could remain as another and fixed variety. It would remain constant unless it is further crosses with the original stock or dissimilar variety. Even with a mutation, change does not continue to change in a gradated linear positive direction. It is sheer speculation that this process would create a new species or kind, such as a dog from a cat, etc.

Paley:

"The hook in the wing of a bat is strictly mechanical, and also a compensating contrivance... At the angle of its wing there is a bent claw, exactly in the form of a hook, by which the bat attaches itself to the sides of rocks, caves, and buildings, laying hold of crevices, joining, chinks, and roughnesses It hooks itself by this claw; remains suspended by this hold; takes its flight from this position: which operations compensate for the decrepitude of its legs and feet. Without her hook, the bat would be the most helpless of all animals. She can neither run upon her feet, nor raise herself from the ground. These inabilities are made up to her by the contrivance [device] in her wing: and in placing a claw on that part, the Creator has deviated from the analogy observed in winged animals. —A singular defect required a singular substitute." (Paley W., Natural Theology or Evidences of the Existence and Attributes of the Deity, 1829, pp. 160-161)

As has already been stated, Mendelian genetics creates change such as crossing different varieties of the same creature. A mutation also creates change. It is all genetic.

SPECIFIC CHARACTERS MORE VARIABLE THAN GENERIC CHARACTERS

Darwin:

"On the ordinary view of each species having been independently created, why should that part of the structure, which differs from the same part in other independently-created species of the same genus, be more variable than those parts which are closely alike in the several species? I do not see that any explanation can be given. But on the view that species are only strongly marked and fixed varieties, we might expect often to find them still continuing to vary in those parts of their structure which have varied within a moderately recent period, and which have thus come to differ…

…On the other hand, the points in which species differ from other species of the same genus are called specific characters; and as these specific characters have varied and come to differ since the period when the species branched off from a common progenitor, it is probable that they should still often be in some degree variable,—at least more variable than those parts of the organisation which have for a very long period remained constant." … (Darwin C., 1872, pp. 122-123)

Whether labeled as specific or generic characters [traits], neither would have a tendency to be more variable in a linear direction. If a mutation occurs, it would not begin a long series of favorable mutation in a linear direction. Genetics just does not work this way.

Darwin did not know genetics. Hybridization and mutations create change, and to assume that God would not create independent creatures with an ability to change is presumptuous. As has already been stated, mutations and hybridization create change but not in a slow systematic step-by step linear fashion from generation to generation. In addition, an organ or part does not change by "Use or disuse of parts". As has already been stated, selecting animals with favourable traits or characteristics would assure these animals and traits survival, but a selected trait would not further change in a linear way after it is selected and a part neglected would not change because it is not used.

Darwin:

"Secondary Sexual Characters Variable. —I think it will be admitted by naturalists, without my entering on details, that secondary sexual characters are highly variable. It will also be admitted that species of the same group differ from each other more widely in their secondary sexual characters, than in other parts of their organisation: compare, for instance, the amount of difference between the males of gallinaceous [heavy-bodied ground-feeding] birds, in which secondary sexual characters are strongly displayed, with the amount of difference between the females. The cause of the original variability of these characters is not manifest; but we can see why they should not have been rendered as constant and uniform as others, for they are accumulated by sexual selection, which is less rigid in its action than ordinary selection, as it does not entail death, but only gives fewer offspring to the less favoured males. Whatever the cause may be of the variability of secondary sexual characters, as they are highly variable, sexual selection will have had a wide scope for action, and may thus have succeeded in giving to the species of the same group a greater amount of difference in these than in other respects." ... (Ibid 123)

The secondary sexual characters vary only to the extent that genetics allows, and sexual selection can only pick what already exists. It is interesting that human males on are average larger than females, and yet we would not consider this difference to be caused by sexual selection. Human mothers often give birth to sons who grow much larger than themselves, and daughters equivalent.

A conceivable example of Darwinian sexual selection follows: breasts of women are very different from woman to women and thus according to Darwin would be highly variable. Thus, there will be women in the future who will have breasts even bigger than what is in existence today. If men pick their partners with bigger and then biggest breasts while ignoring others, there would be change, there would be 'evolution'. (As we know, this does not happen). The breast sizes of women are determined by genetics and as a result, secure.

Darwin:

"Distinct Species present analogous Variations, so that a Variety of one Species often assumes a Character proper to an allied Species, or reverts to some of the Characters of an early Progenitor. —These propositions will be most readily understood by looking to our domestic races. The most distinct breeds of the pigeon …

With pigeons, however, we have another case, namely, the occasional appearance in all the breeds, of slaty-blue birds with two black bars on the wings, white loins, a bar at the end of the tail, with the outer feathers externally edged near their bases with white. As all these marks are characteristic of the parent rock-pigeon, I presume that no one will doubt that this is a case of reversion, and not of a new yet analogous variation appearing in the several breeds. We may, I think, confidently come to this conclusion, because, as we have seen, these coloured marks are eminently liable to appear in the crossed offspring of two distinct and differently coloured breeds; and in this case there is nothing in the external conditions of life to cause the reappearance of the slaty-blue, with the several marks, beyond the influence of the mere act of crossing on the laws of inheritance.

No doubt it is a very surprising fact that characters should reappear after having been lost for many, probably for hundreds of generations. But when a breed has been crossed only once by some other breed, the offspring occasionally show for many generations a tendency to revert in character to the foreign breed—some say, for a dozen or even a score of generations. After twelve generations, the proportion of blood, to use a common expression, from one ancestor, is only 1 in 2048; and yet, as we see, it is generally believed that a tendency to reversion is retained by this remnant of foreign blood. In a breed which has not been crossed, but in which *both* parents have lost some character which their progenitor possessed, the tendency, whether strong or weak, to reproduce the lost character might, as was formerly remarked, for all that we can see to the contrary, be transmitted for almost any number of generations.

When a character which has been lost in a breed, reappears after a great number of generations, the most probable hypothesis is, not that one individual suddenly takes after an ancestor removed by some hundred generations, but that in each successive generation the character in question has been lying latent, and at last, under unknown favourable conditions, is developed. With the barb-pigeon, for instance, which very rarely produces a blue bird, it is probable that there is a latent tendency in each generation to produce blue plumage. The abstract improbability of such a tendency being transmitted through a vast number of generations, is not greater than that of quite useless or rudimentary organs being similarly transmitted. A mere tendency to produce a rudiment is indeed sometimes thus inherited." … (Darwin C., 1872, pp. 125-126)

As has already been stated, change is "genetic", and thus change is only as far as genetically possible. There could be a comparison between Mendel's peas and Darwin's pigeons. Mendel picked tall and short peas and all the hybrids in the F1 cross were tall. In the F2 results, the tall were in a ratio of three to one. Darwin did not know genetics but it is evident that he recognized its effect. Darwin states: "There may truly be said to be a constant struggle going on between, on the one hand, the tendency to reversion to a less perfect state, as well as an innate tendency to new variations, and, on the other hand, the power of steady selection to keep the breed true". With genetics, purebreds if crossed remain true, and new hybrids are created by crossing existing varieties. 'Reversion' could be recessive traits being expressed.

Darwin:

… "What now are we to say to these several facts? We see several distinct species of the horse-genus becoming, by simple variation, striped on the legs like a zebra, or striped on the shoulders like an ass. In the horse we see this tendency strong whenever a dun tint appears—a tint which approaches to that of the general colouring of the other species of the genus. The appearance of the stripes is not accompanied by any change of form or by any other new character. We see this tendency to become striped most strongly displayed in hybrids from between several of the most distinct species. Now observe the case of the several breeds of pigeons: they are descended from a pigeon (including two or three sub-species or geographical races) of a bluish colour, with certain bars and other marks; and when any breed assumes by simple variation a bluish tint, these bars and other marks invariably reappear; but without any other change of form or character. When the oldest and truest breeds of various colours are crossed, we see a strong tendency for the blue tint and bars and marks to reappear in the mongrels.

I have stated that the most probable hypothesis to account for the reappearance of very ancient characters, is—that there is a *tendency* in the young of each successive generation to produce the long-lost character, and that this tendency, from unknown causes, sometimes prevails. And we have just seen that in several species of the horse-genus the stripes are either plainer or appear more commonly in the young than in the old. Call the breeds of pigeons, some of which have bred true for centuries, species; and how exactly parallel is the case with that of the species of the horse-genus! For myself, I venture confidently to look back thousands on thousands of generations, and I see an animal striped like a zebra, but perhaps otherwise very differently constructed, the common parent of our domestic horse (whether or not it be descended from one or more wild stocks) of the ass, the hemionus, quagga, and zebra.

He who believes that each equine [horse] species was independently created, will, I presume, assert that each species has been created with a tendency to vary, both under nature and under domestication, in this particular manner, so as often to become striped like the other species of the genus; and that each has been created with a strong tendency, when crossed with species inhabiting distant quarters of the world, to produce hybrids resembling in their stripes, not their own parents, but other species of the genus. To admit this view is, as it seems to me, to reject a real for an unreal, or at least for an unknown, cause. It makes the works of God a mere mockery and deception; I would almost as soon believe with the old and ignorant cosmogonists, that fossil shells had never lived, but had been created in stone so as to mock the shells living on the sea-shore." ... (Darwin C., 1872, pp. 130-131)

The horse family or genus consists of horses, donkeys, zebras etc. They all belong to the same genus [kind], thus they possess many physical characteristics in common. It is apparent that they are all part of the horse family with mutual lineage and not fashioned as separate entities.

Rather a strange conclusion shows Darwin's unawareness concerning genetics in his position that if species were independently created, that there would not be variability. This view is not correct. It is observable that species are not rigged in their inheritance, and recessive genes are often expressed [Darwin's reversion]. There is no denying the fact that there is change by means of cross breeding and of course mutations, all of which does not deny Intelligent Design.

Edward Robinson

Darwin's Summary:

"Summary. —Our ignorance of the laws of variation is profound. Not in one case out of a hundred can we pretend to assign any reason why this or that part has varied. But whenever we have the means of instituting a comparison, the same laws appear to have acted in producing the lesser differences between varieties of the same species, and the greater differences between species of the same genus.

… Whatever the cause may be of each slight difference between the offspring and their parents—and a cause for each must exist—we have reason to believe that it is the steady accumulation of beneficial differences which has given rise to all the more important modifications of structure in relation to the habits of each species." (Darwin C., 1872, pp. 131-133)

How many step by step positive beneficial changes are needed to create a new species [kind] from an existent one? Genetic change does not work this way. Mutations are not all in a linear step-by-step beneficial direction; if there is a mutation, it may never express itself, or if it does, it can be more often harmful rather than beneficial. With Darwinian evolution, there has to be a tremendous amount of positive mutations with the removal of all or most of the old in favour of the new and improved. Thus, Darwinian evolution is problematic

DIFFICULTIES OF THE THEORY

Darwin:

... "These difficulties and objections may be classed under the following heads: —First, why, if species have descended from other species by fine gradations, do we not everywhere see innumerable transitional forms? Why is not all nature in confusion, instead of the species being, as we see them, well defined?

Secondly, is it possible that an animal having, for instance, the structure and habits of a bat, could have been formed by the modification of some other animal with widely-different habits and structure? Can we believe that natural selection could produce, on the one hand, an organ of trifling importance, such as the tail of a giraffe, which serves as a fly-flapper, and, on the other hand, an organ so wonderful as the eye?

Thirdly, can instincts be acquired and modified through natural selection? What shall we say to the instinct which leads the bee to make cells, and which has practically anticipated the discoveries of profound mathematicians?

Fourthly, how can we account for species, when crossed, being sterile and producing sterile offspring, whereas, when varieties are crossed, their fertility is unimpaired? ...

... *"On the Absence or Rarity of Transitional Varieties.* —As natural selection acts solely by the preservation of profitable modifications, each new form will tend in a fully-stocked country to take the place of, and finally to exterminate, its own less improved parent-form and other less-favoured forms with which it comes into competition. Thus, extinction and natural selection go hand in hand. Hence, if we look at each species as descended from some unknown form, both the parent and all the transitional varieties will generally have been exterminated by the very process of the formation and perfection of the new form. ...

… But, as by this theory innumerable transitional forms must have existed, why do we not find them embedded in countless numbers in the crust of the earth? It will be more convenient to discuss this question in the chapter on the Imperfection of the Geological Record; and I will here only state that I believe the answer mainly lies in the record being incomparably less perfect than is generally supposed. The crust of the earth is a vast museum; but the natural collections have been imperfectly made, and only at long intervals of time." … (Darwin 133-134)

With genetics there is more as it were 'Love not War'. The Métis of Canada are an example of this process. Humans are always mingling. The same process is happening with animals and plants as well. In reality the genes of parents exist in their offspring — variety begets variety. The original parentage may no longer physically exist, but their genes are in hybrids, and these hybrids that do exist, are creating other hybrids and thus new varieties. A cat and a dog do not cross nor an ape with human kind. Their genetics are just too dissimilar.

Scientists today are still looking for intermediate forms and on occasion do find unusual species. The early ancestors of the modern horses are believed to be the descendent of smaller animals that walked on several spread-out toes. Who is to say that these are not just other varieties of the horse family or other species or varieties that did not adapt and are now extinct as the Passenger Pigeon, or the archaeopteryx bird?

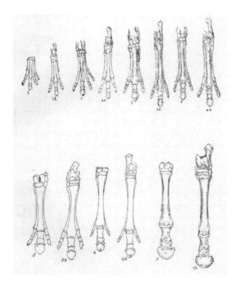

From "The Outline of Science":

Diagram showing seven stages in the evolution of the fore-limbs and hind-limbs of the ancestors of the modern horse, beginning with the earliest known predecessors of the horse and culminating with the horse of today.

1 and 1A, fore-limb and hind-limb of Eohippus; 2 and 2A, Orohippus; 3 and 3A, Mesohippus; 4 and 4A, Hypohippus; 5 and 5A, Merychippus; 6 and 6A, Hipparion; 7 and 7A, the modern horse. Note how the toes shorten and disappear. (Thomson A. J., 1922)

It is debatable whether the above shows the development of the modern horse family. With Mandolin genetics, the crossing of varieties creates change. Consequently, the above could be examples of variety change and not one species changing into another. The modern horse family are in all shapes and sizes such as Miniature Horses, donkeys, zebras, mules etc. Thus their lineage could have been in all shapes and sizes as well.

Darwin:

"To sum up, I believe that species come to be tolerably well-defined objects, and do not at any one period present an inextricable chaos of varying and intermediate links: first, because new varieties are very slowly formed, for variation is a slow process, and natural selection can do nothing until favourable individual differences or variations occur, and until a place in the natural polity of the country can be better filled by some modification of some one or more of its inhabitants. And such new places will depend on slow changes of climate, or on the occasional immigration of new inhabitants, and, probably, in a still more important degree, on some of the old inhabitants becoming slowly modified, with the new forms thus produced and the old ones acting and reacting on each other. So that, in any one region and at any one time, we ought to see only a few species presenting slight modifications of structure in some degree permanent; and this assuredly we do see.

Secondly, areas now continuous must often have existed within the recent period as isolated portions, in which many forms, more especially amongst the classes which unite for each birth and wander much, may have separately been rendered sufficiently distinct to rank as representative species. In this case, intermediate varieties between the several representative species and their common parent, must formerly have existed within each isolated portion of the land, but these links during the process of natural selection will have been supplanted and exterminated, so that they will no longer be found in a living state.

Thirdly, when two or more varieties have been formed in different portions of a strictly continuous area, intermediate varieties will, it is probable, at first have been formed in the intermediate zones, but they will generally have had a short duration. For these intermediate varieties will, from reasons already assigned (namely from what we know of the actual distribution of closely allied or representative species, and likewise of acknowledged varieties), exist in the intermediate zones in lesser numbers than the varieties which they tend to connect. From this cause alone the intermediate varieties will be liable to accidental extermination; and during the process of further modification through natural selection, they will almost certainly be beaten and supplanted by the forms which they connect; for these from existing in greater numbers will, in the aggregate, present more varieties, and thus be further improved through natural selection and gain further advantages.

Lastly, looking not to any one time, but to all time, if my theory be true, numberless intermediate varieties, linking closely together all the species of the same group, must assuredly have existed; but the very process of natural selection constantly tends, as has been so often remarked, to exterminate the parent-forms and the intermediate links. Consequently, evidence of their former existence could be found only amongst fossil remains, which are preserved, as we shall attempt to show in a future chapter, in an extremely imperfect and intermittent record." (Darwin C., 1872, pp. 137-138)

As already stated, genetic change does not happen in a slow step-by-step process from one kind of creature into another. Also, climate does not bring change unless it induces a mutation and intermediate forms between species are lacking in the fossil record. The above is not confusing when we consider what happens with Mendelian genetics. With Darwin's absence of genetic knowledge, he doesn't take into account crosses of varieties as the main reason for change (where varieties are not detached species) nor the expression of recessive traits. With Mendelian genetics, if two varieties of a species are, perhaps in the middle of an area where they mingle, there would be a hybrid created that is different from either parent. This new hybrid in the intermediate zones in lesser numbers would not necessarily be beaten and supplanted, when a new and different hybrid or variety is created. It is not a transitional or intermediate form leading one kind of animal to become another, such as a cat to a dog etc.

(Looking at you - taken at Lion Safari Cambridge Ontario)

Job: 39:13-18

13 "The wings of the ostrich wave proudly,
But are her wings and pinions like the kindly storks?
14 For she leaves her eggs on the ground, and warms them in the dust;
15 She forgets that a foot may crush them, or that a wild beast may break them.
16 She treats her young harshly, as if they were not hers; Her labor is in vain, without concern.
17 Because God has deprived her of wisdom, And did not endow her with understanding.

18 "When she lifts herself on high, She scorns the horse and its rider." ... (NKJV)

Darwin:

"On the Origin and Transitions of Organic Beings with peculiar Habits and Structure.—It has been asked by the opponents of such views as I hold, how, for instance, could a land carnivorous animal have been converted into one with aquatic habits; for how could the animal in its transitional state have subsisted? It would be easy to show that there now exist carnivorous animals presenting close intermediate grades from strictly terrestrial to aquatic habits;

and as each exists by a struggle for life, it is clear that each must be well adapted to its place in nature. ...

Look at the family of squirrels; here we have the finest gradation from animals with their tails only slightly flattened, and from others, as Sir J. Richardson has remarked, with the posterior part of their bodies rather wide and with the skin on their flanks rather full, to the so-called flying squirrels; and flying squirrels have their limbs and even the base of the tail united by a broad expanse of skin, which serves as a parachute and allows them to glide through the air to an astonishing distance from tree to tree. We cannot doubt that each structure is of use to each kind of squirrel in its own country, by enabling it to escape birds or beasts of prey, to collect food more quickly, or, as there is reason to believe, to lessen the danger from occasional falls. But it does not follow from this fact that the structure of each squirrel is the best that it is possible to conceive under all possible conditions. Let the climate and vegetation change, let other competing rodents or new beasts of prey immigrate, or old ones become modified, and all analogy would lead us to believe that some at least of the squirrels would decrease in numbers or become exterminated, unless they also became modified and improved in structure in a corresponding manner. Therefore, I can see no difficulty, more especially under changing conditions of life, in the continued preservation of individuals with fuller and fuller flank-membranes, each modification being useful, each being propagated, until, by the accumulated effects of this process of natural selection, a perfect so-called flying squirrel was produced." ... (Darwin C., 1872, pp. 138-139)

Flying or gliding squirrels are squirrels of a different variety — they are all squirrels. If there is a variety (or species of squirrel) that cannot interbreed with other varieties of squirrels, they may very well be a hybrid of existent squirrels, just as the Liger is a hybrid of a lion and tiger. Another illustration is the peppered moth. The predominant moth before the industrial revolution were light-colored, and during the revolution, they were dark. They were one or the other—black or white. These are just two existing varieties of the same species. The white peppered moth did not slowly turn into the black or black to white. This change does not change in a gradated step-by-step manner from one variety or species into another. Other examples are the Andalusia fowl created by the crossing of white and black birds and obtaining a blue hybrid. The blue hybrid was not created in a step-by step manner from white to black and then blue. This also illustrates incomplete dominance. Another example is the four o'clock garden flower, which are either red or white and the hybrid pink. The flower did not change from white to red then pink and then pinker still. Genetics just does not work this way. Also, a changed condition does not change a variety - genetics does. However, changed conditions can pick out the best fitted variety for a condition.

Darwin:

"If about a dozen genera of birds were to become extinct, who would have ventured to surmise that birds might have existed which used their wings solely as flappers, like the logger-headed duck (Micropterus of Eyton); as fins in the water and as front-legs on the land, like the penguin; as sails, like the ostrich; and functionally for no purpose, like the Apteryx [Kiwi]? Yet the structure of each of these birds is good for it, under the conditions of life to which it is exposed, for each has to live by a struggle; but it is not necessarily the best possible under all possible conditions. It must not be inferred from these remarks that any of the grades of wing-structure here alluded to, which perhaps may all be the result of disuse, indicate the steps by which birds actually acquired their perfect power of flight; but they serve to show what diversified means of transition are at least possible.

Seeing that a few members of such water-breathing classes as the Crustacea and Mollusca are adapted to live on the land; and seeing that we have flying birds and mammals, flying insects of the most diversified types, and formerly had flying reptiles, it is conceivable that flying-fish, which now glide far through the air, slightly rising and turning by the aid of their fluttering fins, might have been modified into perfectly winged animals. If this had been effected, who would have ever imagined that in an early transitional state they had been the inhabitants of the open ocean, and had used their incipient organs of flight exclusively, as far as we know, to escape being devoured by other fish?" ... (Darwin C., 1872, p. 140)

Flight is very complex. Structure and instincts are species specific and both are needed to fly. The flight of a bird is much more complicated than just flapping wings, thus a flying squirrel will never become a bird or a bat or vice versa. Likewise, for a fish to live out of water and fly it needs more than just developing wings; along with structure, it also needs proper instincts. The terrestrial Homo sapiens have been trying to fly long before the airplane and have yet to acquire the bodily structures to do so. By flapping our arms, we will never develop feathers. If God created both the birds, penguins and the kiwi, why couldn't He create them separately while having commonality? None of the above disproves the existence of a Creator God. Without instincts, we would be no better than a scarecrow in a cornfield!

We learn to walk upright while apes move on all fours. Consequently, how can both structure and instincts in humans originate from that of monkeys or ape like creature? Their genetic makeup is just too diverse.

The Archaeopteryx has often been conveyed as a transitional creature between reptile and bird. Is it not just another unusual extinct creature created by God?

A good restoration of the oldest known bird, Archæopteryx (Jurassic Era). It was about the size of a crow; it had teeth on both jaws; it had claws on the thumb and two fingers; and it had a long lizard-like tail. But it had feathers, proving itself a true bird. (Thomson A. J., 1922, p. 90)

Wings of a bird, showing the arrangement of the feathers:

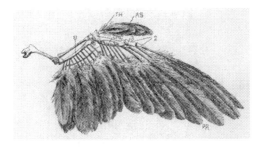

The longest feathers or primaries (PR) are borne by the two fingers (2 and 3), and their palm-bones (CMC); the second longest or secondaries are borne by the ulna bone (U) of the fore-arm; there is a separate tuft (AS) on the thumb (TH). borne by the ulna bone (U) of the fore-arm; there is a separate tuft (AS) on the thumb (TH). (Thomson 91)

Genesis 1:21

So God created great sea creatures and every living thing that moves, with which the waters abounded, according to their kind, and every winged bird according to its kind. And God saw that it was good. (NKJV)

Paley:

"The *covering of birds* cannot escape the most vulgar observation. Its lightness, Its smoothness, its warmth;—the disposition of the feathers all inclined backward, the down about their stem, the overlapping of their tips, their different configuration in different parts, not to mention the variety of their colors, constitute a vestment for the body, so beautiful, and so appropriate to the life which the animal is to lead, as that, I think, we should have had no conception of anything equally perfect, if we had never seen it, or can now imagine anything more so. Let us suppose (what is possible only in supposition) a person who had never seen a bird, to be presented with a plucked pheasant, and bid to set his wits to work, how to contrive [arrange] for it a covering which shall unite the qualities of warmth, levity [lightness], and least resistance to the air, and the highest degree of each; giving it also as much of beauty and ornament as he could afford. He is the person to behold the work of the Deity, in this part of his creation, with the sentiments which are due to it." … (Paley W., Natural Theology or Evidences of the Existence and Attributes of the Deity, 1829, p. 125)

Paley:

… "In comparing the bones of different animals, we are struck, in the bones of birds, with a propriety, which could only proceed from the wisdom of an intelligent and designing Creator. In the bones of an animal which is to fly, the two qualities required are strength and lightness. Wherein, therefore, do the bones of birds (I speak of the cylindrical bones) differ in these respects from the bones of quadrupeds? In three properties; first, their cavities are much larger in proportion to the weight of the bone than in those of quadrupeds; secondly, these cavities are empty; thirdly, the shell is of a firmer texture than the substance of other bones. It is easy to observe those particulars, even in picking the wing or leg of a chicken. Now, the weight being the same, the diameter, it is evident, will be greater in a hollow bone than in a solid one, and with the diameter, as every mathematician can prove, is increased, *coeteris paribiis,* the strength of the cylinder, or its resistance to breaking. In a word, a bone of the same weight would not have been so strong in any other form; and to have made it heavier, would have incommoded the animal's flight. Yet this form could not be acquired by use, or the bone become hollow and tubular by exercise. What appetency [strong desire] could excavate a bone? …

… A principal topic of comparison between animals, is in their instruments of motion. These come before us under three divisions; feet, wings, and fins. I desire any man to say, which of the three is best fitted for its use; or whether the same consummate art be not conspicuous in them all. The constitution of the elements in which the motion is to be performed, is very different. The animal action must necessarily follow that constitution. The different situations, for different difficulties; yet the purpose is accomplished not less successfully in one case than in the other; and, as between wings and the corresponding limbs of quadrupeds, it is accomplished without deserting the general idea. The idea is modified, not deserted. Strip awing of its feathers, and it bears no obscure resemblance to the fore leg of a quadruped. The articulations at the shoulder and the cubitus are much alike; and, what is a closer circumstance, in both cases the upper part of the limb consists of a single bone, the lower part of two.

But fitted up with its furniture of feathers and quills, it becomes a wonderful instrument, more artificial than its first appearance indicates, though that be very striking: at least, the use which the bird makes of its wings in flying is more complicated, and more curious, than is generally known. One thing is certain, that if the flapping of the wings in flight were no more than the reciprocal motion of the same surface in opposite directions, either upwards and downwards, or estimated in any oblique line, the bird would lose as much by one motion as she gained by another. The skylark could never ascend by such an action as this; for, though the stroke upon the air by the underside of her wing would carry her up, the stroke from the upper side, when she raised her wing again, would bring her down. In order, therefore, to account for the advantage which the bird derives from her wing, it is necessary to suppose that the surface of the wing, measured upon the same plane, is contracted whilst the wing is drawn up; and let out to its full expansion, when it descends upon the air for the purpose of moving the body by the reaction of that element." … (Paley W., Natural Theology or Evidences of the Existence and Attributes of the Deity, 1829, pp. 132-135)

Darwin:

"I will now give two or three instances both of diversified and of changed habits in the individuals of the same species. In either case it would be easy for natural selection to adapt the structure of the animal to its changed habits, or exclusively to one of its several habits. It is, however, difficult to decide, and immaterial for us, whether habits generally change first and structure afterwards; or whether slight modifications of structure lead to changed habits; both probably often occurring almost simultaneously" … (Darwin C., 1872, p. 141)

Darwin states that: "it would be easy for natural selection to adapt the structure of an animal to its changed habit, or one of several habits" … "and immaterial for us, whether habits generally change first and structure afterwards; or whether slight modifications of structure lead to changed habits;" … If a horse gained teeth as that of a lion, would it begin to devour chickens? Instinct and structure are species specific: The lion and the wildebeest are very different in structure and instinct, and we would never contemplate a reversal of behaviour. When scientists examine dinosaurs, they can tell whether they were predator or pray by examining their teeth. Did a dinosaur realize it had teeth for grasping its prey and tell itself it will act in a predatory manor, or teeth for cutting and chewing and a stomach for digesting vegetables and thus tell itself that it will eat grass? The instincts of animals are often co-related to their very existence and the balance of nature moreover depends on it. The wildebeest are very productive and the lions, which are few, keep the wildebeest numbers in check. The teeth are tied into predator or prey, tied into instinct, and tied into birth rate. Can all this organization exist without an "Organizer"?

Edward Robinson

Darwin:

... "As we sometimes see individuals following habits different from those proper to their species and to the other species of the same genus, we might expect that such individuals would occasionally give rise to new species, having anomalous habits, and with their structure either slightly or considerably modified from that of their type. And such instances occur in nature. Can a more striking instance of adaptation be given than that of a woodpecker for climbing trees and seizing insects in the chinks of the bark? Yet in North America there are woodpeckers which feed largely on fruit, and others with elongated wings which chase insects on the wing. On the plains of La Plata, where hardly a tree grows, there is a woodpecker (Colaptes campestris) which has two toes before and two behind, a long pointed tongue, pointed tail-feathers, sufficiently stiff to support the bird in a vertical position on a post, but not so stiff as in the typical woodpeckers, and a straight strong beak. The beak, however, is not so straight or so strong as in the typical woodpeckers, but it is strong enough to bore into wood. Hence this Colaptes in all the essential parts of its structure is a woodpecker." ... (Darwin C., 1872, pp. 141-142)

At first thought, it seems that the woodpeckers have changed; on second thought, they have become different varieties of the same species suited to the environment which they populate. With our "Sulimov Dog", instincts and appearance were a product of breeding and genetics, not learned behaviour or habit leading to changed instincts.

In the above, we have varied varieties of woodpecker and perhaps these varieties would cross and we could have even more diversified woodpecker varieties with different habits and instincts. They are all woodpeckers – no more – and no less.

Darwin:

"He who believes that each being has been created as we now see it, must occasionally have felt surprise when he has met with an animal having habits and structure not in agreement. What can be plainer than that the webbed feet of ducks and geese are formed for swimming? Yet there are upland geese with webbed feet which rarely go near the water; and no one except Audubon has seen the frigate-bird, which has all its four toes webbed, alight on the surface of the ocean. On the other hand, grebes and coots are eminently aquatic, although their toes are only bordered by membrane. What seems plainer than that the long toes, not furnished with membrane of the Grallatores are formed for walking over swamps and floating plants?—the water-hen and landrail are members of this order, yet the first is nearly as aquatic as the coot, and the second nearly as terrestrial as the quail or partridge. In such cases, and many others could be given, habits have changed without a corresponding change of structure. The webbed feet of the upland goose may be said to have become almost rudimentary [developing] in function, though not in structure. In the frigate-bird, the deeply scooped membrane between the toes shows that structure has begun to change.

He who believes in separate and innumerable acts of creation may say, that in these cases it has pleased the Creator to cause a being of one type to take the place of another type; but this seems to me only re-stating the fact in dignified language. He who believes in the struggle for existence and in the principle of natural selection, will acknowledge that every organic being is constantly endeavouring to increase in numbers; and that if any one being varies ever so little, either in habits or structure, and thus gains an advantage over some other inhabitant of the same country, it will seize on the place of that inhabitant, however different that may be from its own place. Hence it will cause him no surprise that there should be geese and frigate-birds with webbed feet, living on the dry land and rarely alighting on the water; that there should be long-toed corncrakes, living in meadows instead of in swamps; that there should be woodpeckers where hardly a tree grows; that there should be diving thrushes and diving Hymenoptera, and petrels with the habits of auks." (Darwin C., 1872, pp. 142-143)

With added knowledge of genetics, there should be no surprise that many different varieties of species live in various areas of the world inhabiting environments that are not totally suited to their state – like ducks in a farmer's barnyard that never see open water. We should marvel that ducks and geese have webbed feet in the first place.

Paley:

"The crane kind are to live and seek their food amongst the waters; yet, having no web-feet, are incapable of swimming. To make up for this deficiency, they are furnished with long legs for wading, or long bills for groping; or usually with both. This is compensation. But I think the true reflection upon the present instance is, how every part of nature is tenanted [occupied] by appropriate inhabitants. Not only is the surface of deep waters peopled by numerous tribes of birds that swim, but marshes and shallow pools are furnished with hardly less numerous tribes of birds that wade." (Paley W., Natural Theology or Evidences of the Existence and Attributes of the Deity, 1829, p. 161)

Out with the old, In with the new, for Darwinian evolution to be valid there has to be a slow and continues gradated change from one species into another with most if not all the intermediate disappearing. Can a very irreducible flying fish species turn into a bird with wings and feathers? Where are the intermediates? Where is the evidence?

ORGANS OF EXTREME PERFECTION AND COMPLICATION

Darwin:

"To suppose that the eye with all its inimitable contrivances for adjusting the focus to different distances, for admitting different amounts of light, and for the correction of spherical and chromatic aberration, could have been formed by natural selection, seems, I freely confess, absurd in the highest degree. When it was first said that the sun stood still and the world turned round, the common sense of mankind declared the doctrine false; but the old saying of *Vox populi, vox Dei,* [voice of people, voice of God,] as every philosopher knows, cannot be trusted in science. Reason tells me, that if numerous gradations from a simple and imperfect eye to one complex and perfect can be shown to exist, each grade being useful to its possessor, as is certainly the case; if further, the eye ever varies and the variations be inherited, as is likewise certainly the case; and if such variations should be useful to any animal under changing conditions of life, then the difficulty of believing that a perfect and complex eye could be formed by natural selection, though insuperable by our imagination, should not be considered as subversive of the theory How a nerve comes to be sensitive to light, hardly concerns us more than how life itself originated; but I may remark that, as some of the lowest organisms, in which nerves cannot be detected, are capable of perceiving light, it does not seem impossible that certain sensitive elements in their sarcode should become aggregated and developed into nerves, endowed with this special sensibility.

The simplest organ which can be called an eye consists of an optic nerve, surrounded by pigment-cells and covered by translucent skin, but without any lens or other refractive body. We may, however, according to M. Jourdain, descend even a step lower and find aggregates of pigment-cells, apparently serving as organs of vision, without any nerves, and resting merely on sarcodic tissue. Eyes of the above simple nature are not capable of distinct vision, and serve only to distinguish light from darkness. In certain star-fishes, small depressions in the layer of pigment which surrounds the nerve are filled, as described by the author just quoted, with transparent gelatinous matter, projecting with a convex surface, like the cornea in the higher animals. He suggests that this serves not to form an image, but only to concentrate the luminous rays and render their perception more easy. In this concentration of the rays we gain the first and by far the most important step towards the formation of a true, picture-forming eye; for we have only to place the naked extremity of the optic nerve, which in some of the lower animals lies deeply buried in the body, and in some near the surface, at the right distance from the concentrating apparatus, and an image will be formed on it. ...

When we reflect on these facts, here given much too briefly, with respect to the wide, diversified, and graduated range of structure in the eyes of the lower animals; and when we bear in mind how small the number of all living forms must be in comparison with those which have become extinct, the difficulty ceases to be very great in believing that natural selection may have converted the simple apparatus of an optic nerve, coated with pigment and invested by transparent membrane, into an optical instrument as perfect as is possessed by any member of the Articulate Class.

He who will go thus far, ought not to hesitate to go one step further, if he finds on finishing this volume that large bodies of facts, otherwise inexplicable, can be explained by the theory of modification through natural selection; he ought to admit that a structure even as perfect as an eagle's eye might thus be formed, although in this case he does not know the transitional states. It has been objected that in order to modify the eye and still preserve it as a perfect instrument, many changes would have to be effected simultaneously, which, it is assumed, could not be done through natural selection; but as I have attempted to show in my work on the variation of domestic animals, it is not necessary to suppose that the modifications were all simultaneous, if they were extremely slight and gradual. Different kinds of modification would, also, serve for the same general purpose" ... (Darwin C., 1872, pp. 143-145)

Was the human eye developed from something as simple as heat being detected on the back of a hand, or better still a forehead? A very complicated structure described as extremely simple! If the structure of the eye was the only thing necessary for sight, it would look like the Darwinian premise for the creation of sight has perhaps a little merit, but the eyeball alone is filled with irreducible complexity. (Keep in mind that with every forward mutation or step there should be as many backward or harmful). As already been stated, sight is vastly irreducibly complex and needs many essentials to function. Thus, a Darwinian step-by-step process from simple to the very complex becomes problematic in explaining the development of the eye. Expressly problematic when we consider how genetics works where 'each new step' forward has to be a mutation with the disappearing of the old.

Both William Paley and Charles Darwin used the telescope as an analogy for sight. Mankind created the telescope and God or natural selection created the eye?

Paley:

"I know no better method of introducing; so large a subject, than that of comparing a single thing with a single thing; an eye, for example, with a telescope. As far as the examination of the instrument goes, there is precisely the same proof that the eye was made for vision, as there is that the telescope was made for assisting it. They are made upon the same principles; both being adjusted to the laws by which the transmission and refraction of rays of light are regulated. I speak not of the origin of the laws themselves; but such laws being fixed, the construction, in both cases, is adapted to them. For instance; these laws require, in order to produce the same effect, that the rays of light, in passing from water into the eye, should be refracted by a more convex surface than when it passes out of air into the eye. Accordingly we find, that the eye of a fish, in that part of it called the crystalline lens, is much rounder than the eye of terrestrial animals. What plainer manifestation of design can there be than this difference? What could a mathematical instrument-make; have done more, to show his knowledge of his principle, his application of that knowledge, his suiting of his means to his end. …

… To some it may appear a difference sufficient to destroy all similitude between the eye and the telescope, that the one is a perceiving organ, the other an unperceiving instrument. The fact is, that they are both instruments. And, as to the mechanism, at least as to mechanism being employed, and even as to the kind of it, this circumstance varies not the analogy at all. For, observe what the constitution of the eye is. It is necessary in order to produce distinct vision, that an image or picture of the object be formed at the bottom of the eye. Whence this necessity arises, or how the picture is connected with the sensation, or contributes to it, it may be difficult, nay we will confess, if you please, impossible for us to search out. ...

... In the example before us, it is a matter of certainty, because it is a matter which experience and observation demonstrate, that the formation of an image at the bottom of the eye is necessary to perfect vision. The image itself can be shown. Whatever affects the distinctness of the image, affects the distinctness of the vision. The formation then of such an image being necessary (no matter how) to the sense of sight, and to the exercise of that sense, the apparatus by which it is formed is constructed and put together, not only with infinitely more art, but upon the selfsame principles of art, as in the telescope or the camera-obscura. The perception arising from the image may be laid out of the question; for the production of the image, these are instruments of the same kind. The end is the same; the means are the same. The purpose in both is alike, the contrivance for accomplishing that purpose is in both alike. The lenses of the telescope, and the humours of the eye, bear a complete resemblance to one another, in their figure, their position, and in their power over the rays of light, viz. in bringing each pencil to a point at the right distance from the lens; namely, in the eye, at the exact place where the membrane is spread to receive it. How is it possible, under circumstances of such close affinity, and under the operation of equal evidence, to exclude contrivance from the one, yet to acknowledge the proof of contrivance having been employed, as the plainest and clearest of all propositions, in the other? ...

... But farther; there are other points, not so much perhaps of strict resemblance between the two, as of superiority of the eye over the telescope, which being found in the laws that regulate both, may furnish topics of fair and just comparison. Two things were wanted, to the eye, which were not wanted (at least in the same degree) to the telescope: and these were the adaptation of the organ, first to different degrees of light; and, secondly, to the vast diversity of distance at which objects are viewed by the naked eye, viz. from a few inches to as many miles. These difficulties present not themselves to the maker of the telescope. He wants all the light he can get; and he never directs his instrument to objects near at hand. In the eye, both these cases were to be provided for; and for the purpose of providing for them a subtle and appropriate mechanism is introduced.

In order to exclude excess of light, when it is excessive, and to render objects visible under obscurer degrees of it, when no more can be had, the hole or aperture in the eye, through which the light enters, is so formed, as to contract or dilate itself for the purpose of admitting a greater or less number of rays at the same time. The chamber of the eye is a camera obscura, which, when the light is too small, can enlarge its opening; when too strong, can again contract it; and that without any other assistance than that of its own exquisite machinery. …

The second difficulty which has been stated, was the suiting of the same organ to the perception of objects that lie near at hand, within a few inches, we will suppose, of the eye, and of objects which are placed at a considerable distance from it, that, for example, of as many furlongs; (I speak in both cases of the distance at which distinct vision can be exercised.) Now this, according to the principles of optics, that is, according to the laws by which the transmission of light is regulated, (and these laws are fixed,) could not be done without the organ itself undergoing an alteration and receiving an adjustment. …

… I say, that whenever the eye is directed to a near object, three changes are produced in it at the same time, all severally contributing to the adjustment required. The cornea, or outermost coat of the eye, is rendered more round and prominent; the crystalline lens underneath is pushed forwards; and the axis of vision, as the depth of the eye is called, is elongated. These changes in the eye vary its power over the rays of light in such a manner and degree as to produce exactly the effect which is wanted, viz. the formation of an image upon the retina, whether the rays come to the eye in a state of divergency, which is the case when the object is near to the eye, or come parallel to one another, which is the case when the object is placed at a distance. Can anything be more decisive of contrivance [gadget] than this is? The most secret laws of optics must have been known to the author of a structure endowed with such a capacity of change. It is as though an optician, when he had a nearer object to view, should rectify his instrument by putting in another glass, at the same time drawing out also his tube to a different length. …

… Thus, in comparing the eyes of different kinds of animals, we see, in their resemblances and distinctions, one general plan laid down, and that plan varied with the varying exigencies [needs] to which it is to be applied. There is one property, however, common, I believe, to all eyes, at least to all which

211

have been examined, namely, that the optic nerve enters the bottom of the eye, not in the centre or middle, but a little on one side; not in the point where the axis of the eye meets the retina, but between that point and the nose. The difference which this makes is, that no part of an object is unperceived by both eyes at the same time." ... (Paley W., Natural Theology or Evidences of the Existence and Attributes of the Deity, 1829, pp. 13-21)

Darwin:

... "It is scarcely possible to avoid comparing the eye with a telescope. We know that this instrument has been perfected by the long-continued efforts of the highest human intellects; and we naturally infer that the eye has been formed by a somewhat analogous process. But may not this inference be presumptuous? Have we any right to assume that the Creator works by intellectual powers like those of man? If we must compare the eye to an optical instrument, we ought in imagination to take a thick layer of transparent tissue, with spaces filled with fluid, and with a nerve sensitive to light beneath, and then suppose every part of this layer to be continually changing slowly in density, so as to separate into layers of different densities and thicknesses, placed at different distances from each other, and with the surfaces of each layer slowly changing in form. Further we must suppose that there is a power, represented by natural selection or the survival of the fittest, always intently watching each slight alteration in the transparent layers; and carefully preserving each which, under varied circumstances, in any way or in any degree, tends to produce a distincter image. We must suppose each new state of the instrument to be multiplied by the million; each to be preserved until a better one is produced, and then the old ones to be all destroyed. In living bodies, variation will cause the slight alterations, generation will multiply them almost infinitely, and natural selection will pick out with unerring skill each improvement. Let this process go on for millions of years; and during each year on millions of individuals of many kinds; and may we not believe that a living optical instrument might thus be formed as superior to one of glass, as the works of the Creator are to those of man?" (Darwin C., 1872, p. 146)

Darwin writes, "We must suppose each new state of the instrument to be multiplied by the million; each to be preserved until a better one is produced, and then the old ones to be all destroyed." Is this scenario statistically possible?

Darwin:

… "If it could be demonstrated that any complex organ existed, which could not possibly have been formed by numerous, successive, slight modifications, my theory would absolutely break down. But I can find out no such case. No doubt many organs exist of which we do not know the transitional grades, more especially if we look to much-isolated species, round which, according to the theory, there has been much extinction. Or again, if we take an organ common to all the members of a class, for in this latter case the organ must have been originally formed at a remote period, since which all the many members of the class have been developed; and in order to discover the early transitional grades through which the organ has passed, we should have to look to very ancient ancestral forms, long since become extinct." (ibid pp 146-147)

Darwin, in his own admission, states that his theory would totally break down: "If it could be demonstrated that any complex organ existed, which could not possibly have been formed by numerous, successive, slight modifications." The cell on which all life is based is a very irreducible complex structure which needs all of its independent parts (organelles) functioning for its existence, therefore Darwin's theory in his own admission is not correct. This was demonstrated by Michael Behe in his book, "Darwin's Black Box". (Behe, p. 42)

Gradations exist; we have many animals that are separated into countless varieties. They can all be arranged from the smallest to the largest or from the foulest to the loveliest, but gradation does not explain the original origin of species with all their complexity.

It would be a rash man to say that the human male sex organ developed through gradation. They do come in all shapes and sizes, but does one derive from the other? We need sex organs for our very existence; therefore this complex organ's existence could not have been created by numerous successive, slight modifications. Thus, with Charles Darwin's own statement, his theory breaks down.

Both Darwin and Paley illustrated the swim bladder in fish.

Darwin:

"The illustration of the swimbladder in fishes is a good one, because it shows us clearly the highly important fact that an organ originally constructed for one purpose, namely, flotation, may be converted into one for a widely different purpose, namely, respiration. The swimbladder has, also, been worked in as an accessory to the auditory organs of certain fishes. All physiologists admit that the swimbladder is homologous, or "ideally similar" in position and structure with the lungs of the higher vertebrate animals: hence there is no reason to doubt that the swimbladder has actually been converted into lungs, or an organ used exclusively for respiration." ...

"According to this view it may be inferred that all vertebrate animals with true lungs are descended by ordinary generation from an ancient and unknown prototype, which was furnished with a floating apparatus or swimbladder. We can thus, as I infer from Owen's interesting description of these parts, understand the strange fact that every particle of food and drink which we swallow has to pass over the orifice of the trachea, [windpipe] with some risk of falling into the lungs, notwithstanding the beautiful contrivance by which the glottis is closed." ... Darwin 147-148

Some people believe that there is something inherently wrong with the trachea (windpipe) and likewise dismiss the existence of God because they believe that an Intelligent Creator would not make the trachea this way. They are in essence dismissing the existence of God because He does not fit into their own impression of aptness. However, to assume that there is something innately wrong with the trachea is imprudent. We can eat. We can drink. We can breathe. We can sing. We can smell etc. Thus, the trachea functions very well.

Paley:

"The air-bladder also of a fish affords a plain and direct instance, not only of contrivance [thing made with purpose], but strictly of that species of contrivance which we denominate mechanical. It is a philosophical [rational] apparatus in the body of an animal. The principle of the contrivance is clear; the application of the principle is also clear. The use of the organ to sustain, and, at will, also to elevate the body of the fish in the water, is proved by observing, what has been tried, that, when the bladder is burst, the fish grovels at the bottom; and also, that flounders, soles, skates, which are without the air-bladder, seldom rise in the water, and that, with effort. The manner in which the purpose is attained, and the suitableness of the means to the end, are not difficult It to be apprehended. The rising and sinking of a fish in water, so far as it is independent of the stroke of the fins and tail, can only be regulated by the specific gravity of the body. ... A diving machine might be made to ascend and descend, upon the like principle, namely, by introducing into the inside of it an air-vessel, which by its contraction would diminish, and by its distension enlarge, the bulk of the machine itself, and thus render it specifically heavier, or specifically lighter, than the water which surrounds it. Suppose this to be done, and the artist to solicit a patent for his invention: the inspectors of the model, whatever they might think of the use of value of the contrivance, could, by no possibility, entertain a question in their minds, whether it were a contrivance [thing made with purpose] or not. No reason has ever been assigned. No reason can be assigned, why the conclusion is not as certain in the fish as it is in the machine; why the argument is not as firm in one case as the other.

It would be very worthy of inquiry, if it were possible to discover, by what method an animal, which lives constantly in water, is able to supply a repository of air. The expedient, whatever it be, forms part, and perhaps the most curious part, of the provision. Nothing similar to the air bladder, is found in land-animals; and a life in the water has no natural tendency to produce a bag of air. Nothing can be farther from an acquired organization than this is.

These examples mark the attention of the Creator to the three great kingdoms of his animal creation, and to their constitution as such" ... (Paley W., pp. 140-142)

Whether a creature develops a swim bladder or lunges is determined through genetics at conception. There are some similarities with the swim bladder and lungs but the swim bladder and lungs are vastly different and extremely complex structures, and to assume that one developed into the other is highly speculative.

Frogs are amazing creatures. They go through an astonishing change from a one celled egg to tadpoles and eventually become frogs: A female frog lays thousands of eggs, and when fertilized become embryos. The embryos then attach to weeds in the water and change into tadpoles with long tails and gills. The tadpoles then change into frogs, losing their gills and tails and developing legs. A frog does not evolve from one creature into another. What frog eggs are determined to become are (frogs) specified by genetics at conception. The egg the tadpole and the frog are all just the same creature in different stages of development.

Two solitudes, same facts, different conclusions – all life should and does have similarities. However, similarity does not mean same. Gradation does not explain complexity, nor does it explain where a species derived in the first place. There is no proof that species did not possess the ability for variability from the beginning. We were not there at creation and to claim that all life is a product of evolution is a denial of the bible and can even deny the very existence of a Creator God.

Darwin:

… "In the higher Vertebrata the branchiae [gills] have wholly disappeared— but in the embryo the slits on the sides of the neck and the loop-like course of the arteries still mark their former position. But it is conceivable that the now utterly lost branchiae might have been gradually worked in by natural selection for some distinct purpose: for instance, Landois has shown that the wings of insects are developed from the tracheae; it is therefore highly probable that in this great class organs which once served for respiration have been actually converted into organs for flight." … (Darwin C., 1872, p. 148)

The above is absolute nonsense, and guesswork. The higher Vertebrata, such as humans, never ever had gills or gill slits; it is highly fabricated that gill slits would have changed into folds in an embryos neck in a step-by-step fashion over time. This is Lamarckian, and genetics just does not generate change this way. Gill slits are gill slits and wrinkles in an embryos neck are wrinkles – no more and no less. What a creature is to become is determined at conception.

DEVELOPMENT AND
EMBRYOLOGY

Darwin:

"It has already been stated that various parts in the same individual which are exactly alike during an early embryonic period, become widely different and serve for widely different purposes in the adult state. So again, it has been shown that generally the embryos of the most distinct species belonging to the same class are closely similar, but become, when fully developed, widely dissimilar. A better proof of this latter fact cannot be given than the statement by Von Baer that "the embryos of Mammalia, of birds, lizards, and snakes, probably also of chelonia, are in their earliest states exceedingly like one another, both as a whole and development of their parts; so much so, in fact, that we can often distinguish the embryos only by their size." …

… "As all the organic beings, extinct and recent, which have ever lived, can be arranged within a few great classes; and as all within each class have, according to our theory, been connected together by fine gradations, the best, and, if our collections were nearly perfect, the only possible arrangement, would be genealogical [ancestral]; descent being the hidden bond of connexion which naturalists have been seeking under the term of the Natural System. On this view we can understand how it is that, in the eyes of most naturalists, the structure of the embryo is even more important for classification than that of the adult. In two or more groups of animals, however much they may differ from each other in structure and habits in their adult condition, if they pass through closely similar embryonic stages, we may feel assured that they all are descended from one parent-form, and are therefore closely related." (Darwin C., 1872, pp. 387-397)

Similar in appearance does not mean same. To look at the stars in the sky at night in appearance with the naked eye, they have much in common, but under closer inspection they are vastly different. The embryos of some creatures (including humans) may look-alike with the naked eye, but are vastly different microscopically. From the beginning, what a species is to become is determined at conception, and every species DNA is unique. Also, we should not be surprised with similarities among many creatures since the same Creator made them all.

Darwin:

There is another possible mode of transition, namely, through the acceleration or retardation of the period of reproduction. This has lately been insisted on by Prof. Cope and others in the United States. It is now known that some animals are capable of reproduction at a very early age, before they have acquired their perfect characters; and if this power became thoroughly well developed in a species, it seems probable that the adult stage of development would sooner or later be lost; and in this case, especially if the larva differed much from the mature form, the character of the species would be greatly changed and degraded. Again, not a few animals, after arriving at maturity, go on changing in character during nearly their whole lives. With mammals, for instance, the form of the skull is often much altered with age, of which Dr. Murie has given some striking instances with seals; every one knows how the horns of stags become more and more branched, and the plumes of some birds become more finely developed, as they grow older. Prof. Cope states that the teeth of certain lizards change much in shape with advancing years; with crustaceans not only many trivial, but some important parts assume a new character, as recorded by Fritz Müller, after maturity. In all such cases, —and many could be given, —if the age for reproduction were retarded, the character of the species, at least in its adult state, would be modified; nor is it improbable that the previous and earlier stages of development would in some cases be hurried through and finally lost. Whether species have often or ever been modified through this comparatively sudden mode of transition, I can form no opinion; but if this has occurred, it is probable that the differences between the young and the mature, and between the mature and the old, were primordially [primary, or first in sequence] acquired by graduated steps." (Darwin C., 1872, p. 149)

How and when a species reproduces is fixed in its DNA at conception. The statement, "if the age for reproduction were retarded, the character of the species, at least in its adult state, would be modified" is ridiculous. (If a baby could have a baby, then we would all be baby-like!)

SPECIAL DIFFICULTIES OF THE THEORY OF NATURAL SELECTION

Darwin:

… Finally then, although in many cases it is most difficult even to conjecture by what transitions organs have arrived at their present state; yet, considering how small the proportion of living and known forms is to the extinct and unknown, I have been astonished how rarely an organ can be named, towards which no transitional grade is known to lead. It certainly is true, that new organs appearing as if created for some special purpose, rarely or never appear in any being;—as indeed is shown by that old, but somewhat exaggerated, canon in natural history of "Natura non facit saltum." ["Nature does not jump"- slow not sudden] We meet with this admission in the writings of almost every experienced naturalist; or as Milne Edwards has well expressed it, Nature is prodigal [extravagant] in variety, but niggard [stingy] in innovation. Why, on the theory of Creation, should there be so much variety and so little real novelty [newness]? Why should all the parts and organs of many independent beings, each supposed to have been separately created for its proper place in nature, be so commonly linked together by graduated steps? Why should not Nature take a sudden leap from structure to structure? On the theory of natural selection, we can clearly understand why she should not; for natural selection acts only by taking advantage of slight successive variations; she can never take a great and sudden leap, but must advance by short and sure, though slow steps." (Darwin C., 1872, pp. 155-156)

It is presumptuous to state that God did not create distinct species with the ability to change. If God created original kinds, then species and hybrids produced from existing varieties are of God as well.

Darwin assumes that change is a slow step-by-step process, but genetics does not work this way. For instance, recessive genes from both parents can produce albinism; albinism was not developed in a step-by-step fashion, or by sexual selection. Today, we humans have big heads but there is no proof that our head size developed in a step-by-step fashion from very small to larger and larger over immense time. Here again there is the false assumption that Christians believe that God created species and their varieties in a fixed state where and as we see them presently.

Darwin:

Utilitarian Doctrine, how far true:

"The foregoing remarks lead me to say a few words on the protest lately made by some naturalists, against the utilitarian doctrine that every detail of structure has been produced for the good of its possessor. They believe that many structures have been created for the sake of beauty, to delight man or the Creator (but this latter point is beyond the scope of scientific discussion), or for the sake of mere variety, a view already discussed. Such doctrines, if true, would be absolutely fatal to my theory." ... (Ibid 159-160)

Has any structure been created for the sake of beauty? Can we not look at ourselves and marvel at beauty and design? How can one explain the fact that our bodies are so symmetrical (left to right) while our internal organs and appendages [arms etc.] are not so? We cannot split an arm, an ear or a leg in two identical haves. Also our head's left and right hemispheres are symmetrical, while some brain functions are in different regions of the brain.

Paley:

The human, or indeed the animal frame, considered as a mass or assemblage, exhibits in its composition three properties, which have long struck my mind as indubitable evidences, not only of design, but of a great deal of attention and accuracy in prosecuting [arranging] the design. ...

... The first is, the exact correspondence of the two sides of the same animal; the right hand answering to the left, leg to leg, eye to eye, one side of the countenance to the other. ...

... The next circumstance to be remarked is, that whilst the cavities of the body are so configured, as externally to exhibit the most exact correspondence of the opposite sides, the contents of these cavities have no such correspondence. ...

Similar also to this, is the third observation; that at, internal inequality in the feeding vessels is so managed, as to produce no inequality in parts which were intended to correspond. ... (Paley W., pp. 141-148)

Darwin:

... "I fully admit that many structures are now of no direct use to their possessors, and may never have been of any use to their progenitors; but this does not prove that they were formed solely for beauty or variety. No doubt the definite action of changed conditions, and the various causes of modifications, lately specified, have all produced an effect, probably a great effect, independently of any advantage thus gained. But a still more important consideration is that the chief part of the organisation of every living creature is due to inheritance; and consequently, though each being assuredly is well fitted for its place in nature, many structures have now no very close and direct relation to present habits of life. Thus, we can hardly believe that the webbed feet of the upland goose or of the frigate-bird are of special use to these birds; we cannot believe that the similar bones in the arm of the monkey, in the fore-leg of the horse, in the wing of the bat, and in the flipper of the seal, are of special use to these animals. We may safely attribute these structures to inheritance. But webbed feet no doubt were as useful to the progenitor of the upland goose and of the frigate-bird, as they now are to the most aquatic of living birds. So we may believe that the progenitor of the seal did not possess a flipper, but a foot with five toes fitted for walking or grasping; and we may further venture to believe that the several bones in the limbs of the monkey, horse, and bat, were originally developed, on the principle of utility [usefulness], probably through the reduction of more numerous bones in the fin of some ancient fish-like progenitor of the whole class. It is scarcely possible to decide how much allowance ought to be made for such causes of change, as the definite action of external conditions, so-called spontaneous variations, and the complex laws of growth; but with these important exceptions, we may conclude that the structure of every living creature either now is, or was formerly, of some direct or indirect use to its possessor." ... (Darwin C., 1872, p. 160)

All organic life has much commonality, but similar does not mean same. Humans share substantially with the ape and chimpanzee, and since this is so, there should be no surprise that our genetic makeup or blueprint as it were to other organisms would have much in common as well. Even our domestic dogs and cats have much in common, but all life has vast differences as well. Since all life was molded by a common designer and maker, these facts should not be surprising.

We should not be surprised that webbed footed birds live far from water, but that they have webbed feet in the first place.

BEAUTY HOW ACQUIRED

Beauty is in the eye of the beholder. A fruit full of maggots is disgusting to us but delightful to a bird.

Darwin:

… "With respect to the belief that organic beings have been created beautiful for the delight of man,—a belief which it has been pronounced is subversive of my whole theory,—I may first remark that the sense of beauty obviously depends on the nature of the mind, irrespective of any real quality in the admired object; and that the idea of what is beautiful, is not innate or unalterable. We see this, for instance, in the men of different races admiring an entirely different standard of beauty in their women. If beautiful objects had been created solely for man's gratification, it ought to be shown that before man appeared, there was less beauty on the face of the earth than since he came on the stage. Were the beautiful volute and cone shells of the Eocene epoch, and the gracefully sculptured ammonites of the Secondary period, created that man might ages afterwards admire them in his cabinet? Few objects are more beautiful than the minute siliceous cases of the diatomaceae: were these created that they might be examined and admired under the higher powers of the microscope? The beauty in this latter case, and in many others, is apparently wholly due to symmetry of growth. Flowers rank amongst the most beautiful productions of nature; but they have been rendered conspicuous [visible] in contrast with the green leaves, and in consequence at the same time beautiful, so that they may be easily observed by insects. … (Darwin C., 1872, pp. 160-161)

… On the other hand, I willingly admit that a great number of male animals, as all our most gorgeous birds, some fishes, reptiles, and mammals, and a host of magnificently coloured butterflies, have been rendered beautiful for beauty's sake; but this has been effected through sexual selection, that is, by the more beautiful males having been continually preferred by the females, and not for the delight of man. So it is with the music of birds. We may infer from all this that a nearly similar taste for beautiful colours and for musical sounds runs through a large part of the animal kingdom. When the female is as beautifully coloured as the male, which is not rarely the case with birds and butterflies, the cause apparently lies in the colours acquired through sexual selection having been transmitted to both sexes, instead of to the males alone. How the sense of beauty in its simplest form—that is, the reception of a peculiar kind of pleasure from certain colours, forms and sounds—was first developed in the mind of man and of the lower animals, is a very obscure [unclear] subject. The same sort of difficulty is presented, if we enquire how it is that certain flavours and odours give pleasure, and others displeasure. Habit in all these cases appears to have come to a certain extent into play; but there must be some fundamental cause in the constitution of the nervous system in each species.

Natural selection cannot possibly produce any modification in a species exclusively for the good of another species; though throughout nature one species incessantly takes advantage of, and profits by, the structures of others. But natural selection can and does often produce structures for the direct injury of other animals, as we see in the fang of the adder, and in the ovipositor of the ichneumon, by which its eggs are deposited in the living bodies of other insects. If it could be proved that any part of the structure of any one species had been formed for the exclusive good of another species, it would annihilate my theory, for such could not have been produced through natural selection.

Although many statements may be found in works on natural history to this effect, I cannot find even one which seems to me of any weight. It is admitted that the rattlesnake has a poison-fang for its own defence and for the destruction of its prey; but some authors suppose that, at the same time, it is furnished with a rattle for its own injury, namely, to warn its prey. I would almost as soon believe that the cat curls the end of its tail when preparing to spring, in order to warn the doomed mouse. It is a much more probable view that the rattlesnake uses its rattle, the cobra expands its frill, and the puff-adder swells whilst hissing so loudly and harshly, in order to alarm the many birds and beasts which are known to attack even the most venomous species. Snakes act on the same principle which makes the hen ruffle her feathers and expand her wings when a dog approaches her chickens; but I have not space here to enlarge on the many ways by which animals endeavour to frighten away their enemies. Natural selection will never produce in a being any structure more injurious than beneficial to that being, for natural selection acts solely by and for the good of each. No organ will be formed, as Paley has remarked, for the purpose of causing pain or for doing an injury to its possessor. If a fair balance be struck between the good and evil caused by each part, each will be found on the whole advantageous. After the lapse of time, under changing conditions of life, if any part comes to be injurious, it will be modified; or if it be not so, the being will become extinct as myriads [many] have become extinct.

Natural selection tends only to make each organic being as perfect as, or slightly more perfect than, the other inhabitants of the same country with which it comes into competition. And we see that this is the standard of perfection attained under nature. The endemic [native] productions of New Zealand, for instance, are perfect, one compared with another; but they are now rapidly yielding before the advancing legions of plants and animals introduced from Europe. Natural selection will not produce absolute perfection, nor do we always meet, as far as we can judge, with this high standard under nature." ... (Ibid 161-164)

The creation of hybrids by the crossing of existing varieties does not necessarily create an improved species, and as has already been stated, hybrids are not new 'kinds'.

If one believes in a Creator God, then there is room for parts of structures of species, and whole species created for the good of other species. Nature has many checks and balances. For an example, the lion is helpful towards the wildebeests by keeping its numbers in check, thus the well-being of the lion is helpful for another creature - the wildebeest. Also, the wildebeest is essential for the lion as food, thus the creation of the wildebeest is essential for the good of the lion.

Paley:

"A third general property of animal forms is beauty. I do not mean relative beauty, or that of one individual above another of the same species, or of one species compared with another species; but I mean generally, the provision which is made in the body of almost every animal, to adapt its appearance to the perception of the animals with which it converses. In our own species, for example, only consider what the parts and materials are, of which the fairest body is composed; and no farther observation will be necessary to show, how well these things are wrapped up, so as to form a mass, which shall be capable of symmetry in its proportion, and of beauty in its aspect; how the bones are covered, the bowels concealed, the roughnesses of the muscles smoothed and softened; and how over the whole is drawn an integument [cover], which converts the disgusting materials of a dissecting-room into an object of attraction to the sight, or one upon which it rests, at least, with ease and satisfaction. Much of this effect is to be attributed to the intervention of the cellular or adipose [fat] membrane, which lies immediately under the skin; is a kind of lining to it; is moist, soft, slippery, and compressible; everywhere filling up the interstices of the muscles, and forming thereby the roundness and flowing line, as well as the evenness and polish of the whole surface.

… All which seems to be a strong indication of design and of a design studiously directed to this purpose. And it being once allowed, that such a purpose existed with respect to any of the productions of nature, we may refer, with a considerable degree of probability, other particulars to the same intention; such as the tints of flowers, the plumage of birds, the furs of beasts, the bright scales of fishes, the painted wings of butterflies and beetles, the rich colors and spotted lustre of many tribes of insects.

There are parts also of animals ornamental, and the properties by which they are so, not subservient, that we know of, to any other purpose. The *irides* [plural for iris] of most animals are very beautiful, without conducing at all, by their beauty, to the perfection of vision; and nature in no part have employed her pencil to so much advantage, because no part presents itself so conspicuously to the observer, or communicates so great an effect to the whole aspect. …

A ground, I know, of objection, has been taken against the whole topic of argument, namely, that there is no such thing as beauty at all: in other words, that whatever is useful and familiar, comes of course to be thought beautiful; and that things appear to be so, only by their alliance with these qualities. Our idea of beauty is capable of being so modified by habit, by fashion, by the experience of advantage or pleasure, and by associations arising out of that experience, that a question has been made, whether it be not altogether generated by these causes, or would have any proper existence without them. …

… I do not however know, that the argument which alleges beauty as a final-cause [ultimate or last goal], rests upon this concession. We possess a sense of beauty, however we come by it. It in fact exists. Things are not indifferent to this sense; all objects do not suit it; many, which we see, are agreeable to it; many others disagreeable. It is certainly not the effect of habit upon the particular object, because the most agreeable objects are often the most rare; many, which are very common, continue to be offensive. If they be made supportable by habit, it is all which habit can do; they never become agreeable. If this sense, therefore, be acquired, it is a result; the produce of numerous and complicated actions of external objects upon the senses, and of the mind upon its sensations. With this result, there must be a certain congruity [agreement] to enable any particular object to please; and that congruity, we contend, is consulted in the *aspect* [part]which is given to animal and vegetable bodies." … (Paley W., Natural Theology or Evidences of the Existence and Attributes of the Deity, 1829, pp. 115-118)

"Beauty is in the eye of the beholder": A baby alligator is beautiful to its mother and an attractive dinner for its father.

The monarch butterfly is regarded as extremely beautiful. The advent of its beauty would be difficult or impossible to explain through Natural and or sexual selection.

For the female widow spider, the male is seen as both her sex companion and a feast. Widow spiders are so named because after mating they have been observed devouring her much smaller male companion – unless he can escape quickly!

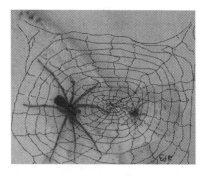

Female on left and male spider on right:

MISCELLANEOUS OBJECTIONS TO THE THEORY OF NATURAL SELECTION

Darwin:

… "A distinguished zoologist, Mr. St. George Mivart, has recently collected all the objections which have ever been advanced by myself and others against the theory of natural selection, as propounded by Mr. Wallace and myself, and has illustrated them with admirable art and force. When thus marshalled, they make a formidable array; and as it forms no part of Mr. Mivart's plan to give the various facts and considerations opposed to his conclusions, no slight effort of reason and memory is left to the reader, who may wish to weigh the evidence on both sides. When discussing special cases, Mr. Mivart passes over the effects of the increased use and disuse of parts, which I have always maintained to be highly important, and have treated in my 'Variation under Domestication' at greater length than, as I believe, any other writer. He likewise often assumes that I attribute nothing to variation, independently of natural selection, whereas in the work just referred to I have collected a greater number of well-established cases than can be found in any other work known to me. My judgment may not be trustworthy, but after reading with care Mr. Mivart's book, and comparing each section with what I have said on the same head, I never before felt so strongly convinced of the general truth of the conclusions here arrived at, subject, of course, in so intricate a subject, to much partial error.

All Mr. Mivart's objections will be, or have been, considered in the present volume. The one new point which appears to have struck many readers is, "that natural selection is incompetent to account for the incipient [initial] stages of useful structures." This subject is intimately connected with that of the gradation of characters, often accompanied by a change of function, —for instance, the conversion of a swim-bladder into lungs, —points which were discussed in the last chapter under two headings. Nevertheless, I will here consider in some detail several of the cases advanced by Mr. Mivart, selecting those which are the most illustrative, as want of space prevents me from considering all." ... (Ibid 176-177)

Darwin:

... Man has modified some of his animals, without necessarily having attended to special points of structure, by simply preserving and breeding from the fleetest individuals, as with the race-horse and greyhound, or as with the game-cock, by breeding from the victorious birds. So under nature with the nascent [emerging] giraffe, the individuals which were the highest browsers and were able during dearths to reach even an inch or two above the others, will often have been preserved; for they will have roamed over the whole country in search of food. That the individuals of the same species often differ slightly in the relative lengths of all their parts may be seen in many works of natural history, in which careful measurements are given. These slight proportional differences, due to the laws of growth and variation, are not of the slightest use or importance to most species. But it will have been otherwise with the nascent [emerging] giraffe, considering its probable habits of life; for those individuals which had some one part or several parts of their bodies rather more elongated than usual, would generally have survived. These will have intercrossed and left offspring, either inheriting the same bodily peculiarities, or with a tendency to vary again in the same manner; whilst the individuals, less favoured in the same respects, will have been the most liable to perish."

"We here see that there is no need to separate single pairs, as man does, when he methodically improves a breed: natural selection will preserve and thus separate all the superior individuals, allowing them freely to intercross, and will destroy all the inferior individuals. By this process long-continued, which exactly corresponds with what I have called unconscious selection by man, combined no doubt in a most important manner with the inherited effects of the increased use of parts, it seems to me almost certain that an ordinary hoofed quadruped might be converted into a giraffe.

To this conclusion Mr. Mivart brings forward two objections. One is that the increased size of the body would obviously require an increased supply of food, and he considers it as "very problematical whether the disadvantages thence arising would not, in times of scarcity, more than counterbalance the advantages." But as the giraffe does actually exist in large numbers in S. Africa, and as some of the largest antelopes in the world, taller than an ox, abound there, why should we doubt that, as far as size is concerned, intermediate gradations could formerly have existed there, subjected as now to severe dearths. ... (Ibid 177-178)

To assume that the giraffe's neck was advanced in a step-by-step [systematic] fashion is guesswork. The giraffe as a species is extremely irreducibly complex and requires a whole collection of structures and systems that need to be in place to accommodate its long neck. The giraffe's vertebrae are large and bound together with ball-and-socket joints. It has large elastic like ligament (nuchal ligament) in the back of its neck aiding in holding its neck and head in an upright position. To pump blood to its head, the giraffe's heart is large and muscular developing very high blood presser for an animal of its size. This is only a sample of the giraffe's complexity.

'Use and disuse of parts' played heavily in Darwin's explanation for change, more so in his sixth edition than in earlier versions of 'Origin of Species'. As has already been stated, the Lamarckian theory of "use and disuse" was totally debunked by a German biologist. August Weismann, at the University of Freiburg in1813. Weismann cut off the tails of mice up to the twenty second generation. The offspring of these mice were still being born with tails thus demonstrating that the theory of "use and disuse" is false. It has been discredited by modern science as well; Genetic change does not work this way. A weak man, through exercise becoming strong, cannot pass on his new-found strength through his genes to his sons, nor can his sons pass on their new found strength to their sons to become stronger still.

Darwin:

... Objections of the same nature as the foregoing have been advanced by many writers. In each case various causes, besides the general ones just indicated, have probably interfered with the acquisition through natural selection of structures, which it is thought would be beneficial to certain species. One writer asks, why has not the ostrich acquired the power of flight? But a moment's reflection will show what an enormous supply of food would be necessary to give to this bird of the desert force to move its huge body through the air. Oceanic islands are inhabited by bats and seals, but by no terrestrial mammals; yet as some of these bats are peculiar species, they must have long inhabited their present homes. Therefore Sir C. Lyell asks, and assigns certain reasons in answer, why have not seals and bats given birth on such islands to forms fitted to live on the land? But seals would necessarily be first converted into terrestrial carnivorous animals of considerable size, and bats into terrestrial insectivorous [eating insects] animals; for the former there would be no prey; for the bats ground-insects would serve as food, but these would already be largely preyed on by the reptiles or birds, which first colonise and abound on most oceanic islands. Gradations of structure, with each stage beneficial to a changing species, will be favoured only under certain peculiar conditions. A strictly terrestrial animal, by occasionally hunting for food in shallow water, then in streams or lakes, might at last be converted into an animal so thoroughly aquatic as to brave the open ocean. But seals would not find on oceanic islands the conditions favourable to their gradual reconversion into a terrestrial form. Bats, as formerly shown, probably acquired their wings by at first gliding through the air from tree to tree, like the so-called flying-squirrels, for the sake of escaping from their enemies, or for avoiding falls; but when the power of true flight had once been acquired, it would never be reconverted back, at least for the above purposes, into the less efficient power of gliding through the air. Bats might, indeed, like many birds, have had their wings greatly reduced in size, or completely lost, through disuse; but in this case it would be necessary that they should first have acquired the power of running quickly on the ground, by the aid of their hind legs alone, so as to compete with birds or other ground animals; and for such a change a bat seems singularly ill-fitted. These conjectural remarks have been made merely to show that a transition of structure, with each step beneficial, is a highly complex affair; and that there is nothing strange in a transition not having occurred in any particular case.

Lastly, more than one writer has asked, why have some animals had their mental powers more highly developed than others, as such development would be advantageous to all? Why have not apes acquired the intellectual powers of man? Various causes could be assigned; but as they are conjectural [theoretical], and their relative probability cannot be weighed, it would be useless to give them. A definite answer to the latter question ought not to be expected, seeing that no one can solve the simpler problem why, of two races of savages, one has risen higher in the scale of civilisation than the other; and this apparently implies increased brain-power." ... (Darwin C., 1872, pp. 178-181)

Interesting speculations! Necessity or circumstances has never ever changed a species. Darwin also refers to brain power. There is the common belief that over time, humankind has increased head size. Did we grow bigger heads because we needed more brain power than that of our ancestry? Necessity does not command change and natural selection can only select what has already changed. Darwin places a great deal of emphasis for change to Lamarck's "use and disuse of parts" and gradation in which a large change takes place over time from many small changes. Genetic change just does not work this way. For example, the liger is a hybrid cross between a male lion and a female tiger. Hybrids are never created in a slow step by step method.

Mankind can only select what nature provides. Therefore, the race horse will have a limit on speed; the dray horse on size; the greyhound on sleekness. Variation happens through hybridization and mutation, and for a Christian who believes in "Intelligent Design", change does not extend to the development of "kinds" formed through time from other "kinds" like an ape to human.

Darwin:

... "With respect to the baleen, Mr. Mivart remarks that if it "had once attained such a size and development as to be at all useful, then its preservation and augmentation within serviceable limits would be promoted by natural selection alone. But how to obtain the beginning of such useful development?" In answer, it may be asked, why should not the early progenitors of the whales with baleen[25] are possessed a mouth constructed something like the lamellated beak of a duck? Ducks, like whales, subsist by sifting the mud and water; and the family has sometimes been called *Criblatores,* or sifters. I hope that I may not be misconstrued into saying that the progenitors of whales did actually possess mouths lamellated like the beak of a duck. I wish only to show that this is not incredible, and that the immense plates of baleen in the Greenland whale might have been developed from such lamellae by finely graduated steps, each of service to its possessor. ...

... We thus see that a member of the duck family, with a beak constructed like that of the common goose and adapted solely for grazing, or even a member

---

[25] Some whales strain food from water.

with a beak having less well-developed lamellae, might be converted by small changes into a species like the Egyptian goose,—this into one like the common duck,—and, lastly, into one like the shoveller, provided with a beak almost exclusively adapted for sifting the water; for this bird could hardly use any part of its beak, except the hooked tip, for seizing or tearing solid food. The beak of a goose, as I may add, might also be converted by small changes into one provided with prominent, recurved teeth, like those of the Merganser (a member of the same family), serving for the widely different purpose of securing live fish." (Ibid 183-185)

William Paley could place the different types of duck beaks as having been created by God for their particular service, while Darwin places their differences and development to Natural Selection.

Need cannot create, neither does small changer leading to a large advancement without numerous defects. Mendelian genetics does not make change in a gradated fashion. For example, every time a male lion and a female tiger cross, it creates a liger. A liger was not created in a step-by-step manner.

What follows is a reduced rendition of the development of the flounder-fish by Charles Darwin.

"The Pleuronectidae, or Flat-fish, are remarkable for their asymmetrical bodies. They rest on one side,—in the greater number of species on the left, but in some on the right side; and occasionally reversed adult specimens occur. The lower, or resting-surface, resembles at first sight the ventral surface of an ordinary fish. …

… But the eyes offer the most remarkable peculiarity; for they are both placed on the upper side of the head. During early youth, however, they stand opposite to each other, and the whole body is then symmetrical, with both sides equally coloured. Soon the eye proper to the lower side begins to glide slowly round the head to the upper side; but does not pass right through the skull, as was formerly thought to be the case. …

… Mr. Mivart has taken up this case, and remarks that a sudden spontaneous transformation in the position of the eyes is hardly conceivable, in which I quite agree with him. He then adds: "if the transit was gradual, then how such transit of one eye a minute fraction of the journey towards the other side of the head could benefit the individual is, indeed, far from clear. It seems, even, that such an incipient [initial] transformation must rather have been injurious." But he might have found an answer to this objection in the excellent observations published in 1867 by Malm. The Pleuronectidae, whilst very young and still symmetrical, with their eyes standing on opposite sides of the head, cannot long retain a vertical position, owing to the excessive depth of their bodies, the small size of their lateral fins, and to their being destitute of a swimbladder. Hence soon growing tired, they fall to the bottom on one side. Whilst thus at rest they often twist, as Malm observed, the lower eye upwards, to see above them; and they do this so vigorously that the eye is pressed hard against the upper part of the orbit. The forehead between the eyes consequently becomes, as could be plainly seen, temporarily contracted in breadth. On one occasion Malm saw a young fish raise and depress the lower eye through an angular distance of about seventy degrees....

… We should keep in mind, as I have before insisted, that the inherited effects of the increased use of parts, and perhaps of their disuse, will be strengthened by natural selection. For all spontaneous variations in the right direction will thus be preserved; as will those individuals which inherit in the highest degree the effects of the increased and beneficial use of any part. How much to attribute in each particular case to the effects of use, and how much to natural selection, it seems impossible to decide.

I may give another instance of a structure which apparently owes its origin exclusively to use or habit. The extremity of the tail in some American monkeys has been converted into a wonderfully perfect prehensile organ, and serves as a fifth hand. A reviewer who agrees with Mr. Mivart in every detail, remarks on this structure: "It is impossible to believe that in any number of ages the first slight incipient tendency to grasp could preserve the lives of the individuals possessing it, or favour their chance of having and of rearing offspring." But there is no necessity for any such belief. Habit, and this almost implies that some benefit great or small is thus derived, would in all probability suffice for the work. Brehm saw the young of an African monkey (Cercopithecus) clinging to the under surface of their mother by their hands, and at the same time they hooked their little tails round that of their mother. Professor Henslow kept in confinement some harvest mice (Mus messorius) which do not possess a structurally prehensile tail; but he frequently observed that they curled their tails round the branches of a bush placed in the cage, and thus aided themselves in climbing. I have received an analogous account from Dr. Günther, who has seen a mouse thus suspend itself. If the harvest mouse had been more strictly arboreal, it would perhaps have had its tail rendered structurally prehensile, as is the case with some members of the same order. Why Cercopithecus, considering its habits whilst young, has not become thus provided, it would be difficult to say. It is, however, possible that the long tail of this monkey may be of more service to it as a balancing organ in making its prodigious leaps, than as a prehensile organ." (Darwin C., 1872, pp. 186-189)

The above is interesting conjecture. As we know today, the Pleuronectidae, or Flatfish's shape, size, and behaviour, as well as prehensile tails in some American monkeys, are all governed by genetics acquired at conception. In other words, what a creature is to become is determined by Its DNA, and not its surroundings - unless its environment induces mutations. There would have to have been countless mutations in a positive direction. Necessity 'like magic' does not create, thus the creation of the flatfish in this way is problematic.

Darwin gives abundant credence to "use and disuse of parts" as causes for change. Can a giraffe make his neck longer by stretching? Can a lazy father who sits around watching television day and night pass on his laziness to his son or does a son become lazy by just watching his dad? As we know, a father cannot change his own genetic makeup and every species has a given range of possibilities within its genetic mix. This theory of "use and disuse of parts" is an example of taking a concept and stating it as fact.

MAMMARY GLANDS

Paley:

... "The attraction of the calf or lamb to the teat of the dam, is not explained by simply referring it to the sense of smell. What made the scent of milk so agreeable to the lamb, that it should follow it up with its nose, or seek with its mouth the place from which it proceeded? No observation, no experience, no argument could teach the new dropped animal, that the substance from which the scent issued, was the material of its food. It had never tasted milk before its birth. None of the animals, which are not designed for that nourishment, ever offer to suck, or to seek out any such food. What is the conclusion, but that the spumescent [syrupy] parts of animals are fitted for their use, and the knowledge of that use put into them?" … (Paley W., Natural Theology or Evidences of the Existence and Attributes of the Deity, 1829, pp. 179-180)

The breasts are optimally placed containing the milk glands enclosed in sacks of skin with the important nipples. The mammary glands or breast are irreducibly complex; each part of the whole has to function correctly and at the optimal time.

If one holds a finger on a baby's cheek, the baby will turn and try to suck it. Without a baby's instinct for sucking combined with its physical ability to suck, there would be no future generation.

Darwin:

"The development of the mammary glands would have been of no service, and could not have been effected through natural selection, unless the young at the same time were able to partake of the secretion. There is no greater difficulty in understanding how young mammals have instinctively learnt to suck the breast, than in understanding how unhatched chickens have learnt to break the egg-shell by tapping against it with their specially adapted beaks; or how a few hours after leaving the shell they have learnt to pick up grains of food. In such cases the most probable solution seems to be, that the habit was at first acquired by practice at a more advanced age, and afterwards transmitted to the offspring at an earlier age. But the young kangaroo is said not to suck, only to cling to the nipple of its mother, who has the power injecting milk into the mouth of her helpless, half-formed offspring. On this head Mr. Mivart remarks: "Did no special provision exist, the young one must infallibly be choked by the intrusion of the milk into the windpipe. But there *is* a special provision. The larynx is so elongated that it rises up into the posterior end of the nasal passage, and is thus enabled to give free entrance to the air for the lungs, while the milk passes harmlessly on each side of this elongated larynx, and so safely attains the gullet behind it." Mr. Mivart then asks how did natural selection remove in the adult kangaroo (and in most other mammals, on the assumption that they are descended from a marsupial form), "this at least perfectly innocent and harmless structure?" It may be suggested in answer that the voice, which is certainly of high importance to many animals, could hardly have been used with full force as long as the larynx entered the nasal passage; and Professor Flower has suggested to me that this structure would have greatly interfered with an animal swallowing solid food." (Darwin C., 1872, p. 190)

Where did instincts, such as a baby's sucking or a chick breaking its eggshell come from? How can habit become instinct at a later age and be transferred to younger and younger offspring when this instinct is needed for existence in the first place? How can the development from nothing to a larger and larger functioning female breast be explained by natural selection, since it is necessary for the very survival of an infant at birth? Also, with natural selection, this continually improved organ would have to be passed on to at least one daughter whose mammary glands would develop – not for herself – but for her future offspring; giving milk would be of no use to the mother who is being drained for the sake of someone other than herself – the child.

Paley:

"It is not very easy to conceive a more evidently prospective [yet to come] contrivance than that which, in all viviparous animals, is found in the milk of the female parent. At the moment the young animal enters the world, there is its maintenance ready for it. The particulars to be remarked in this economy are neither few nor slight. We have, first, the nutritious quality of the fluid, unlike, in this respect every other excretion of the body; and in which nature hitherto remains unimitated, neither cookery nor chemistry having been able to make milk out of grass, we have secondly, the organ for its reception and retention; we have, thirdly, the excretory duct, annexed to it: and we have, lastly, the determination of the milk to the breast, at the particular juncture when it is about to be wanted. We have all these properties in the subject before us; and they are all indications of design. The last circumstance is the strongest of any. If I had been to guess beforehand, I should have conjectured, that at the time when there was an extraordinary demand for nourishment in one part of the system, there would be the least likelihood of a redundancy to supply another part. The advanced pregnancy of the female has no intelligible tendency to fill the breast with milk. The lacteal system is a constant wonder: and it adds to other causes of our admiration, that the number of the teats and paps in each species is found to bear a proportion to the number of the young. In the sow, the bitch, the rabbit, the cat, that, which have numerous litters, the paps are numerous, and are disposed along the whole length of the belly; in the cow and mare they are few. The most simple account of this, is to refer it to a designing Creator." (p-148)

Without gradation, [a step-by-step progression] and without habit becoming instinct, Charles Darwin's assumptions are not correct.

Are we related to the domestic barnyard cows since they are also mammals? Amazing speculation! The other explanation is that the same Creator created all life distinct having commonality.

After eating an apple, do we never marvel at how it is constructed with its seeds and shells in its core? Is the apple tree a species that has beaten down others for survival, or a wonder of design by a Creator God?

What is worse than seeing a worm in our apple? – (Seeing half a worm!)

CLIMBING PLANTS

Darwin:

"We will now turn to climbing plants. These can be arranged in a long series, from those which simply twine round a support, to those which I have called leaf-climbers, and to those provided with tendrils. In these two latter classes the stems have generally, but not always, lost the power of twining, though they retain the power of revolving, which the tendrils likewise possess. The gradations from leaf-climbers to tendril-bearers are wonderfully close, and certain plants may be indifferently placed in either class. But in ascending the series from simple twiners to leaf-climbers, an important quality is added, namely sensitiveness to a touch, by which means the foot-stalks of the leaves or flowers, or these modified and converted into tendrils, are excited to bend round and clasp the touching object. He who will read my memoir on these plants will, I think, admit that all the many gradations in function and structure between simple twiners and tendril-bearers are in each case beneficial in a high degree to the species. For instance, it is clearly a great advantage to a twining plant to become a leaf-climber; and it is probable that every twiner which possessed leaves with long foot-stalks would have been developed into a leaf-climber, if the foot-stalks had possessed in any slight degree the requisite sensitiveness to a touch." ...

...It is a more important fact that according to the high authority of Hofmeister, the young shoots and leaves of all plants move after being shaken; and with climbing plants it is, as we know, only during the early stages of growth that the foot-stalks and tendrils are sensitive. It is scarcely possible that the above slight movements, due to a touch or shake, in the young and growing organs of plants, can be of any functional importance to them. But plants possess, in obedience to various stimuli, powers of movement, which are of manifest importance to them; for instance, towards and more rarely from the light, —in opposition to, and more rarely in the direction of, the attraction of gravity. ...

... So with plants it appears that, from having the power of movement in obedience to certain stimuli, they are excited in an incidental manner by a touch, or by being shaken. Hence there is no great difficulty in admitting that in the case of leaf-climbers and tendril-bearers, it is this tendency which has been taken advantage of and increased through natural selection. It is, however, probable, from reasons which I have assigned in my memoir, that this will have occurred only with plants which had already acquired the power of revolving, and had thus become twiners.

I have already endeavoured to explain how plants became twiners, namely, by the increase of a tendency to slight and irregular revolving movements, which were at first of no use to them; this movement, as well as that due to a touch or shake, being the incidental result of the power of moving, gained for other and beneficial purposes. Whether, during the gradual development of climbing plants, natural selection has been aided by the inherited effects of use, I will not pretend to decide; but we know that certain periodical movements, for instance the so-called sleep of plants, are governed by habit." (Darwin C., 1872, pp. 196-198)

The above is sheer speculation. Why would twinging plants be developed by the inherited effects of use, or why would touch or shaking have anything to do with the development of twiners? Is it posable that twining can be changed by natural selection in a step by step method? Mendelian Genetics does not work this way,

Paley:

"In all subjects, the most common observations are the best, when it is their truth and strength which have made them common. There are, of this sort *two* concerning plants, which it falls within our plan to notice. The *first* relates to what has already been touched upon, their germination. When a grain of corn is cast into the ground, this is the change which takes place. From one end of the grain issues a green sprout; from the other, a number of white fibrous threads. How can this be explained? Why not sprouts from both ends? Why not fibrous threads from both ends? To what is the difference to be referred, but to design; to the different uses which the parts are thereafter to serve; uses which discover themselves in the sequel of the process? The sprout, or plumule, struggles into the air; and becomes the plant, of which, from the first, it contained the rudiments; the fibres shoot into the earth; and thereby both fix the plant to the ground, and collect nourishment from the soil for its support. Now, what is not a little remarkable, the parts issuing from the seed take their respective directins, into whatever position the seed itself happens to be cast. …

… Our second observation is upon a general property of climbing plants, which is strictly mechanical. In these plants, from each knot or joint, or as botanists call it, axilla, of the plant, issue, close to each other, two shoots; one bearing the flower and fruit, the other, drawn out into a wire, a long, tapering, spiral tendril, that twists itself round anything which lies within its reach. Considering, that in this class two purposes are to be provided for, (and together,) fructification and support, the fruitage of the plant, and the sustentation of the stalk, what means could be used more effectual, or, as I have said, more mechanical, than what this structure presents to our eyes? Why, or how, without a view to this double purpose, do two shoots, of such different and appropriate forms, spring from the same joint, from contiguous points of the same stalk? It never happens thus in robust plants, or in trees. "We see not, says Ray, so much as one tree, or shrub, or herb, that hath a firm and strong stem, and that is able to mount up and stand alone without assistance, *furnished with these tendrils.*" Make only so simple a comparison as that between a pea and its bean. Why does the pea put forth tendrils, the bean not; but because the stalk of the pea cannot support itself, the stalk of the bean can; We may add also, as a circumstance not to be overlooked, that in the pea tribe these clasps do not make their appearance, till they are wanted;

till the plant has grown to a height to stand in need of support. This word "support" suggests to us a reflection upon the property of grasses, of corn, and canes. The hollow stems of these classes of plants are set, at certain intervals, with joints. These joints are not found in the trunks of trees, or in the solid stalks of plants. There maybe other uses of these joints; but the fact is, and it appears to be at least one purpose designed by them, that they *corroborate* the stem; which, by its length and hollowness, would otherwise be too liable to break or bend." (Paley W., Natural Theology or Evidences of the Existence and Attributes of the Deity, 1829, pp. 203-207)

My wife has often told me that her garden plants seem to be alive in their movement in seeking out something to climb. Habit does not create twining plants – genetics does. I have often worked in our family garden and never seen any of the plants that were not twiners with a tendency to twine. We can never take a plant as a potato stock and force it to become a twiner. In 'Letty's garden', the ability of twining was due to inheritance. Also, the crossing of sitting and twining plants acquired something entirely different from either parent and this difference was not created over generations in a slow step-by-step fashion, or from the environment, such as shaking or touching.

We can observe the tremendous ability of houseplants in seeking out the direction of sunlight, which can be comparable to sunflowers orientating in the direction of the sun in an open field.

Maybe there is something in talking and singing to your plants, but don't do that too boisterously or your neighbours might question your sanity. Furthermore, I am not about to apologize to a carrot before eating it!

INSTINCTS

Darwin:

"… If we suppose any habitual action to become inherited—and it can be shown this does sometimes happen—then the resemblance between what originally was a habit and an instinct becomes so close as not to be distinguished. If Mozart, instead of playing the pianoforte at three years old with wonderfully little practice, had played a tune with no practice at all, he might truly be said to have done so instinctively. But it would be a serious error to suppose that the greater number of instincts have been acquired by habit in one generation, and then transmitted by inheritance to succeeding generations. It can be clearly shown that the most wonderful instincts with which we are acquainted, namely, those of the hive-bee and of many ants, could not possibly have been acquired by habit.

It will be universally admitted that instincts are as important as corporeal structures for the welfare of each species, under its present conditions of life. Under changed conditions of life, it is at least possible that slight modifications of instinct might be profitable to a species; and if it can be shown that instincts do vary ever so little, then I can see no difficulty in natural selection preserving and continually accumulating variations of instinct to any extent that was profitable. It is thus, as I believe, that all the most complex and wonderful instincts have originated. As modifications of corporeal structure arise from, and are increased by, use or habit, and are diminished or lost by disuse, so I do not doubt it has been with instincts. But I believe that the effects of habit are in many cases of subordinate importance to the effects of the natural selection of what may be called spontaneous variations of instincts; —that is of variations produced by the same unknown causes which produce slight deviations of bodily structure.

No complex instinct can possibly be produced through natural selection, except by the slow and gradual accumulation of numerous slight, yet profitable, variations. Hence, as in the case of corporeal structures, we ought to find in nature, not the actual transitional gradations by which each complex instinct has been acquired—for these could be found only in the lineal ancestors of each species—but we ought to find in the collateral lines of descent some evidence of such gradations; or we ought at least to be able to show that gradations of some kind are possible; and this we certainly can do. I have been surprised to find, making allowance for the instincts of animals having been but little observed except in Europe and North America, and for no instinct being known amongst extinct species, how very generally gradations, leading to the most complex instincts, can be discovered. Changes of instinct may sometimes be facilitated by the same species having different instincts at different periods of life, or at different seasons of the year, or when placed under different circumstances, &c.; in which case either the one or the other instinct might be preserved by natural selection. And such instances of diversity of instinct in the same species can be shown to occur in nature.

Again, as in the case of corporeal structure, and conformably to my theory, the instinct of each species is good for itself, but has never, as far as we can judge, been produced for the exclusive good of others. ... (Darwin C., 1872, pp. 206-207)

There is no proof that any habit ever changed into instinct. Instincts are genetically inherited while habits are learned after birth. Genetics never changes a species because of necessity or habit.

Our cat is so cute and yet so deadly. Nonetheless, we realize that her ability to stalk squirrels and mice is instinctive, because other cats in the neighborhood manifest this same behavior. Our cat also learned to open the patio screen door to our back yard. If our cat ever had kittens they would be born with the same instincts to stock and hunt but without an inherent aptitude for opening screen doors.

Some instincts are necessary for survival, and many instincts and structures are species' specific. (Which makes Darwinian evolution even more problematic?) A lion or tiger has teeth to kill and not to eat grass; without their instinct to stalk and kill, they would not exist. The lion and the wildebeest are very different in structure and instinct, and we would never contemplate a reversal of behaviour.

As stated earlier, when scientists examine dinosaurs, they often tell whether it was predator or prey by examining its teeth. Did a dinosaur realize it had teeth for grasping its prey and so decide to act in a predatory manor? Or teeth for cutting and chewing and a stomach for digesting vegetables, therefore decide that to eat grass?

Where does the instinct of love and devotion come from? The beginning of love and devotion would be difficult to explain through Darwinism because they are often for the betterment of others and not for the well-being of the possessor. Many mothers would starve or even die for their own children. (Love covers a multitude of sins).

My wife and I met a woman who had four cats. She treated them as if they were her family even to the extent of creating a seat at her table for one of them. She also told us that when one of her cats died, she had it cremated and kept its ashes in an urn in her house. She also said that when she dies, she wants to be cremated and the ashes of her cats mixed with her remains. To most of us, this is very bizarre.

Doesn't the very existence of instincts advance the credence of a creator God?

Instincts are inherited and not derived generationally in a slow step by way.

Paley:

… "An instinct is a propensity prior to experience, and independent of instruction. We contend, that it is by instinct that the sexes of animals seek each other; that animals cherish their offspring; that the young quadruped is directed to the teat of its dam; that birds build their nests, and brood with so much patience upon their eggs; that insects which do not sit upon their eggs, deposit them in those particular situations, in which the young, when hatched, find their appropriate food; that it is instinct which carries the salmon, and some other fish, out of the sea into rivers, for the purpose of shedding their spawn in fresh water.

We may select out of this catalogue the incubation of eggs. I entertain no doubt, but that a couple of sparrows hatched in an oven, and kept separate from the rest of their species, would proceed as other sparrows do, in every office which related to the production and preservation of their brood. Assuming this fact, the thing is inexplicable upon any other hypothesis than that of an instinct impressed upon the constitution of the animal. For, first, what should induce the female bird to prepare a nest before she lays her eggs? It is in vain to suppose her to be possessed of the faculty of reasoning; for no reasoning will reach the case. The fullness or distention which she might feel in a particular part of her body, from the growth and solidity of the egg within her, could not possibly inform her, that she was about to produce something, which, when produced, was to be preserved and taken care of. Prior to experience, there was nothing to lead to this inference, of to this suspicion. The analogy was all against it; for, in every other instance, what issued from the body, was cast out and rejected." …

… But admit the sparrow by some means to know, that within that egg was concealed the principle of a future bird, from what chemist was she to learn, that warmth was necessary to bring it to maturity, or that the degree of warmth, imparted by the temperature of her own body, was the degree required?

To suppose, therefore, that the female bird acts in this process from a sagacity [knowledge] and reason of her own, is to suppose her to arrive at conclusions which there are no premises to justify. If our sparrow, sitting upon her eggs, expect young sparrows to come out of them, she forms, I will venture to say, a wild and extravagant expectation, in opposition to present appearances, and to probability. She must have penetrated into the order of nature, farther than any faculties of ours will carry us; and it hath been well observed, that this deep sagacity [knowledge], if it be sagacity, subsists in conjunction with great stupidity, even in relation to the same subject. "A chemical operation, "says Addison," could not be followed with greater art or diligence, than is seen in hatching a chicken; yet is the process carried on without the least glimmering of thought or common sense. The hen will mistake a piece of chalk for an egg; is insensible of the increase or diminution of their number; does not distinguish between her own and those of another species; is frightened when her supposititious breed of ducklings take the water."

But it will be said, that what reason could not do for the bird, observation, or instruction, or tradition, might. Now, if it be true, that a couple of sparrows, brought up from the first in a state of separation from all other birds, would build their nest, and brood upon their eggs, then there is an end of this solution. What can be the traditionary knowledge of a chicken hatched in an oven?

Of young birds taken in their nests, a few species breed when kept in cages; and they which do so, build their nests nearly in the same manner as in the wild state, and sit upon their eggs. This is sufficient to prove an instinct, without having recourse to experiments upon birds hatched by artificial heat, and deprived from their birth of all communication with their species; for we can hardly bring ourselves to believe, that the parent bird informed her unfledged pupil of the history of her gestation, her timely preparation of a nest, her exclusion of the eggs, her long incubation, and of the joyful eruption at last of her expected offspring; all which the bird in the cage must have learned in her infancy, if we resolve her conduct into *institution.* ...

... In birds, is it the egg which the hen loves? Or is it the expectation which she cherishes of a future progeny, that keeps her upon her nest? What cause has she to expect delight from her progeny [offspring]? Can any rational answer be given to the question, why, prior to experience, the brooding hen should look for pleasure from her chickens? It does not, I think, appear that the cuckoo ever knows her young; yet, in her way, she is as careful in making provision for them, as any other bird. She does not leave her egg in every hole.

The salmon suffers no surmountable obstacle to oppose her progress up the stream of fresh rivers. And what does she do there: She sheds a spawn, which she immediately quits, in order to return to the sea; and this issue of her body she never afterwards recognises in any shape whatever. Where shall we find a motive for her efforts and her perseverance? Shall we seek it in argumentation [logical reasoning], or in instinct? The violet crab of Jamaica performs a fatiguing march of some months' continuance, from the mountains to the sea side. When she reaches the coast, she casts her spawn into the open sea; and sets out upon her return home. ...

... In this part of the case, the variety of resources, expedients, and materials, which animals of the same species are said to have recourse to, under different circumstances, and when differently supplied, makes nothing against the doctrine of instincts. The thing which we want to account for is the propensity [tendency]. The propensity being there, it is probable enough that it may put the animal upon different actions, according to different exigencies [needs]. And this adaptation of resources may look like the effect of art and consideration, rather than of instinct; but still the propensity [tendency] is instinctive. For instance, suppose what is related of the woodpecker to be true, that, in Europe, she deposits her eggs in cavities, which she scoops out in the trunks of soft or decayed trees, and in which cavities the eggs lie concealed from the eye, and in some sort safe from the hand of man; but that, in the forests of Guinea and the Brazils, which man seldom frequents, the same bird hangs her nest to the twigs of tall trees; thereby placing them out of the reach of *monkeys* and *snakes*; i. e. that in each situation she prepares against the danger which she has most occasion to apprehend: suppose, I say, this to be true, and to be alleged, on the part of the bird that builds these nests, as evidence of a reasoning and distinguishing precaution, still the question returns, whence the propensity to build at all? ...

... I am not ignorant of the theory, which resolves instincts into sensation [feeling]; which asserts, that what appears to have a view and relation to the future, is the result only of the present dispassion of the animal's body, and of pleasure or pain experienced at the time. ...

We assert, secondly, that, even as to the cases in which the hypothesis has the fairest claim to consideration, it does not at all lessen the force of the argument for intention and design. The doctrine of instincts is that appetencies [desire], superadded to the constitution of an animal, for the effectuating of a purpose beneficial to the species. The above-stated solution would derive these appetencies [strong desire] from organization; but then this organization is not less specifically, not less precisely, and, therefore, not less evidently adapted to the same ends, than the appetencies themselves would be upon the old hypothesis. In this way of considering the subject, sensation supplies the place of foresight; but this is the effect of contrivance on the part of the Creator. ...

... In a word ; I should say to the patrons of this opinion, Be it so; be it, that those actions of animals which we refer to instinct, are not gone about with any view to their consequences, but that they are attended in the animal with a present gratification, and are pursued for the sake of that gratification alone; what does all this prove, but that the prospection [foresight], which must be somewhere, is not in the animal, but in the Creator? ... (Paley W., Natural Theology or Evidences of the Existence and Attributes of the Deity, 1829, pp. 172-181)

Darwin:

Inherited Changes of Habit or Instinct in Domesticated Animals

"The possibility, or even probability, of inherited variations of instinct in a state of nature will be strengthened by briefly considering a few cases under domestication. We shall thus be enabled to see the part which habit and the selection of so-called spontaneous variations have played in modifying the mental qualities of our domestic animals. It is notorious how much domestic animals vary in their mental qualities. With cats, for instance, some naturally takes to catching rats, and others mice. These tendencies are known to be inherited. ...

"How strongly these domestic instincts, habits, and dispositions are inherited, and how curiously they become mingled, is well shown when different breeds of dogs are crossed. Thus it is known that a cross with a bull-dog has affected for many generations the courage and obstinacy of greyhounds; and a cross with a greyhound has given to a whole family of shepherd-dogs a tendency to hunt hares. These domestic instincts, when thus tested by crossing, resemble natural instincts, which in a like manner become curiously blended together, and for a long period exhibit traces of the instincts of either parent: for example, Le Roy describes a dog, whose great-grandfather was a wolf, and this dog showed a trace of its wild parentage only in one way, by not coming in a straight line to his master, when called. ...

... Hence, we may conclude, that under domestication instincts have been acquired, and natural instincts have been lost, partly by habit, and partly by man selecting and accumulating, during successive generations, peculiar mental habits and actions, which at first appeared from what we must in our ignorance call an accident. In some cases compulsory [necessary] habit alone has sufficed to produce inherited mental changes; in other cases compulsory habit has done nothing, and all has been the result of selection, pursued both methodically and unconsciously: but in most cases habit and selection have probably concurred." (Darwin C., 1872, pp. 209-212)

Can habit become instinct through natural selection? Does necessity create change? Natural selection can only select what already is in existence, thus by Cross a mild dog with a pit-bull, you might get mild, vicious, or something in-between. This Change would be attained through genetics and not by habit. An example is the 'Russian dog', mentioned earlier, in this book, which is an example of crossing two dissimilar varieties and creating something novel. The instincts of this newly acquired dog variety were not be created by habit.

Edward Robinson

SPECIAL INSTINCTS

Darwin:

"Instincts of the Cuckoo.—It is supposed by some naturalists that the more immediate cause of the instinct of the cuckoo is, that she lays her eggs, not daily, but at intervals of two or three days; so that, if she were to make her own nest and sit on her own eggs, those first laid would have to be left for some time unincubated, or there would be eggs and young birds of different ages in the same nest. If this were the case, the process of laying and hatching might be inconveniently long, more especially as she migrates at a very early period; and the first hatched young would probably have to be fed by the male alone. But the American cuckoo is in this predicament; for she makes her own nest, and has eggs and young successively hatched, all at the same time. ...

... Now let us suppose that the ancient progenitor of our European cuckoo had the habits of the American cuckoo, and that she occasionally laid an egg in another bird's nest. If the old bird profited by this occasional habit through being enabled to migrate earlier or through any other cause; or if the young were made more vigorous by advantage being taken of the mistaken instinct of another species than when reared by their own mother, encumbered as she could hardly fail to be by having eggs and young of different ages at the same time; then the old birds or the fostered young would gain an advantage. And analogy would lead us to believe, that the young thus reared would be apt to follow by inheritance the occasional and aberrant habit of their mother, and in their turn would be apt to lay their eggs in other birds' nests, and thus be more successful in rearing their young. By a continued process of this nature, I believe that the strange instinct of our cuckoo has been generated. It has, also, recently been ascertained on sufficient evidence, by Adolf Müller, that the cuckoo occasionally lays her eggs on the bare ground, sits on them, and feeds her young. This rare event is probably a case of reversion to the long-lost, aboriginal instinct of nidification [to build a nest]." ...With respect to the means by which this strange and odious instinct was acquired, if it were of great importance for the young cuckoo, as is probably the case, to receive as much food as possible soon after birth, I can see no special difficulty in its having gradually acquired, during successive generations, the blind desire, the strength, and structure necessary for the work of ejection; for those young cuckoos which had such habits and structure best developed would be the most securely reared. The first step towards the acquisition of the proper instinct might have been mere unintentional restlessness on the part of the young bird, when somewhat advanced in age and strength; the habit having been afterwards improved, and transmitted to an earlier age." ... (pp. 212- 214)

The American and European cuckoos could be hybrids of the same species. The cuckoo birds can only develop into what genetics and the environment in which they are exposed. They are all cuckoos, no more or any less. It is cuckoo [not correct] to state that habit become instinct. Genetics does not create this way.

It is tremendous guesswork, to assume that change of structure and instinct of the cuckoo might be caused in a step-by-step gradated process from unintentional restlessness to the odd instinctive behaviour of ejecting other species' eggs from their nest. Necessity does not change a species genetic makeup. For example, the 'passenger pigeon' mentioned earlier became extinct rather than changed. The above is mostly Lamarckian and not correct.

Darwin:

"*Cell-making instinct of the Hive-Bee.* —I will not here enter on minute details on this subject, but will merely give an outline of the conclusions at which I have arrived. He must be a dull man who can examine the exquisite structure of a comb, so beautifully adapted to its end, without enthusiastic admiration. We hear from mathematicians that bees have practically solved a recondite [complex] problem, and have made their cells of the proper shape to hold the greatest possible amount of honey, with the least possible consumption of precious wax in their construction. ...

Let us look to the great principle of gradation, and see whether Nature does not reveal to us her method of work. At one end of a short series we have humble-bees, which use their old cocoons to hold honey, sometimes adding to them short tubes of wax, and likewise making separate and very irregular rounded cells of wax. At the other end of the series we have the cells of the hive-bee, placed in a double layer: each cell, as is well known, is an hexagonal prism, with the basal edges of its six sides bevelled so as to join an inverted pyramid, of three rhombs.

… In the series between the extreme perfection of the cells of the hive-bee and the simplicity of those of the humble-bee we have the cells of the Mexican Melipona domestica, carefully described and figured by Pierre Huber. The Melipona itself is intermediate in structure between the hive and humble bee, but more nearly related to the latter; it forms a nearly regular waxen comb of cylindrical cells, in which the young are hatched, and, in addition, some large cells of wax for holding honey. …

Hence we may safely conclude that, if we could slightly modify the instincts already possessed by the Melipona, and in themselves not very wonderful, this bee would make a structure as wonderfully perfect as that of the hive-bee. We must suppose the Melipona to have the power of forming her cells truly spherical, and of equal sizes; and this would not be very surprising, seeing that she already does so to a certain extent, and seeing what perfectly cylindrical burrows many insects make in wood, apparently by turning round on a fixed point. We must suppose the Melipona to arrange her cells in level layers, as she already does her cylindrical cells; and we must further suppose, and this is the greatest difficulty, that she can somehow judge accurately at what distance to stand from her fellow-labourers when several are making their spheres; but she is already so far enabled to judge of distance, that she always describes her spheres so as to intersect to a certain extent; and then she unites the points of intersection by perfectly flat surfaces. By such modifications of instincts which in themselves are not very wonderful, —hardly more wonderful than those which guide a bird to make its nest, —I believe that the hive-bee has acquired, through natural selection, her inimitable architectural powers. … (Darwin C., 1872, pp. 212-222)

Darwin assumes that natural selection changes species from the very simple to the complex in a step-by-step fashion. Darwin shows humble-bees, at one end of a series, which use their old cocoons to hold honey and sometimes adding to them short tubes of wax. At the other end of the series, we have the well-developed cells of the hive-bee. There are many varieties of hive-bee but to assume that the hive-bee became more and more complex from generation to generation is total conjecture. Instincts and the physical capacity to build are separate entities. Where did the instincts and ability of the bee to make wax and honey come from in the first place?

Darwin gives a great deal of information defending natural selection leading to change. He does not explain the bees' origin and their immense irreducible complex structures that are co-related to their instincts. Does an individual bee in a beehive think beyond its immediate task? Can it reason [think] to the extent that a change in action will create a better and more efficient beehive—not likely! Does a hive-bee born in the summer think to itself, "winter is coming, and if I don't work hard, I will starve"? These instincts for preparing for winter are all necessary survival instincts. A hive bee's ability to build and the division of labor are all derived through inheritances, and also are irreducible complex. Does all this not further indicate the existence of Intelligent Design?

We had a barbeque in our back yard that we kept covered when not in use. When the weather began to get colder in the fall, we noticed a young squirrel was getting up under the BBQ's cover and taking the padding. We assumed this little squirrel was destroying our BBQ cover to build her own nest for the winter. How could this young squirrel that never felt cold previously know that it had to prepare a worm nest for winter?

Paley:

"Bees, under one character or other, have furnished every naturalist with a set of observations. I shall in this place confine myself to one; and that is, the *relation* which obtains between the wax and the honey. No person who has inspected a bee-hive, can forbear remarking how commodiously the honey is bestowed in the comb, and amongst other advantages, how effectually the fermentation of the honey is prevented by distributing it into small cells. The fact is, that when the honey is separated from the comb, and put into jars, it runs into fermentation, with a much less degree of heat than what takes place in a hive. This may be reckoned a nicety; but, independently of any nicety in the matter, I would ask, what could the bee do with the honey if it had not the wax? How, at least, could it store it up for winter? The wax, therefore, answers a purpose with respect to the honey; and the honey constitutes that purpose with respect to the wax. This is the relation between them. But the two substances, though together of the greatest use, and without each other of little, come from a different origin. The bee finds the honey, but makes the wax. The honey is lodged in the nectaria of flowers, and probably undergoes little alteration; is merely collected: whereas the wax is a ductile, tenacious paste, made out of a dry powder, not simply by kneading it with a liquid, but by a digestive process in the body of the bee. What account can be rendered of facts so circumstanced, but that the animal, being intended to feed upon honey, was, by a peculiar external configuration, enabled to procure it? that, moreover, wanting the honey when it could not be procured at all, it was farther endued with the no less necessary faculty of constructing repositories for its preservation? which faculty, it is evident, must depend primarily, upon the capacity of providing suitable materials. Two distinct functions go to make up the ability. First, the power in the bee, with respect to wax, of loading the farina of flowers upon its thighs. Microscopic observers speak of the spoon-shaped appendages with which the thighs of bees are beset for this very purpose; but, inasmuch as the art and will of the bee may be supposed to be concerned in this operation, there is, secondly, that which doth not rest in art or will — a digestive faculty which converts the loose powder into a stiff substance. This is a just account of the honey and the honey-comb, and this account, through every part, carries a creative intelligence along with it. The sting; also of the bee has this relation to the honey, that it is necessary for the protection of a treasure which invites so many robbers." ... (Paley, Natural Theology or Evidences of the Existence and Attributes of the Deity, 1829, pp. 189-190)

The Honey bee is optimally designed to collect nectar and make wax for honey-combs. The very survival of the honey bee is dependent on many factors which are complex and irreducible which indicates Intelligent Design.

MORPHOLOGY - STRUCTURE OF ORGANISMS

Darwin:

"We have seen that the members of the same class, independently of their habits of life, resemble each other in the general plan of their organisation. This resemblance is often expressed by the term "unity of type;" or by saying that the several parts and organs in the different species of the class are homologous. The whole subject is included under the general term of

Morphology. This is one of the most interesting departments of natural history, and may almost be said to be its very soul. What can be more curious than that the hand of a man, formed for grasping, that of a mole for digging, the leg of the horse, the paddle of the porpoise, and the wing of the bat, should all be constructed on the same pattern, and should include similar bones, in the same relative positions? How curious it is, to give a subordinate though striking instance, that the hind-feet of the kangaroo, which are so well fitted for bounding over the open plains,—those of the climbing, leaf-eating koala, equally well fitted for grasping the branches of trees,—those of the ground-dwelling, insect or root eating, bandicoots,—and those of some other Australian marsupials,—should all be constructed on the same extraordinary type, namely with the bones of the second and third digits extremely slender and enveloped within the same skin, so that they appear like a single toe furnished with two claws. Notwithstanding this similarity of pattern, it is obvious that the hind feet of these several animals are used for as widely different purposes as it is possible to conceive. The case is rendered all the more striking by the American opossums, which follow nearly the same habits of life as some of their Australian relatives, having feet constructed on the ordinary plan. Professor Flower, from whom these statements are taken, remarks in conclusion: "We may call this conformity to type, without getting much nearer to an explanation of the phenomenon;" and he then adds "but is it not powerfully suggestive of true relationship, of inheritance from a common ancestor?"

… Nothing can be more hopeless than to attempt to explain this similarity of pattern in members of the same class, by utility [usefulness] or by the doctrine of final causes [purpose or goal]. The hopelessness of the attempt has been expressly admitted by Owen in his most interesting work on the 'Nature of Limbs.' On the ordinary view of the independent creation of each being, we can only say that so it is; —that it has pleased the Creator to construct all the animals and plants in each great class on a uniform plan; but this is not a scientific explanation. … (Darwin C., 1872, p. 382)

… On the theory of natural selection, we can, to a certain extent, answer these questions. We need not here consider how the bodies of some animals first became divided into a series of segments, or how they became divided into right and left sides, with corresponding organs, for such questions are almost beyond investigation." … (Darwin C., 1872, pp. 382-384)

If the same Creator made all creatures, then why would we not expect to find "unity of type"? As has already been stated, our left and right side of our bodies are homogenous one to the other, and yet if any of our appendages were divided in half, these two halves would never be identical. How can evolution explain that the outside of our bodies are uniform from side to side but not so, from front to back; our hands and feet are mirror images from left to right but a hand cannot be divided homogenously? How can evolution explain that our head is a mirror image, left to right and yet our brain has many distinct areas of function? In addition, organs within our bodies are not all homogenous. These facts are unexplainable with Darwinian evolution but are understandable with faith in a Creator God; a Creator who made each species [kind] distinct and yet fabricated on a similar pattern. We should not marvel that we share much in common with other species but that we exist as an irreducible multipart structure in the first place.

RECAPITULATION
AND CONCLUSION

The following is a skeleton of Charles Darwin's and William Paley's original but I tried to retain the core aspects.

CHARLES DARWIN

… "That many and serious objections may be advanced against the theory of descent with modification through variation and natural selection, I do not deny. I have endeavoured to give to them their full force. Nothing at first can appear mor e difficult to believe than that the more complex organs and instincts have been perfected, not by means superior to, though analogous with, human reason, but by the accumulation of innumerable slight variations, each good for the individual possessor. Nevertheless, this difficulty, though appearing to our imagination insuperably great, cannot be considered real if we admit the following propositions [ideas], namely, that all parts of the organisation and instincts offer, at least, individual differences—that there is a struggle for existence leading to the preservation of profitable deviations of structure or instinct—and, lastly, that gradations in the state of perfection of each organ may have existed, each good of its kind. The truth of these propositions cannot, I think, be disputed." … (Darwin C., pp. 404-405)

The existence of a Creator God does not negate the facts that there is gradation in which all species and varieties of species differ. There is no denying that evolution [change] happens. New varieties are created - all the time and varieties and whole species are becoming extinct - all the time. These changes do not disprove the genuineness that in the beginning, God created species [kinds] autonomously.

Darwin:

"Turning to geographical distribution, the difficulties encountered on the theory of descent with modification are serious enough. All the individuals of the same species, and all the species of the same genus, or even higher group, are descended from common parents; and therefore, in however distant and isolated parts of the world they may now be found, they must in the course of successive generations have travelled from some one point to all the others. We are often wholly unable even to conjecture how this could have been effected. Yet, as we have reason to believe that some species have retained the same specific form for very long periods of time, immensely long as measured by years, too much stress ought not to be laid on the occasional wide diffusion of the same species; for during very long periods there will always have been a good chance for wide migration by many means. A broken or interrupted range may often be accounted for by the extinction of the species in the intermediate regions (Ibid p-406)

Darwin is comparing apples to apples not apples to oranges. He is observing variety change, not species change when he compares island to island and island to mainland. Crossing varieties of the same species creates variety change.

Differences with species and varieties of species – island to nearest mainland - are explainable through Mendelian genetics, where varieties cross with other varieties creating other varieties. These 'other varieties' may have been produced on an island, and or mainland and, with the possibility of parental extinction, there would be change on an island or mainland or both. These processes do not negate the belief in a Creator God who created individual species and varieties of species that have migrated to diverse parts of the globe.

Darwin:

On this doctrine of the extermination of an infinitude of connecting links, between the living and extinct inhabitants of the world, and at each successive period between the extinct and still older species, why is not every geological formation charged with such links? Why does not every collection of fossil remains afford plain evidence of the gradation and mutation of the forms of life? Although geological research has undoubtedly revealed the former existence of many links, bringing numerous forms of life much closer together, it does not yield the infinitely many fine gradations between past and present species required on the theory; and this is the most obvious of the many objections which may be urged against it. Why, again, do whole groups of allied species appear, though this appearance is often false, to have come in suddenly on the successive geological stages? Although we now know that organic beings appeared on this globe, at a period incalculably remote, long before the lowest bed of the Cambrian system was deposited, why do we not find beneath this system great piles of strata stored with the remains of the progenitors of the Cambrian fossils? For on the theory, such strata must somewhere have been deposited at these ancient and utterly unknown epochs of the world's history.

I can answer these questions and objections only on the supposition that the geological record is far more imperfect than most geologists believe. The number of specimens in all our museums is absolutely as nothing compared with the countless generations of countless species which have certainly existed. (Ibid 408)

Darwin believed that with the passage of time, the geological record would be filled in to align with his tree of life depiction, but it has not happened. Scientists are still looking for missing links.

Darwin:

"Now let us turn to the other side of the argument. Under domestication we see much variability, caused, or at least excited, by changed conditions of life; but often in so obscure a manner, that we are tempted to consider the variations as spontaneous [unplanned]. Variability is governed by many complex laws, —by correlated growth, *compensation, the increased use and disuse of parts, and the definite action of the surrounding* conditions. There is much difficulty in ascertaining how largely our domestic productions have been modified; but we may safely infer that the amount has been large, and that modifications can be inherited for long periods. As long as the conditions of life remain the same, we have reason to believe that a modification, which has already been inherited for many generations, may continue to be inherited for an almost infinite number of generations. On the other hand, we have evidence that variability when it has once come into play, does not cease under domestication for a very long period; nor do we know that it ever ceases, for new varieties are still occasionally produced by our oldest domesticated productions.

Variability is not actually caused by man; he only unintentionally exposes organic beings to new conditions of life, and then nature acts on the organisation and causes it to vary. But man can and does select the variations given to him by nature, and thus accumulates them in any desired manner. He thus adapts animals and plants for his own benefit or pleasure." ... (ibid 410-411)

Creation is more credible then evolution: Much of what Darwin expresses as change is variation and not species change; Mutations occur in plants and animals, but mutations can be more often harmful than helpful; Conditions do not change a species unless it causes a mutation in the reproductive or sex cell, and a mutation change is never continuous in a step-by-step process. Evolution does not happen through correlated growth - this idea is disproven by Mendel's law of independent assortment. And what has already been stated, 'physical conditions' or 'necessity' does not create a variety or a species, and neither can 'use and disuse of parts'. Lamarck's theory of change over time by means of 'use and disuse of parts. has been discredited. Farmers have continuously chosen the best that nature provides, and never generated a single new species.

Darwin:

"The complex and little known laws governing the production of varieties are the same, as far as we can judge, with the laws which have governed the production of distinct species. In both cases physical conditions seem to have produced some direct and definite effect, but how much we cannot say. Thus, when varieties enter any new station, they occasionally assume some of the characters proper to the species of that station. With both varieties and species, use and disuse seem to have produced a considerable effect; for it is impossible to resist this conclusion when we look, for instance, at the logger-headed duck, which has wings incapable of flight, in nearly the same condition as in the domestic duck; or when we look at the burrowing tucu-tucu,(sic) [tuco-tuco] If yes, then so be it. which is occasionally blind, and then at certain moles, which are habitually blind and have their eyes covered with skin; or when we look at the blind animals inhabiting the dark caves of America and Europe. With varieties and species, correlated variation seems to have played an important part, so that when one part has been modified other parts have been necessarily modified. With both varieties and species, reversions to long-lost characters occasionally occur. How inexplicable on the theory of creation is the occasional appearance of stripes on the shoulders and legs of the several species of the horse-genus and of their hybrids! How simply is this fact explained if we believe that these species are all descended from a striped progenitor, in the same manner as the several domestic breeds of the pigeon are descended from the blue and barred rockpigeon! On the ordinary view of each species having been independently created, why should specific characters, or those by which the species of the same genus differ from each other, be more variable than generic characters in which they all agree?" (Ibid 415-416)

It is obvious that Charles Darwin did not know Mendelian genetics in which most of the above can be explainable. The lager is an example of tremendous change that is possible when existing varieties are crossed. Reappearances of long-lost traits or characteristics as the occasional appearance of stripes on shoulders and legs of horses could be the result of recessive genes being expressed. Correlated variation could be traits expressed simultaneously. Also, no 'specific' or 'generic' characters continue to vary in a step-by-step fashion. Genetics just does not work this way. As has already been stated, Darwin's facts don't disprove the existence of a Creator God that made species autonomous with their ability for variation.

Darwin:

"Glancing at instincts, marvellous as some are, they offer no greater difficulty than do corporeal structures on the theory of the natural selection of successive, slight, but profitable modifications. We can thus understand why nature moves by graduated steps in endowing different animals of the same class with their several instincts." (Ibid P 425)

Species and all organic life share much in common, but each species is unique and irreducibly complex as well. Structures and instincts are co related and species specific; they match the physical state of the animal possessing them. For examples, humans need human instincts and structure in learning to walk upright, while apes move on all fours; the lion has teeth, claws and other characters that make it a perfect predator, and a stomach to digest their prey. Without the instincts as a stalker to hunt and kill, their physical characteristics are useless and the lion would starve. The lion's prey is not so.

Their instincts are fear and escape and their stomachs are co-related to their instincts for eating grasses. Since instincts and bodily structures are co-related and irreducibly complex, and as a result, their development is problematic as explained by Darwinian evolution through graduated steps, but easy to explain with belief in a Creator God.

What a species is to become is determined at conception. Embryos, even if some look alike to the naked eye, are vastly different genetically; similar in appearance with the naked eye does not mean same. A cow embryo becomes a cow and a giraffe becomes a giraffe. Humans do not flap their arms as birds flap their wings or wish to climb trees as monkeys or jump from limb to limb as flying squirrels. We should not marvel that much of organic life is built on a similar framework, since the same Maker made all.

Darwin:

"It can hardly be supposed that a false theory would explain, in so satisfactory a manner as does the theory of natural selection, the several large classes of facts above specified. It has recently been objected that this is an unsafe method of arguing; but it is a method used in judging of the common events of life, and has often been used by the greatest natural philosophers". ... (Darwin C., The Origin of Species by Means of Natural Selection. 6th ed., 1872, p. 421)

Many of Darwin's facts for his theory of evolution by Natural Selection are correct; there is no denying the obvious, evolutionary change takes place by means of mutations and or hybridization, however, there is a great deal that Darwinian evolution cannot explain which is understood through the existence of a creator God.

'Charles Darwin had a great lack of faith evident in what follows from Darwin's autobiography edited by his son Francis: "The passages which here follow are extracts, somewhat abbreviated, from a part of the Autobiography, written in 1876, in which my father gives the history of his religious views: —

"During these two years I was led to think much about religion. Whilst on board the *Beagle* I was quite orthodox, and I remember being heartily laughed at by several of the officers (though themselves orthodox) for quoting the Bible as an unanswerable authority on some point of morality. I suppose it was the novelty of the argument that amused them. But I had gradually come by this time, *i.e.* 1836 to 1839, to see that the Old Testament was no more to be trusted than the sacred books of the Hindoos. The question then continually rose before my mind and would not be banished,—is it credible that if God were now to make a revelation to the Hindoos, he would permit it to be connected with the belief in Vishnu, Siva, &c., as Christianity is connected with the Old Testament? This appeared to me utterly incredible.

By further reflecting that the clearest evidence would be requisite to make any sane man believe in the miracles by which Christianity is supported,—and that the more we know of the fixed laws of nature the more incredible do miracles become,—that the men at that time were ignorant and credulous to a degree almost incomprehensible by us,—that the Gospels cannot be proved to have been written simultaneously with the events,—that they differ in many important details, far too important, as it seemed to me, to be admitted as the usual inaccuracies of eye-witnesses;—by such reflections as these, which I give not as having the least novelty or value, but as they influenced me, I gradually came to disbelieve in Christianity as a divine revelation. The fact that many false religions have spread over large portions of the earth like wild-fire had some weight with me." (Charles, The Life and Letters of Charles Darwin, including an autobiographical Chapter, 1885, p. 308)

The above is a tremendous lack of faith which is often expressed even today. The trustworthiness of the Christian bible is addressed in the last chapter of this work. Also since God created the universe and all living creatures, the laws of nature and miracles are within His grasp as well.

WILLIAM PALEY

In contrast to Charles Darwin, William Paley had tremendous faith. What follows are portions derived from William Paley's conclusion to, "Natural theology or Evidences of the Existence and Attributes of the Deity, Collected from the Appearances of Nature".

Edward Robinson

Paley:

... "There is no subject in which the tendency to dwell upon select or single topics is so usual, because there is no subject, of which, in its full extent, the latitude [scope - freedom] is so great, as that of natural history applied to the proof of an intelligent Creator. For my part, I take my stand in human anatomy; and the examples of mechanism I should be apt to draw out from the copious [abundant] catalogue which it supplies, are the pivot upon which the head turns the ligament within the socket of the hip joint, the pulley or trochlear muscles of the eye, the epiglottis, the bandages which tie down the tendons of the wrist and instep, the slit or perforated muscles at the hands and feet, the knitting of the intestines to the mesentery, the course of the chyle [fluid in small intestine] into the blood, and the constitution of the sexes as extended throughout the whole of the animal creation." ... (Paley W., 1829, pp. 295-296)

"The works of nature want only to be contemplated. When contemplated, they have everything in them which can astonish by their greatness: for, of the vast scale of operation through which our discoveries carry us, at one end we see an intelligent Power arranging planetary systems, fixing, for instance, the trajectory of Saturn, or constructing a ring of two hundred thousand miles diameter to surround his body, and be suspended like a magnificent arch over the heads of his inhabitants; and, at the other, bending a hooked tooth, concerting and providing an appropriate mechanism, for the clasping and reclasping of the filaments of the feather of the humming bird. We have proof, not only of both these works proceeding from an intelligent agent, but of then proceeding from the same agent: for, in the first place, we can trace an identity of plan, a connexion of system, from Saturn to our own globe: and when arrived upon our globe, we can, in the second place, pursue the connexion through all the organized, especially the animated, bodies which it supports. We can observe marks of a common relation, as well to one another as to the elements of which their habitation is composed Therefore one mind hath planned or at least hath prescribed, a general plan for all these productions One Being has been concerned in all.

Under this stupendous Being we live. Our happiness, our existence, is in his hands. All we expect must come from him. Nor ought we to feel our situation insecure. In every nature, and in every portion of nature, which we can describe, we find attention bestowed upon even the minutest parts. The hinges in the wings of an earwig, and the joints of its antennas, are as highly wrought, as if the Creator had nothing else to finish. We see no signs of diminution of care by multiplicity of objects, or of distraction of thought by variety. We have no reason to fear, therefore, our being forgotten, or overlooked, or neglected.

The existence and character of the Deity, is, in every view, the most interesting of all human speculations. In none, however, is it more so, than as it facilitates the belief of the fundamental articles of *Revelation*. It is a step to have it proved, that there must be something in the world more than what we see. It is a farther step to know, that amongst the invisible things of nature, there must be an intelligent mind, concerned in its production, order, and support. These points being assured to us by Natural Theology, we may well leave to Revelation …

But above every other article of revealed religion, does the anterior belief of a Deity bear with the strongest force upon that grand point, which gives indeed interest and importance to all the rest — the resurrection of the human dead. The thing might appear hopeless, did we not see a power at work adequate to the effect, a power under the guidance of an intelligent will, and a power penetrating the inmost recesses of all substance. I am far from justifying the opinion of those, who "thought it a thing incredible that God should raise the dead:" but I admit, that it is first necessary to be persuaded, that there is a God to do so.

This being thoroughly settled in our minds, there seems to be nothing in this process (concealed and mysterious as we confess it to be) which need to shock our belief." … (Ibid 297-299)

"Upon the whole; in everything which respects this awful, but, as we trust, glorious change, we have a wise and powerful Being (the author, in nature, of infinitely various expedients, for infinitely various ends) upon whom to rely for the choice and appointment of means, adequate to the execution of any plan which his goodness or his justice may have formed, for the moral and accountable part of his terrestrial creation. That great office rests with him: be it ours to hope and to prepare, under a firm and settled persuasion, that, living and dying, we are his; that life is passed in his constant presence, that death resigns us to His merciful disposal." (Ibid 301-302)

William Paley believed that we could see the working of a creator God through His creation: "Upon the whole; after all the schemes and struggles of a reluctant Philosophy, the necessary resort is to a Deity. The marks of design are too strong to be gotten over Design must have had a designer. That designer must have been a person. That person is God." (Paley W., Natural Theology or Evidences of the Existence and Attributes of the Deity, 1829, pp. 241-246)

Romans 1:20-21:

"For since the creation of the world His invisible attributes are clearly seen, being understood by the things that are made, even His eternal power and Godhead, so that they are without excuse, because, although they knew God They did not glorify Him as God, nor were thankful, but their foolish hearts were darkened."(NKJV)

CAN WE TRUST THE JUDAIC CHRISTIAN BIBLE?

Many skeptics have claimed that the Judaic Christian Bible has been altered and corrupted through time, but the discovery of the Dead Sea Scrolls would refute this assumption. The Dead Sea Scrolls were discovered between 1946 and 1956 in eleven caves in the Judean Desert of the West Bank. They were mostly written in Hebrew and contained remains of every book of the (Old Testament) except Esther.

According to Dr. Bryant Wood, "Probably the Dead Sea Scrolls have had the greatest Biblical impact. They have provided Old Testament manuscripts approximately 1,000 years older than our previous oldest manuscript. The Dead Sea Scrolls have demonstrated that the Old Testament was accurately transmitted during this interval. In addition, they provide a wealth of information on the times leading up to, and during, the life of Christ." (Verner, 2008)

We can be assured that the current Old Testament and also the New Testament are consistent, because when comparing the text of the Dead Sea scrolls to the contemporary Old Testament and also the many quotes in the New Testament referenced to the Old, they are uncannily similar. Consequently, the Dead Sea Scrolls assures us that our current bible [Old and New Testament] was copied with great care and precision.

FULFILLMENT OF PROPHECY

We can also have confidence in the Christian bible and our faith, because of fulfilled prophesies. For example, the prophet Isaiah prophesied about the birth, death on the cross, and resurrection of Jesus Christ, hundreds of years before Christ was born in a manger in Bethlehem. [26]

---

[26] The prophet Micah foretold that the Messiah would come from the small town of Bethlehem: Micah 5: 2-5

Isaiah 53:1-13:

1 Who has believed our report? And to whom has the arm of the Lord been revealed?

2 For He shall grow up before Him as a tender plant, And as a root out of dry ground. He has no form or comeliness; And when we see Him, There is no beauty that we should desire Him.

3 He is despised and rejected by men, A Man of sorrows and acquainted with grief. And we hid, as it were, our faces from Him; He was despised, and we did not esteem Him.

4 Surely He has borne our griefs And carried our sorrows; Yet we esteemed Him stricken, Smitten by God, and afflicted.

5 But He was wounded for our transgressions, He was bruised for our iniquities; The chastisement for our peace was upon Him, And by His stripes we are healed.

6 All we like sheep have gone astray; We have turned, every one, to his own way; And the Lord has laid on Him the iniquity of us all.

10 Yet it pleased the Lord to bruise Him; He has put Him to grief. When You make His soul an offering for sin, He shall see His seed, He shall prolong His days, And the pleasure of the Lord shall prosper in His hand.

11 He shall see the labor of His soul, and be satisfied. By His knowledge My righteous Servant shall justify many, For He shall bear their iniquities.

12 Therefore I will divide Him a portion with the great, And He shall divide the spoil with the strong, Because He poured out His soul unto death, And He was numbered with the transgressors, And He bore the sin of many, And made intercession for the transgressors. (NKJV)

MORE THAN A CARPENTER

The most indispensable portion of the Christian message is the Cross. The gospel (good news) message is the suffering, death and resurrection of Jesus Christ for atonement for our sins. By confessing our wrong doing, we can be as it were, "Born Again", and have a new life as a follower of Jesus

This same Jesus, being fully human (Son of Man), and also fully God [son of God] could call God His Father, because He had no earthly father. he was born in the flesh by means of a virgin.

1 Corinthians 15:1-4:

1 Now I make known to you, brethren, the gospel which I preached to you, which also you received, in which also you stand,

2 by which also you are saved, if you hold fast the word which I preached to you, unless you believed in vain.

3 For I delivered to you as of first importance what I also received, that Christ died for our sins according to the Scriptures,

4 and that He was buried, and that He was raised on the third day according to the Scriptures, (NKJV)

CHRIST HAS RISEN

What follows is an encounter with the resurrected Jesus on the road to Emmaus.

Luke 24:13-27+44

13 Now behold, two of them were traveling that same day to a village called Emmaus, which was seven miles from Jerusalem.

14 And they talked together of all these things which had happened.

15 So it was, while they conversed and reasoned, that Jesus Himself drew near and went with them.

16 But their eyes were restrained, so that they did not know Him.

17 And He said to them, "What kind of conversation is this that you have with one another as you walk and are sad?"

18 Then the one whose name was Cleopas answered and said to Him, "Are You the only stranger in Jerusalem, and have You not known the things which happened there in these days?"

19 And He said to them, "What things?" So they said to Him, "The things concerning Jesus of Nazareth, who was a Prophet mighty in deed and word before God and all the people,

20 and how the chief priests and our rulers crucified Him.

21 But we were hoping that it was He who was going to redeem Israel. Indeed, besides all this, today is the third day since these things happened.

22 Yes, and certain women of our company, who arrived at the tomb early, astonished us.

23 When they did not find His body, they came saying that they had also seen a vision of angels who said He was alive.

24 And certain of those who were with us went to the tomb and found it just as the women had said; but Him they did not see."

25 Then He said to them, "O foolish ones, and slow of heart to believe in all that the prophets have spoken!

26 Ought not the Christ to have suffered these things and to enter into His glory?"

27 And beginning at Moses and all the Prophets, He expounded to them in all the Scriptures the things concerning Himself.

44 Then He said to them, "These are the words which I spoke to you while I was still with you, that all things must be fulfilled which were written in the Law of Moses and the Prophets and the Psalms concerning Me in the Law of Mosses and the Prophets and the Psalms must be fulfilled." (NKJV)

SALVATION IN CHRIST

The death and resurrection of Jesus Christ is the center of our faith as Christians.

Romans 10:8-11

8 But what does it say? "The word is near you, in your mouth and in your heart" (that is, the word of faith which we preach):

9 that if you confess with your mouth the Lord Jesus and believe in your heart that God has raised Him from the dead, you will be saved.

10 For with the heart one believes unto righteousness, and with the mouth confession is made unto salvation.

11 For the Scripture says, "Whoever believes on Him will not be put to shame." NKJV

Without the cross, I wouldn't know the tremendous love of God for mankind. With the suffering of Jesus on the cross, I realize that by confessing my transgressions, however horrible, I can be forgiven, because Christ died on a cross and received the punishment due me. With God's forgiveness, I can have a relationship with God and others.

MY BOSS IS MORE THAN A CARPENTER

The Gospel message of Jesus Crist is more than salvation; we can also have friendship with the very maker of the universe.

John 1:5-10:

5 This is the message which we have heard from Him and declare to you, that God is light and in Him is no darkness at all.

6 If we say that we have fellowship with Him, and walk in darkness, we lie and do not practice the truth.

7 But if we walk in the light as He is in the light, we have fellowship with one another, and the blood of Jesus Christ His Son cleanses us from all sin. (NKJV)

Romans 10:17:

"So then faith *comes* by hearing, and hearing by the word of God." (NKJV)[27]

---

[27] All Scripture taken from the New King James Version®. Copyright © 1982 by Thomas Nelson. Used by permission. All rights reserved. (Unless otherwise marked)

FINAL CONCLUSION

There has been a tremendous increase in scientific knowledge since Charles Darwin first published *"On the Origin of Species by Means of Natural Selection or The Preservation of Favours Races in the Struggle for Life"*, and William Paley's *"Natural Theology, or Evidences of the Existence and Attributes of the Deity"*. Today, the two main world views for creation still exist; the one that all life derived through pre-existent life forms and the other that organic life was created by Intelligent Design. Increased scientific knowledge has not negated faith, and for believers, science and faith are not autonomous. For believers in a creator God, further discoveries in science just add to the awe and wonder of His creation.

Darwin's "natural selection and survival of the fittest is not a difficult hypothesis.

Darwin:

… "I think it inevitably follows, that as new species in the course of time are formed through natural selection, others will become rarer and rarer, and finally extinct. The forms which stand in closest competition with those undergoing modification and improvement, will naturally suffer most. And we have seen in the chapter on the Struggle for Existence that it is the most closely-allied forms,—varieties of the same species, and species of the same genus or of related genera,—which, from having nearly the same structure, constitution, and habits, generally come into the severest competition with each other; consequently, each new variety or species, during the progress of its formation, will generally press hardest on its nearest kindred, and tend to exterminate them. We see the same process of extermination amongst our domesticated productions, through the selection of improved forms by man. investigation." … (Darwin C., 1872, pp. 86-87)

Darwinism cannot explain the origin and progression of the following:

- Amazing genes, e.g. genes can be turned on and off.
- Sexual characteristics and their development - sexual features - has to be in existence for any future generations.

- Irreducible complexity - many biological structures are just too composite to begin by chance, and their very existence is contingent on independent parts functioning applicable. An example is the cell which is the smallest unit of organic life.
- Consciousness - it cannot be reduced merely to the physical brain.-I think, therefore I am. The bible states that humans were created in God's image, thus our consciousness was created by a higher consciousness.
- Empathy for departed relatives – it does not have any survival benefits, thus problematic to explain its origin by means of Darwinism.
- Survival instincts - they have to be in existence from the beginning. - An example is a chick breaking out of an egg shell.
- Many Instincts and biological structures are irreducible complex - blinking our eyes involves muscles nerves and brain activity.

Darwin, in his own admission, stated that his theory would totally break down if it could be demonstrated that any complex organ existed, which could not possibly have been formed by numerous, successive, slight modifications.

"Irreducible-complexity" is a term used in Michael Behe's book "Darwin's *Black Box*" (1996). The principal that Behe makes is that many systems with irreducible complexity needs all their parts in place in order to function. Since Darwin's theory is built on numerous successive slight modifications, his theory is problematic.

"The smallest unit of all organic life is the cell. The cell functions as a composite unit comprised of specialised and essential subunits called (organelles). Each organelle is essential for the function of the whole; take away any essential part of the cell and it does not function. Thus, the cell cannot be formed by numerous, successive, slight modifications.

Our bodies comprise many complex and irreducible parts; each part functions for the purpose of the whole organism. (Who can exist without a heart or kidney etc.?) If we combine sight, walking, hearing, chewing, and the great organization of our brain as just a small sample of the complexity of a whole body, does this not indicate that there must be an organizer, and this organizer must stand as a Creator God?

Since all organic life was made by the same Creator God, there should be no surprise that we share much in common with all life forms.

Darwinian evolution can only infer that an ape like creator evolved into humans. With Darwinian evolution, each forward step has to be a favourable mutation and the new is to replace the former. Statistically there should be as many or more negative or harmful mutations as positive. (Keep in mind that with Darwinian evolution, an irreducibly complex ape like creature first has to be in existence to become human.) With Mendelian genetics, varieties change, not species and not in a gradated step by step fashion.

In addition, the fossil evidence (meager as it is) also shows that deviation is a normal process. There is plenty of evidence confirming that varieties change; crossing of existing varieties continually creates new varieties. In meiosis, the process of crossing over creates change. A mutation also creates change. And also, species and varieties are becoming extinct – all the time. Today, there may be more diversity in modern humans then in the fossil record.

Finally, there is overwhelming evidence demonstrating the existence of an Everlasting Creator God. The creation and existence of all of the above can be explained in light of this reality. As stated by William Paley. "Upon the whole; after all the schemes and struggles of a reluctant "Philosophy, the necessary resort is to a Deity. The marks of design are too strong to be gotten over".

There is also evidence showing the reliability of the Judaic Christian Bible. The discovery of the Dead Sea Scrolls in 1948 demonstrates that the bible was accurately copied through the centuries. Fulfillment of prophecy (prior knowledge of future events) also demonstrates that the bible is the emphatic word of a living God. The bible teaches that God is an everlasting Loving Intelligent Being at the head of all creation. The bible also conveys that we were created by God in His image; we were created for Him and by Him.

Christians have faith, but our faith is not a blind faith. There is overwhelming evidence demonstrating the existence of an everlasting, loving, intelligent and Creative God. We know that our salvation is made possible by the death and resurrection of our Lord and saviour Jesus Christ. As followers of Jesus, we look forward to eternal life and fellowship with other believers and with the everlasting Creator of all things.

WORKS CITED

Allen. (2004, November). From the Editor. *National Geography*, p. n.pag.

Aris, B. (2002). Russians Breed Superdog With Jackal's Nose for Boms and Drugs. *The Telegraph Europe*. Retrieved 11 25, 2016, from http://www. telegraph.co.uk/news/worldnews/europe/russia/1416227/Russians-breed-superdog-with-a-jackals-nose-for-bombs-and-drugs.html

Bateson, W. (1902). *Mendel's Principles of Heredity a Diffence*. (w. Bateson, Ed.) London, England: Cambridge University press. Retrieved from <http://www.archive.org/details/mendelsprinciple1902bate>

Bateson, W. (1902). *Mendel's Principles of Heredity a Diffence*. (w. Bateson, Ed.) London, England: Cambridge University press.

Behe, M. (1996). *Darwin's Black Box* (Paperback Edition 2003 ed.). New York: The free press.

Behe, M. (2000, July 31). *A Mousetrap Defended: Reswponse to Critics*. Retrieved 6 8, 2012, from Access Research Network: http://www.arn. org/docs/behe/mb_mousetrapdefended.htm

Campbell, N. A. (1993). BIOLOGY. In Third (Ed.). Redwood, California: The Benjamin / Cummings.

Charles, D. (1885). *The Life and Letters of Charles Darwin, including an autobiographical Chapter*, Volume 1. (F. Darwin, Editor) Retrieved 06 21, 2017, from Darwin Online: http://darwin-online.org.uk/content/ frameset?pageseq=326&itemID=F1452.1&viewtype=side

Charles, D. (1885). *The Life and Letters of Charles Darwin, including an autobiographical Chapter*. Retrieved 06 21, 2017, from Darwin Online.

Darwin. (1860, May 22). *Darwin Correspondence Database, entry-2814*. Retrieved June 28, 2016, from University of Cambridge: http://www. darwinproject.ac.uk/entry-2814

Darwin. (1887). *The life and letters of Charles Darwin,* London: John Murray. Volume 1. (F. e. Darwin, Editor) Retrieved 05 08, 2017, from DARWIN ONLINE: http://darwin-online.org.uk/content/ frameset?itemID=F1452.1&viewtype=text&pageseq=1

Darwin, C. (1866, December 28). *Darwin Correspondence Database, entry-5307*. Retrieved October 28, 2019, from University of Cambridge: http://www.darwinproject.ac.uk/entry-5307

Darwin, C. (1868). *TheVariation of Animals and Plants Under Domestication.* New York, 245 Broadway: Orange Judd and Company.

Darwin, C. (1872). *The Origin of Species by Means of Natural Selection. 6th ed.* London: John Murray.

Darwin, C. (1875). *Animals and Plants Under Domestication* (Vol. 1). London, England: John Murray. Retrieved March 31, 2012, from The complete Work of Charles Darwin Online: http://darwin-online.org.uk/content/ frameset?viewtype=text&itemID=F880.1&pageseq=2

Darwin, C. (1876, July 7). *Darwin Correspondence Database, entry-12041*. Retrieved March 26, 2012, from darwinCorrespondence Project: http:// www.darwinproject.ac.uk/entry-12041

Darwin, C. (1881, July 3). *Darwin Correspondence Project*. Retrieved 10 27, 2016, from University of Cambridge: http:www.darwinproject.ac.uk/ entry-13230

Darwin, C. (1887). *The life and letters of Charles Darwin, including an autobiographical chapter. London: John Murray. Volume 1.* (F. Darwin, Editor) Retrieved from Darwin Online : http://darwin-online.org.uk/ content/frameset?itemID=F1452.1&viewtype=text&pageseq=1

Darwin, C. (1958). *The Autobiography of Charles Darwin 1809-1882.* (B. Nora, Ed.) London: Collins. Retrieved March 23, 2012, from htt://darwin-online. org.uk/content/frameset?itemd=F1497&viewtype=text&pageseq=1

Darwin, C. (n.d.). *Darwin. Francis ed. 1887.* Retrieved June 5, 2014, from The Victorian Web: http://www.victorian web.org/sc

eee. (1922). *The Outline of Science.* New Yoark London.

Encyclopaedia Britannica. (Last Updated 10-21-2013). *Dmanisi.* Retrieved 09 30, 2014, from http://www.britannica.com/EBchecked/topic/1116131/ Dmanisi

Gerald Karp. (1996). The Cell Nucleus and the Control of Gene Expression. In G. Karp, *Cell and Molecular Biology* (p. 557). New York * Chiechester * Bresbone* Toronto* Singapore: John Wiley and Sons, Inc.

kham, A. (2011, 07 08). Las Angeles Times. Retrieved 07 13, 2012, from http:// articles.latimes.com/2011/jul/08/science/la-sci-polar-bears-20110708

Paley, W. (1829). *"Natural Theology or Evidences of the Existence and Attributes of the Deity".* Boston: Lincoln & Edmands.

Paley, W. (1829). *National Theology or Evidences of the Existence and Attributes of the Deity.* Bosten: Lincoln & Edmonds.

Paley, W. (1829). *Natural Theology or Evidences of the Existence and Attributes of the Deity.* Boston: Lincoln & Edmands.

Raven @ Johnson. (1992). Mechanical Problems in Preservation. In R. @. Johnson, *Biology Third Edition* (p. 425). St Louis, United States : Edward F. Murphy.

Roberts, H. F. (1929). *1900: Rediscovery of Mendel's Work.* Retrieved 11 02, 2016, from National Human Genome Research Institue: https://www.genome. gov/25520238/online-education-kit-1900-rediscovery-of-mendels-work/

Sample, I. (2013, October 17). *Skill of Homo erectus throws story of human evelution int disarray.* Retrieved 12 20, 2013, from The Guardian: http://www.theguardian.com/science/2013/oct/17/skull-homo-erectus-human-evolution

Sanba38. (2006, 09 02). *Sexual dimorphism.* Retrieved 07 30, 2014, from Wikipedia the Free Encyclopedia: http://en.wikipedia.org/wiki/Male_female_differences

Schroeder, K. (2014, June 4). *Wikimedia Commons.* Retrieved Aug. 26, 2016, from Wikipedia The Free Encyclopedia: https://commons.wikimedia.org/wiki/File:Annelid_redone_w_white_background.svg

Statistics Canada. (2011, 09 30). *Mixed Unions Increasing.* Retrieved 07 12, 2012, from Statistics Canada: http://www.statcan.gc.ca/pub/11-402-x/2011000/chap/imm/imm02-eng.htm

Strobel, L. (2004). *The Case For a Creator.* Grand Rapids, Michigan: Zondervan. Retrieved 07 12, 2014

Thomson, A. J. (1922, 04). *The Projet Gutenberg Ebook of The outline of Scienc, Val. 1 (of 4).* Retrieved 11 06, 2012, from Http://www.Gutenberg.org/jiles/20417/20417-h/20417-h.htm

Thomson, J. (1922). *The Outline of Science Vol.1.* New York and London: G.P. Putmam's Sons. Retrieved from http://www.gutenberg.org/files/20417/20417-h/20417-h.htm

Thomson, J. A. (1922). *The Outline of Science Vol. 1.* New York and London: G.P. Putnam's Sona. Retrieved from http://www.gutenberg.org/files/20417/20417-h/20417-h.htm

Thomson, J. A. (January 22, 200). *The Outline of Science, Vol 1.*

U.S. National Library of Medicine. (2012, 10). *Homeobox gene family.* Retrieved 08 20, 2014, from U.S. Hational Library of Medicine: http://ghr.nlm.nih.gov/geneFamily/homeobox

U.S. National Library of Medicine. (2016, 11 01). *Can genes be turned on and off in cells?* Retrieved 11 05, 2016, from U.S. National Library of Medicine: https://ghr.nlm.nih.gov/primer/howgeneswork/geneonoff

U.S. National Library of Medicine. (2016, 11 01). *How do cells divide?* Retrieved 11 o4, 2016, from U.S. National Library of Medicine: https://ghr.nlm.nih.gov/primer/howgeneswork/cellsdivide

U.S. National Library of Medicine. (2016, 11 01). *What is a gene mutation and how do mutations occur?* Retrieved 11 05, 2016, from U.S. National Library of Medicine: https://ghr.nlm.nih.gov/primer/mutationsanddisorders/genemutation

U.S. National library of Medicine. (n.d.). *Genetics Home Reference.* Retrieved 06 26, 2012, from http://ghr.nlm.nih.gov/handbook

U.S. National Library of Medicine. (n.d.). *Genetics Home Reference (Handbook-How genes work).* Retrieved 06 24, 2014, from U.S. National Library of Medicine: http://ghr.nlm.nih.gov/handbook/howgeneswork/makingprotein

Verner, W. (2008, 05 21). *What is the importance of ther Dead Sea Sctolls?* Retrieved 02 09, 2017, from Association for Aiblical Reseatch: http://www.biblearchaeology.org/post/2008/05/21/What-is-the-importance-of-the-Dead-Sea-Scrolls.aspx

Watson, J. D. (2004). *DNA The Secret of Life.* New York: Alfred A Knope.

Wikapedia. (n.d.). *Lucy (Australopithecus).* Retrieved 07 13, 2014, from Wikapedia The Free Encycolopedia : https://en.wikipedia.org/wiki/Lucy_(Australopithecus)

Wikipedia. (1915). *Piltdown Man.* Retrieved 02 24, 2017, from wikipedia The Free Encyclopedia: https://en.wikipedia.org/wiki/Piltdown_Man

Wikipedia. (2012, 12 19). *Neanderthal.* Retrieved 12 19, 2012, from Wikipedia the free Encyclopedia: http://en.wikipedia.org/wiki/Neanderthal

Wikipedia. (2012, 05 18). *The Beothuk People.* Retrieved 07 12, 2012, from Beothuk people - Wikipedia, the free encyclopedia: http://en.wikipedia.org/wiki/Beothuk_people

Wikipedia. (2012, November). *Turnspit Dog.* Retrieved December 17, 2012, from Wikipedia The Free Encyclopedia : http://en.wikipedia.org/wiki/Turnspit_Dog

Wikipedia. (2017, 01 17). *Sulimov dog.* Retrieved 02 22, 2017, from Wikipedia The Free Encyclopedia: https://en.wikipedia.org/wiki/Sulimov_dog

Wikipedia. (2017, 17 01). *Sulimov dog.* Retrieved 02 25, 2017, from Wikipedia The Free Encyclopedia: https://en.wikipedia.org/wiki/Sulimov_dog

Wikipedia. (This page was last modified on 12 March 2017). *Systema Naturae.* Retrieved 04 30, 2017, from Wikipedia the Freee Encyclopedia: https://en.wikipedia.org/wiki/Systema_Naturae

Wikipidia. (2012, September 5). *Category:Extinct dog breeds.* Retrieved 12 17, 2012, from From Wikipedia, the free encyclopedia: http://en.wikipedia.org/wiki/Category:Extinct_dog_breeds

Wingrove, J. (2011, 08 03). Hybrid grizzly-polar bears a worrisome sign of the North's changing climate. *THE GLOBE AND MAIL.* Retrieved from http://www.theglobeandmail.com/news/national/hybrid-grizzly-polar-bears-a-worrisome-sign-of-the-norths-changing-climate/article589290/

Wood, J. (1853). *Wood's Animal Kingdom.* London, England: H.A. Brown and Co.

Yongsheng, L. (2008). A new perspective on Darwin'a Pangenesis. *Cambridge Philosophical Society, 83,* 148-149. Retrieved 11 03, 2016, from http://download.bioon.com.cn/upload/201108/10113502_6033.pdf

Zielinski, S. (2012, october 12). *Neanderthals ... They're Just Like Us?* Retrieved 12 19, 2012, from National Geographic News: http://news.nationalgeographic.com/news/2012/10/121012-neanderthals-science-paabo-dna-sex-breeding-humans/

Printed in the United States
By Bookmasters